THE DIVIDED KINGDOM

By the same author

The Centralist Enemy (1974)
Creative Conflict (1978)
Police Conspiracy? (1984)
The National Question Again (ed.) (1985)
Work in the Future (1986)

John Osmond

THE DIVIDED KINGDOM

Constable · London

305
OSM.

First published in Great Britain 1988
by Constable and Company Limited
10 Orange Street, London WC2H 7EG
Copyright © 1988 John Osmond
Set in Linotron Plantin 11 pt by
Rowland Phototypesetting Limited
Bury St Edmunds, Suffolk
Printed in Great Britain by
St Edmundsbury Press Limited
Bury St Edmunds, Suffolk

British Library CIP data
Osmond, John, *1946*–
The divided kingdom
1. Great Britain. Social inequality
I. Title
305

ISBN 0 09 468210 0
ISBN 0 09 468720 X Pbk

TO THE MEMORY OF
RAYMOND WILLIAMS

A 'region' was once a realm, a distinct society. In its modern sense, by contrast, it is from the beginning a subordinate part of a larger unity . . . What has then happened is that the real and powerful feelings of native place and a native formation have been pressed and incorporated into an essentially political and administrative organization, which has grown from quite different roots . . . Nothing is now more striking, for example, than the images of 'England' which are culturally predominant. Many urban children, when asked what is really 'England', reply with images of the monarchy, of the flag, of the Palace of Westminster and, most interestingly, of 'the countryside', the 'green and pleasant land'. It is here that the element of artifice is most obvious, when the terms of identity flow downwards from a political centre . . .

Raymond Williams, *Towards 2000*

The Celt in all his variants from Builth to
Ballyhoo,
His mental processes are plain – one knows
what he will do,
And can logically predicate his finish by his
start;
But the English – ah, the English! – they are
quite a race apart.

Rudyard Kipling, 'The Puzzler'

Contents

Maps

Acknowledgements

Any work of such ambitious scope as this incurs many debts. My greatest intellectual obligation is to Tom Nairn, who acted as consultant to the HTV Wales television series for Channel 4, first transmitted in the autumn of 1988, which was based on this book. In the mid-1970s, in his pathfinding study of the role of Scottish, Welsh and Ulster nationalism within British political culture, Tom Nairn pointed out that it was in England that the long-term future of the British Isles would be settled: 'The paralytic decline of the old state has given a temporary ascendancy to Scotland and other peripheric problems. Beyond this moment, it is bound to be the post-imperial crisis of the English people itself which takes over . . .'* To a great extent this book is a response to that prediction.

Others who read early drafts of the book and made many helpful suggestions are Owen Dudley Edwards, Peter Madgwick, John Benyon, and Christopher Harvie. I benefited from specific discussions with Henry Drucker, Bernard Crick, R. W. Johnson, Anthony Barnett, Michael Steed, Paddy Scannell, Brian Robson, Robin Reeves and Richard Rose. I have benefited, too, from attending a number of the annual conferences of the UK Politics Work Group of the Political Studies Association during the 1970s and 1980s, and should like to thank all the participants. Most of the Introduction to the book

* Tom Nairn, *The Break-Up of Britain*, Verso edition, 1981, p. 79.

first appeared in *Planet* magazine, and I am grateful to the editors for permission to reprint it here.

Though an early draft of the book was completed before the television project began it was amended to take account of the results of making the series, and the many discussions that took place along the way. Primarily these were with the series director, Colin Thomas, whose distinctive views on British politics sharpened my own. Balance, if not objectivity, was provided by our team of presenters: Kim Howells, Beatrix Campbell, Julian Critchley, A. T. Q. Stewart, and Margo MacDonald. Friends and colleagues at HTV Wales who bore the brunt of translating conceptual ideas about the Divided Kingdom into a television series include Bethan Eames, Angela Graham, Mike Reynolds, Peter Thornton, Paul Gaydon, Maggie Lucas, Sue Lodwig Jones, Mike Parker, Toby Grosvenor, Roger Mitchell, Rob Copeland and many others who, in a way peculiar to television, collaborate as a team. My thanks go as well to my executive producers, Geraint Talfan Davies and Emyr Daniel, and the commissioning editor at Channel 4, Gwynn Pritchard, without whose encouragement and continual support the project could never have come to fruition. Detailed editorial help, as well as her usual forbearance, was provided by my wife, Alphie. Prudence Fay of Constable made many vital suggestions on syntax.

A continual presence in these pages are the ideas of the late Raymond Williams, a native of my own part of Wales, and in whose intellectual shadow I grew up. This book is dedicated to his memory.

J.O.
1988

Introduction: Trying to understand England

A number of constitutional issues – from proportional representation, the future of Northern Ireland, and Scottish devolution to reform of the House of Lords, a Bill of Rights and continued evolution of the European Community – are likely to achieve renewed prominence as the twentieth century draws to a close. Underlying them is a range of territorial and community identities. These include Britishness; Englishness and a variety of regional attachments within England; the Welsh, Scottish and Ulster dimensions; and the more recent addition of a supra-national European political awareness.

Many of these identities are interlocking: thus, for example, it is possible to feel simultaneously Scottish, British and European; Ulster and British; or Welsh and European. But where does the balance between such combinations lie, and does it change according to circumstance? What does being English mean in relation to Britain? Is English regional identity more important in the development of, say, literary culture than Englishness itself? How far does living in the relatively affluent South-east of Britain rather than the relatively impoverished North-west affect attitudes? What is meant by metropolitan and provincial culture and thinking? Can Scottish and Welsh consciousness be understood at least in part as a reaction against such distinctions?

These are questions to be asked of Highland as much as Lowland Scots, Catholic as much as Protestant Ulster people,

Welsh-speaking as much as English-speaking Welsh, Lancastrian as much as Berkshire English. The questions are common enough in Wales, Scotland, and Northern Ireland: in England, however, it is a different matter. Here questions of identity are seldom discussed and rarely in political terms. It is a central contention of this book that owing to circumstances largely beyond their control, the English will increasingly have to face up to these questions in the decades ahead.

The origins of this book lie in the politics of Wales in the 1970s which culminated in a referendum on St David's Day 1979. In that referendum the Welsh people decisively rejected, by a factor of four-to-one, proposals to establish an elected Welsh Assembly in Cardiff. In endeavouring to interpret that result it quickly became obvious that the British dimension of Welsh identity had played a critical role. I, in common with many writers on Wales in the 1970s, had tended to concentrate on the Welshness of the people of Wales, somehow taking their Britishness for granted. Now, however, it was clear that if we were to understand Wales we should have to understand Britain.

In this context the immediate focus, for reasons of proximity if not sheer numbers, was England and the English. But who are the English? Where do they live? Are Sunderland and Surrey both England? Are the English also British? To understand them does one have to examine class consciousness or first a sense of place? Is the essence of Englishness a subtle mix of both?

The fault line of England remains, as it has always been, a boundary drawn between the Severn and the Wash. Somewhere here 'The North' begins, though the signposts keep declaring its imminent arrival as far as the Scottish border, and beyond. In previous centuries this line separated highland from lowland England (and Britain), the fertile land being in the South. The Romans built their Fosse Way to patrol this border.

Today the line encloses those areas within effective commuting distance of London; Peterborough on this count being a border town between North and South. Peterborough is, of course, some kind of Midland town, but this is disputed territory: the East and West Midlands do have a distinctive feel; and where does East Anglia begin? The East Midlands have a more balanced and therefore prosperous economy, drawn by culture and accent towards the South. The West Midlands, following the disastrous collapse of their manufacturing base during the 1980s, have more in common with the North.

An early draft of this book was completed in 1986. During 1987 and into 1988 we travelled throughout Britain and Northern Ireland, filming the Channel 4 series based on it. It was fascinating to discover how far the images we collected confirmed the thesis already developed during research for the book. For our most vivid pictures of Northern and Southern England we were drawn inevitably to the North-east, Northumberland and Durham, and to the South-east, the City and the Home Counties. There was an immediate danger of falling into caricature, cloth caps versus bowlers when very few are left of either. Are these two Englands, in fact, no more different and separate than Gwynedd from Gwent in Wales, between which some of us urge a community of interest?

We took Tom Haddoway, the Tyneside playwright (famous for *When the Boat Comes In*), to show us the Northumberland Miners' Picnic at Bedlington, about ten miles north of Newcastle. On the way he made us pause at Earsdon churchyard to inspect in a quiet overgrown wood the memorial to the Hartley Colliery accident of 1862. Those were the days of single shaft mines, and in the accident the beam of the pumping engine snapped, blocking the shaft with winding gear and rubble, and asphyxiating 204 men and boys (many nine- and ten-year-olds) below.

At that time there were hundreds of collieries across Northumberland and Durham. Now they are all but gone and the Miners' Picnic that pale June day was a thin reminder of a past spectacle. Watching the procession, swelled by the banners of other unions and regiments of gaily uniformed children's kazoo bands, Tom reflected on a disappearing culture. So much of what had made the North, he said, depended on extractive and basic industries like deep-sea fishing, mining, steel-making and shipbuilding: things that men could touch and see under their hands. What could replace this as the core of a distinctive identity?

Further south in the devastated ex-steel town of Consett we spoke about what is left with former steel-worker John Kearney. 'Our culture was one of accommodation to the continuous processes of steel-production,' he said. 'Sex occurred depending which shift you were on.' When steel-making and its 4,000 jobs disappeared in 1980 so, too, did a network of activities and institutions that gave the community meaning – trade unions, social clubs, football teams, even allotments. In their place came a stark vacuum of unemployment, only partially filled by Manpower Services Commission injections of funding and the creation of jobs lacking real substance. It is little wonder that the walls of Consett abound with the symbols of the National Front.

Not far away is the open-air Beamish Museum. Here, linked by working trams, a small town is being constructed complete with shops, dentist's surgery, solicitor's office, pit head, miners' cottages and an old steam railway station. The whole is set as though it were still 1926, but there is no mention of the General Strike. When all the MSC seasonal labour is added in, Beamish is one of the larger employers in Durham. One contractor was paid by a government derelict land scheme to clear a tip further south in the county, and by the Beamish Museum to build it up again. With a jaundiced eye John Kearney described the place as the product of cultural vampirism: 'Objects are drained of their political and social meaning and presented as exhibits in a working-class Disneyland,' he said.

The North-east hopes to attract investment from abroad to create a new manufacturing base, and it is true that more than thirty (mainly Japanese and American) companies established a presence in the region during the 1980s. A problem, however, is that virtually no research and development or decision-making 'brains' have followed. These new factories are all assembly operations, with the machine tools almost wholly imported as well as a large proportion of the components to be assembled.

Working practices have an alien, neo-colonial character. A classic case is the Nissan car assembly plant at Washington. Inside, the atmosphere is one of regimented pressure, with men seeming to race to keep up with the energy of the robots. The Amalgamated Engineering Union, the only one operating in the plant, claims a membership of only 25 per cent amongst the 1000-plus workforce, a number that is expected to double by the early 1990s. There have been complaints about excessive line speeds, staff forced to continue during the lunch break, and attempts to buy out holidays at time-and-a-half – all, it should be said, strenuously denied by the management.

An interesting development in the North-east during the mid-1980s was the formation of the Northern Development Company, a kind of embryonic North-east (though it embraces Cumbria) Development Agency modelled on those in Wales and Scotland. An entirely regionally based initiative, it brought together the local authorities and the Northern TUC and CBI. After protracted negotiations the government was persuaded to allow the Northern Development Company to take over the North of England Development Council and its £650,000 annual budget, an organization previously appointed by Whitehall and responsible for inward investment. The total funds the Development Company could spend in the late 1980s amounted to little more than £2 million a year – a small sum when compared with the £100 million-plus a year wielded by its nearest rival, the Scottish Development Agency. In early 1988 the Northern group of Labour MPs, headed by Durham North MP Giles Radice, published a Parliamentary Bill advocating the establishment of a full-blooded Northern Development Agency, together with a directly elected Assembly for the North.

Like Scotland, the North-east has to face a southern English economy grown fat on generations of investment, both cultural and material, and continuing government-led expenditure. For instance, the £8-billion Ministry of Defence procurement budget in the mid-1980s accounted for half the output of the aerospace industry and 20 per cent of the electronics industries in Britain, and an enormous number of jobs. The regional breakdown of this spending was even more sobering: England south of that line from the Severn to the Wash accounted for 68 per cent of it (the South-west 11 per cent, East Anglia 3 per cent, and the South-east a staggering 54 per cent). The North-east had, by comparison, a miserly 2 per cent; Scotland 6 per cent; and Wales, with Northern Ireland, as usual bottom of the pile with just 1 per cent each.

It was with a prejudice engendered by these figures that we approached the South-east. Where else to begin but Cambridge, now boasting on the edge of the city a rapidly expanding Science Park complete with twenty-first-century mirror-walled buildings, all tubes and curves. Nearer the centre of the city, however, all is still reassuringly ancient, with corniced college towers, stone arches, and water lapping at the punts. Here we spoke with Raymond Williams, walking through the grounds of Jesus College, about the relationships, history and money that combine into the effortless confidence of ruling-class England. He referred to its accent: 'It became a badge not simply of power but of knowledge. There was a curious convention that to speak in that way was to know something, to be more authoritative. I think that is loosening now, but it was a very successful thing for about two hundred years and its effects still haven't gone.'

Cambridge is just one of a large number of affluent towns that ring London in an arc extending to the south coast – Stevenage, St Albans, Oxford, Maidenhead, Basingstoke, Winchester, Guildford, Crawley, Sevenoaks . . . the roll call continues, summoning up that swath of immutable blue on the electoral map. There is, however, a sense of pressure here, of green belts under threat, of agricultural land being lifted to make way for yet more Wimpey-style but expensive estates, more clean-looking factories. Basingstoke contains an extraordinary golden mile of exotic office blocks, the UK bases of high-tech household names of transnational companies. The stretch is known as Basing View. In the early 1980s the office space here doubled in five years to three million square feet. Further south the M27 between Portsmouth and Havant is an arc of growth, with more than thirty high-technology, mainly defence-contracting companies spread like beads along it, with new science and business parks, and new marinas sprouting thousands of yachts.

Closer to the heart of London we cruised in the older, more established, leafy private roads of Virginia Water and its scores of detached, impossibly priced homes hiding behind the shimmering leaves. It was here that R. W. Johnson, an Oxford political scientist who arrived at Magdalen College from Merseyside via South Africa and a Rhodes scholarship, told us a revealing story about Winston Churchill. It was to illustrate the importance of myth in sustaining a sense of national identity, not least for the dominant sensibility of England and Englishness. Churchill, it seems, in those critical months of 1940–41, was poring over the casualty lists of the Battle of Britain pilots, the young men who fell out of the sky over Kent. He complained that the public schools were poorly represented: the fallen came overwhelmingly from grammar schools located in less romantic-sounding northern towns. He was gently reminded that the boys from Harrow, Eton and Winchester tended to join their family regiments. 'This should be put right,' Churchill is reported by Lord Colville to have declaimed. And, of course, it has been, though only by folk-memory.

So we came to the centre, to London and the City. At first we could find very little to see, to film. The Big Bang had already happened, the computers had taken over: everything, it seemed, was now on the screen and not on the Floor; the Stock Exchange was like a morgue. That was, until we found LIFFE – the London Financial Futures Exchange. Here was pure capitalism in action, and colourful action at that, with barrow-boy figures (many of them actually from the East End) dressed up in red, yellow, orange and green-and-white striped jackets, falling over each other on the trading floor in their anxiety to make deals in the future notional value of currencies and commodities. Above them the time clocks of Tokyo and New York, with London's in the middle, signified the fortunate geographical position of the City in the world's daily round of trading: in the morning the East, in the evening the West, Euro-dollars in between.

'I don't think anybody really feels they're part of an English exchange,' the chairman of LIFFE, Brian Williamson told us. 'They feel part of an international exchange.' The City is separate from the rest of England, and certainly from poverty-stricken London boroughs like Brent and Hackney, in that its priorities are determined by the international market place. But its base is still the Home Counties and that intellectual triangle with Oxford and Cambridge at the two other points. Raymond Williams described Oxbridge as London's hinterland: 'In cultural terms there's this sort of back-up of Oxford and Cambridge where people come on their way to formations in London. You see them gathering into political, literary, theatrical formations here and then flying off to London – rather like geese, you know, honking all the way – and they fly along what are still relatively automatic routes to power and disposal of resources, always with those signs of authority and competence which their cultural domination gives.'

In the end, how many Englands are there? On this account, two. But then, since the time of Owain Glyndŵr it has always been a Welsh strategy to divide England this way. Recent developments, however, which are the theme of this book, suggest the old North-South cultural and economic rift is widening and that the English themselves are witnessing the birth of two countries within their own borders.

—1—

Britain – one nation?

One clear image of British identity as the twenty-first century approaches remains a Polaris submarine sailing down the Clyde towards the open sea: Her Britannic Majesty's navy still ruling the waves. A key symbol of Britishness is that the country is a nuclear power and can still in some sense retain 'a seat at the top table'.

The military image is modulated and somehow softened, however, by the attachment of royal insignia, often a royal person, to the army, navy and air force. The emblems of the Crown are important in understanding the way Britain works. In relation to the military, for instance, the monarchy provides a civil and moral authority that is not available to comparable countries. So the British military is able to project a more benign aspect than, say, the militarism or chauvinism of the German or French armed forces. The British monarch's apparently pacific, domestic and curiously non-nationalist symbolism continues to legitimate high defence expenditure and the British bomb.

At the end of the 1980s Britain was spending 5.5 per cent of its national wealth on defence, compared with 4 per cent in France, a little over 3 per cent in West Germany and just 3 per cent in Italy. Yet the standard of living in Britain was behind that of both France and West Germany and, on projected trends, threatened to fall even further in comparative terms.

Britain as a world power has been in decline for something like a hundred years. However, the decline has been relative to other countries. The British people have actually become wealthier. When Britain finally entered the European Economic Community as one of its poorer members in 1973, the mass of its people were better off than they had been in 1900 when British power and economic superiority were still pre-eminent. The hundred years' decline of Britain has been in investment and manufacturing output relative to the rest of the world. In terms of gross domestic product per head, Britain slipped from ninth place in 1961 to eighteenth in 1976 – falling behind not just the United States, Canada and Sweden, but Japan, France, Austria, Finland and Iceland as well.[1]

As the recession bit deeper in the late 1970s and early 1980s the economy was no longer merely in relative decline but actually began contracting. Mass redundancies in manufacturing industry pushed unemployment towards 20 per cent. In some areas of the country relative decline seemed to be turning into absolute decline – in parts of northern England, central Scotland and south Wales, but above all in the English inner cities where riots occurred on an unprecedented scale.

The political impact of the decline has been keenly felt. Most profound has been the break-up of the informal mixed-economy consensus on which the traditional British two-party system has rested. And accompanying the inability of successive governments to halt the economic decline has been an undermining of the authority of the State and public institutions.

The years since the early 1970s have seen a marked ideological polarization between Labour and Conservatives. During this period the Liberal, Social Democrat and nationalist parties increased their support to an extent that at times threatened the two-party system. The competence of the civil service, the impartiality of the media, the relevance of the universities, the professionalism of business, the representativeness of the trade unions, even the spirituality of the church, have all come under attack.

Finally, the unity of the United Kingdom, virtually unchallenged for two hundred years, has come into question. Though the Welsh and Scottish Nationalists have seemed to be in retreat since 1979, the underlying reason for their rise remains – the unwillingness of some in Wales and greater numbers in Scotland to permit their futures to be subordinate to a British identity. The continuing troubles in Northern Ireland tell their own story.

To understand the underlying causes of British decline it is necessary to come to terms with the British character, the British identity. For instance, it is no coincidence that the economic problems and the high defence spending of Britain go hand in hand: high defence spending and low industrial investment are closely related, and it is low investment that is at the heart of Britain's economic difficulties.

Yet what would happen if Britain were to reduce its defence expenditure to the level of, say, Germany or Italy? It would involve fundamental changes in policy, such as ending any pretence at having a world-wide navy, together with huge cuts in the equipment programme and cancelling the purchase of foreign weapons, for instance American Trident nuclear missiles.

The problem here is that to a large extent British nationalism is carried by military, and particularly naval, prowess legitimated, as stated at the outset, by royal authority. British nationalism was born in the Tudor period. It was then that England freed herself from Rome, fought off the danger of becoming a Spanish satellite, and laid the foundations for becoming the world's leading trading country. The country in question at this stage was, of course England and not Britain, though the idea of a British Empire was born in the Tudor period. England's grip on the British Isles as a whole began in this period, too, first with the incorporation of Wales in 1536, and then the troubled relations with Scotland towards the end of the century which set the stage for the Stuart accession. The eventual union of the Parliaments in 1707 can be said to have formally created the British State but it left unclear the idea of a

British nation. Certainly, the Scots never understood it to be such since they retained the foundations, if not the superstructure, of a separate national identity in their Kirk and legal system. As for the English, their conflation of England and Britain is at the core of the questions of identity explored in this book.

Meanwhile, the pattern of victory and uninhibited progress set in the Tudor period continued with the crushing of Napoleon, the imperial adventure of the Victorian era, and then in this century the epic struggles against Germany – especially World War II when 'England' once more stood alone, for a time, against superior forces. Harold Macmillan's description of the spirit of 1940 captures this central feature of the English/British character.

> Even the humblest could feel that they were taking part in the making of history. As the new Armada was being prepared against us, we seemed indeed the heirs of Queen Elizabeth and her captains. All the great figures of the past – Drake, Raleigh, Marlborough, Chatham, Wolfe, Pitt, Nelson, Wellington – seemed alive again and almost standing at our side. The unity of the nation was complete and unshakeable.[2]

Macmillan's selection of military and naval heroes as the great figures of English history is reflected in the monuments and names of buildings, streets and squares to be found in English cities. London, for instance, has Waterloo Station, Trafalgar Square and Nelson's Column; but in striking contrast with, for example, France, few prominent buildings or thoroughfares named after politicians, poets or playwrights. In the media, and in the culture generally, there is a continuous stream of material dealing with war and especially the Second World War. As well as television and film productions, focusing especially on anniversaries (Battle of Britain, D-Day), there is an enormous output of popular fiction; memoirs and diaries; military, political, and social histories; and works of military strategy and technology.

Enmeshed with this military projection of England into the world, filtered through the prism of British imperial identity, is the long evolution of Crown-centred Parliamentary institutions. In contrast with our Continental neighbours, the balance of power between Crown and Parliament was settled early on, in the seventeenth century: well before industrialization, mass democracy and the growth of modern nationalism. This set the stage for Britain's unique, by now four-century-old (1688–1988) continuity of institutions. In the final century of this saga, when the country had reached first the height and now the nadir of its power, it is the monarchy that has played a major role in ensuring stability and acting as a prime focus for British identity.

A momentary reflection on the enormous interest and attention given the monarchy by the popular press and television, let alone the continual outpouring of adulatory books and magazine articles, suggests that it must play a profound role in the people's identification. And, indeed, as Britain's place and influence in the world has declined, the monarchy has taken on an increasingly higher profile.

The sixtieth birthday celebrations of Queen Elizabeth in 1986 provided a perfect example of the royal family's role in preserving stability. Massive coverage in the press and on television came in the immediate aftermath of Mrs Thatcher's decision to let President Reagan use British bases to bomb Libya. It is not a question of royal events being deliberately arranged, as it were, to coincide with moments of crisis, but simply that the interminable round of royal family engagements – births, weddings, deaths, birthdays, visits and other events – means that at any point in the year there is usually something to hand for the media to latch on to, thereby having easily available key symbols of continuity and tradition whenever required. As Rosalind Brunt, who has made a study of this process, remarked on the coverage of the Queen's sixtieth birthday:

Once again the media took the occasion to plug the Queen's biography into key moments of national history, particularly those of the Second World War. So the images replayed: the two princesses on *Children's Hour* encouraging evacuees; the King and Queen in the blitzed East End; Elizabeth in uniform changing a wheel; the family and Churchill on the palace balcony on VE day; enter the gallant naval officer, Philip (40th anniversary of their marriage in 1987) . . . One by one the symbols of love and Britishness were dusted down and restored after Thatcher's unbearable exposure of the nation's political weakness. Our island history, reduced to the role of Yankee aircraft carrier and direct nuclear target, had been a bad dream after all. The birthday celebrations were a dramatic instance of how the monarchy has become almost the sole prop and mainstay of the national identity.[3]

When the particular nature of the survival of England's Parliamentary tradition is joined with the consciousness of an Anglo-British military and imperial extension into the world, and the whole is held in a monarchical embrace, there is a formula for a unique and powerful identity. Its essence is not a specific sense of territory, nor even a cultural sensibility (other than language); but rather an affirmation of position in the world.

This has not been a matter of dispute between the political parties. Thus, when Labour took office in 1945 its Foreign Secretary, Ernest Bevin, proclaimed that it would be a government 'at the centre of a great Empire and Commonwealth of nations which touches all parts of the world'. In 1948, speaking to the Conservative Party conference at Llandudno, Winston Churchill described the three overlapping circles of British interest: the Empire and Commonwealth that stretched round the globe; the English-speaking North Atlantic community; and a united Europe with its Mediterranean. Britain, he said, was the only country to stand at the juncture of all three spheres of interest:

We are the only country which has a great part in every one of them. We stand, in fact, at the very point of junction. And here in this Island, at the centre of the seaways and, perhaps, of the airways also, we have the opportunity of joining them together. If we rise to the occasion in the years that are to come, it may be found that once again we hold the key to opening a safe and happy future for humanity that will gain for us gratitude and fame.[4]

The same perception of spheres of influence remains to this day, with the proviso that since Britain's membership of the EEC the order of priorities had been reversed. The power the sentiment still retains can be gauged by the cross-party support for, and easy mobilization of public opinion behind, the Falklands/Malvinas adventure. In 1982, when Margaret Thatcher went to the House of Commons to announce the news of Argentina's surrender in the Falkland Islands, she told the crowd in Downing Street: 'Today has put the Great back into Britain.'

Mrs Thatcher's pursuit of the Falklands campaign, and also her rejection of post-war, 1945–79 consensus politics, rests on a construction of national identity that resonates with the pre-World War II imperial period, before Britain's decline began in earnest. It resonates, too, with World War II itself, or rather the popular memory of it as defined by Churchillian rhetoric. Thus Thatcher could refer to the Falkland Islanders as 'an island race like us' and speak of their 'British way of life'. The language used to justify the conflict, for instance in the fateful Saturday Parliamentary debate that launched the Task Force, was a straightforward reworking of Churchillian World War II oratory.

So the story starts with a British defeat: democracy is under threat from dictatorship; the 'island race' is 'standing alone' on its 'native soil' threatened by a dictator (for Hitler read Galtieri) and surrounded by 'the cruel sea'. But Britain under strong leadership 'rules the waves' and through 'courage' and 'resolution' 'we' will have victory – 'our finest hour' once again.

Anthony Barnett, author of *Iron Britannia – Why Parliament Waged its Falklands War*, described this national identity as 'Churchillism', a condition so deeply and pervasively a part of England, so natural to its political culture, that it is difficult to see, impossible to smell as something distinct. Like the oxygen in the air we breathe, and which allows flames to burn, it is extraordinarily intangible. Perhaps the Falklands crisis will at last bring the mystery to light . . .[5]

It is at this point that the dichotomy and connection between England and Britain, Englishness/Britishness should be drawn. A clear duality of identity is felt in Wales and Scotland – Welshness and Britishness, Scottishness and Britishness. But is there any sense in which the English share such a duality? Barnett says that for the English 'to be English is to be English; to be British is to be English in the world'[6].

So the English don't appear to think of England having a place in the world; their international persona is British – and, preferably, Great British. The idea has been expressed from a different angle by the Welsh historian Kenneth Morgan who said of the English: 'They are English in their culture, but British in their capacity to rule.'[7]

The English, then, rather than possessing a dual identity like the Welsh or Scottish, have a fused identity which can best be described as Anglo-British. However, Britain's long-term economic decline, coupled with forced abandonment of Empire and latterly entry into the EEC, has placed this Churchillian sense of Anglo-Britishness under great strain.

Churchillian Anglo-Britishness was born in May 1940, a formative moment for two generations in British politics, including Mrs Thatcher's. This moment saw the collapse of Chamberlain's government and the emergence, with crucial Labour support, of Churchill's wartime coalition. It saw, too, Dunkirk – the snatching of victory from the jaws of defeat – which Churchill's rhetoric moulded into a new sense of national unity. Placing the experience of April 1982 alongside that of May 1940, and comparing the effort to articulate once more the 'Dunkirk spirit', provides an effective dramatization of the strain under which contemporary Anglo-Britishness labours. As Anthony Barnett put it:

> Today Churchillism has degenerated into a chronic deformation, the sad history of contemporary Britain. It was Churchillism that dominated the House of Commons on 3 April 1982. All the essential symbols were there: an island people, the cruel seas, a British defeat, Anglo-saxon democracy challenged by a dictator, and, finally, the quintessentially Churchillian posture – we were down but we were not out. The parliamentarians of right, left and centre looked through the mists of time to the Falklands and imagined themselves to be the Grand Old Man. They were, after all, his political children and they too would put the 'Great' back into Britain.[8]

The annual event that symbolizes the military, royal and parliamentary projection of Britain as *one* nation is the Remembrance Day ceremony at the London Cenotaph with its military march-past, the royal laying of a wreath, and the presence of the leaders of the Parliamentary parties, even those from Wales, Scotland and Northern Ireland.

So when Michael Foot turned up as leader of the Labour Party at the 1981 ceremony in a donkey jacket/duffle-coat – there is uncertainty as to precisely which it was – he was destined to provoke controversy, to offend the Establishment view of what the State occasion was about. On 10 November both the *Sun* and the *Daily Telegraph* caricatured Foot as Worzel Gummidge. The *Daily Mail* presented a centrefold of Foot as a cut-out doll and offered the reader costume options (including cloth caps and CND badges): 'Dress Your Own Michael Foot', read the caption.

Foot was being lampooned not just for being slipshod and scruffy, but for in some sense representing an oppositional image to what the Cenotaph ceremony is conventionally held to be about. Whether it was actually a donkey jacket he wore – resonant of sullen proletarianism – or a duffle-coat – with its connotations of the early phase of CND – it challenged the one-nation ethos of the Cenotaph ceremony. Patrick Wright, in his book *On Living in an Old Country* (1985), defined the clash as follows:

> The Establishment mode of remembrance is both militarist and nationalist. Remembrance is a state occasion structured through regimental history and parade; retired generals and admirals speak in grave tones on the BBC World Service . . . Remembrance of this kind does not merely obliterate the 'realities' of war. Its essence lies instead in the *transfiguration* which its ceremonies bring to bear on past war, introducing order, solemnity and meaning where there was chaos, disorder and loss. Acts of commemoration *re-present* the glory of war, its transmutation of destruction into heroism and, above all, that precious sense of nationhood. In its contempt for society at peace, establishment remembrance tends to accuse the post-war present of mediocre survival, of ending up spineless and bent over a stick. These attitudes were implicit in the way the *Daily Telegraph* derided Foot as 'an old man'.
>
> In his green coat, brown shoes and plaid tie Michael Foot stood out from all this. Instead of transfiguration, Foot's image presented a spectacle of peaceful solidarity. Not the uniforms, the ranks, the regiments, nor the specious ceremoniousness: all this was antithetical to Foot who appeared – in public image if not conscious intention – to stand in homage to the ordinary, to the civilians of no particular distinction who were caught up into war, militarized and destroyed, to people whose drive generally was towards justice, socialization and democracy.[9]

In view of Michael Foot's position – standing in a long line of English radical, libertarian thought and action – his role in the Falklands/Malvinas conflict bears eloquent testimony to the power of Anglo-British nationalism to absorb and even co-opt opposition at moments of crisis. For it was Michael Foot, above all, who delivered Labour's support for Mrs Thatcher's adventure, indeed insisted upon it. His speech set the tone in the

Saturday debate in Parliament on 3 April 1982. He denounced the government for failing to be prepared and for failing to protect British people against a threat from dictatorship. The House of Commons, the country, were 'paramountly concerned', he stated:

> . . . about what we can do to protect those who rightly and naturally look to us for protection. So far they have been betrayed. The government must now prove by deeds – they will never be able to do it by words – that they are not responsible for the betrayal and cannot be faced with that charge.

This text conveys little of the atmosphere and tone of the statement, less of its emotional impact. Foot's denunciation had the ring of Henry V at Agincourt and won him cheers from the ultra-patriots on the Tory back benches. As he sat down Edward du Cann, a leading Conservative back-bencher, rose to congratulate him:

> There are times in the affairs of our nation when the House should speak with a single, united voice. This is just such a time. The Leader of the Opposition spoke for us all . . .

Later in the debate Foot was commended by the Tory MP Patrick Cormack who said that he truly 'spoke for Britain' – a fascinating echo of Leo Amery's famous parliamentary intervention on 2 September 1939, literally the eve of World War II, when he shouted across to the acting Labour leader Arthur Greenwood, after Chamberlain had failed to announce an ultimatum for war: 'Speak for England, Arthur!'

Michael Foot's dilemma perfectly illustrated the gap between 'who we are' and 'who we think we are' which afflicts all shades of political opinion caught up in the nexus of British national identity. It is the contradiction at the core of the Divided Kingdom. British national identity, resting on the three-pillar support of military-led world influence, monarchy and Parliament, emerged refashioned by the furnace of World War II and

THE REGIONAL FRAGMENTATION FOLLOWING THE 1987 GENERAL ELECTION

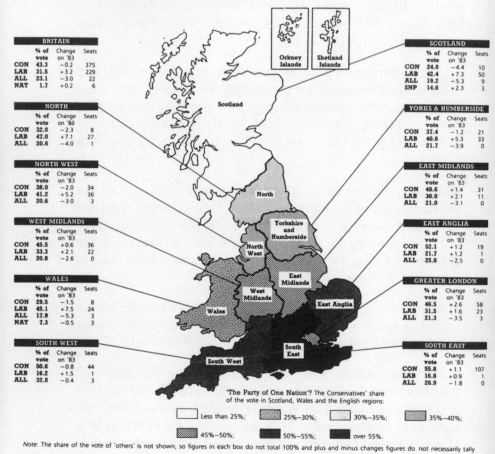

BRITAIN			
	% of vote	Change on '83	Seats
CON	43.3	−0.2	375
LAB	31.5	+3.2	229
ALL	23.1	−3.0	22
NAT	1.7	+0.2	6

NORTH			
	% of vote	Change on '83	Seats
CON	32.0	−2.3	8
LAB	47.0	+7.1	27
ALL	20.8	−4.0	1

NORTH WEST			
	% of vote	Change on '83	Seats
CON	38.0	−2.0	34
LAB	41.2	+5.2	36
ALL	20.6	−3.0	3

WEST MIDLANDS			
	% of vote	Change on '83	Seats
CON	45.5	+0.6	36
LAB	33.3	+2.1	22
ALL	20.8	−2.6	0

WALES			
	% of vote	Change on '83	Seats
CON	29.5	−1.5	8
LAB	45.1	+7.5	24
ALL	17.9	−5.3	3
NAT	7.3	−0.5	3

SOUTH WEST			
	% of vote	Change on '83	Seats
CON	50.6	−0.8	44
LAB	16.2	+1.5	1
ALL	32.8	−0.4	3

SCOTLAND			
	% of vote	Change on '83	Seats
CON	24.0	−4.4	10
LAB	42.4	+7.3	50
ALL	19.2	−5.3	9
SNP	14.0	+2.3	3

YORKS & HUMBERSIDE			
	% of vote	Change on '83	Seats
CON	37.4	−1.2	21
LAB	40.6	+5.3	33
ALL	21.7	−3.9	0

EAST MIDLANDS			
	% of vote	Change on '83	Seats
CON	48.6	+1.4	31
LAB	30.0	+2.1	11
ALL	21.0	−3.1	0

EAST ANGLIA			
	% of vote	Change on '83	Seats
CON	52.1	+1.2	19
LAB	21.7	+1.2	1
ALL	25.8	−2.5	0

GREATER LONDON			
	% of vote	Change on '83	Seats
CON	46.5	+2.6	58
LAB	31.5	+1.6	23
ALL	21.3	−3.5	3

SOUTH EAST			
	% of vote	Change on '83	Seats
CON	55.8	+1.1	107
LAB	16.8	+0.9	1
ALL	26.9	−1.8	0

'The Party of One Nation'? The Conservatives' share of the vote in Scotland, Wales and the English regions:

Less than 25%;   25%–30%;   30%–35%;   35%–40%.

45%–50%;   50%–55%;   over 55%.

Note: The share of the vote of 'others' is not shown, so figures in each box do not total 100% and plus and minus changes figures do not necessarily tally

From the *Social Studies Review*, September 1987 (Philip Allan Publishers)

remained intact until deployed once again during the Falklands crisis. There is no doubt that the enterprise was highly successful at a superficial level. The Churchillian myth caught the public imagination and propelled an audacious Mrs Thatcher through the conflict and on past the 1983 general election.

But the underlying reality is painfully different. The world, and Britain, have moved on since 1940. Relative economic decline that in the inner cities threatens to become absolute has fatally undermined Britain as a world power and is now challenging British identity itself. Reflecting on the myth and reality that have co-existed since 1940, Graham Dawson and Bob West conclude (in the British Film Institute 1984 study *National Fictions*):

All the while, the gap between 'who we are' and 'who we think we are' has steadily widened, so that in recent years 'British national identity' had taken on aspects of fantasy. Despite economic decline, the long withdrawal from Empire and a subordinate relation to the US, 'Britain' has clung to a grandiose world role. The 'White British' inherit a largely untransformed sense of superiority over the rest of the world, and racism has come home to roost. The 'United Kingdom' is held together by the army in Northern Ireland. What post-war Labour apologized for and covered up, Thatcherism now asserts. In re-attributing their former weight to those old imperial elements, it takes Britain into the realm of paranoid delusion. 'The British Nation' has never been more confused about itself.[10]

The confusion has been reflected and promoted by the increasing division of the United Kingdom electorate on territorial lines. Of course, there have always been divides in British politics relating to the separate cultures of Wales, Scotland and Northern Ireland. What is new in the modern period is the scale and growing polarity of the divide between northern and southern England. Together with the growing emergence of a separate Scottish politics, this is what presents the most likely catalyst for constitutional change to accommodate the divided nature of British society.

The Conservatives won in 1979 largely on the votes of the electorate in the southern half of England, south of the line from the Severn to the Wash. The swing to the Conservatives was highest in the southern half of England and in Wales, lowest in northern England and in Scotland. Compared with the 1955 election the party had twenty fewer seats in the North and fourteen fewer in Scotland; conversely, it had thirty-four more in the South and Midlands and five more in Wales. This concentration became even more pronounced in 1983. In the southern half of England, the Labour Party won only three seats outside Greater London, and was largely displaced as the main challenger to the Conservatives by the Alliance. The Labour vote declined least in Scotland, while the Conservative vote declined most in the North-west of England.

In the 1987 election the political separation between the North and West of Britain and the South and East was re-affirmed even more emphatically. Labour's support improved most in Scotland, Wales and parts of northern England. Elsewhere it performed disastrously. It had become a regional class party representing the traditional working class of the council estates, the public sector, industrial Scotland, Wales and the North, and the old industrial unions. It had failed to attract the affluent and expanding working class of the new estates and the new service economy of the South. It could no longer claim, in electoral terms, to be a national party in a British sense.

The Conservatives had a better claim to embrace at least the whole of England, though in Scotland its representation was reduced to an embarrassing rump, with just ten out of seventy-two MPs. In no English region, however, did the Conservatives' share of the vote fall below 32 per cent – twice that which Labour could secure in the whole of the South-east and South-west. Yet in the 1987 election the Conservatives won less than half the number of seats it had won in the larger cities in 1959, the previous period when the party had enjoyed three-figure majorities. In some northern cities decline in its support has been dramatic. In 1959 in the three cities of Glasgow, Liverpool and Manchester, the Conservatives won a total of fifteen seats. In the same three cities in 1983 they won one (in Manchester), and in 1987 none. Like Labour, the Conservatives' claim to be a British 'national' party was becoming less credible: instead, it was looking more and more like a regional class party itself, representing the middle and more affluent sections of the working class in southern England. Pondering the 1987 election results the Scottish historian Christopher Harvie reflected:

After the election results were out the term 'bloody English' was on a lot of lips in Scotland, and I found myself falling into this, probably to the concern of my English friends. 'Thatcher seemed to be hated so intensely north of the Border because she personified every quality we had always disliked in the English: snobbery, bossiness, selfishness and, by our lights, stupidity. And the English seem to have applauded her precisely for these. I sensed an ill-temper and irritation which went beyond politics; not in itself violent but the sort of atmosphere in which recourse to violence could become tolerated.

The Ulster Catholic who hates the IRA but, if he saw a boy from his community on the run from the police or army, wouldn't turn him in. This sort of thing, according to Franz Fanon, provides the 'water in which the fish swim'. Despite our deep structure of legalism, I can now see circumstances where this critical breakdown in law and order could become possible. In his book on the political psychology of the English, the French political scientist Émil Boutmy wrote that even the success of the Empire couldn't mask the lack of affection between the component nationalities of the UK. If this was the case in 1900, how much more aggravated must the situation be today? Yet hatred still presupposes some sort of relationship, and I find that in my own case, it is giving way to a cool distancing. Thatcher just doesn't represent me or my country. If the English want her, well and good. But to use her own words, she isn't 'one of us'.[11]

The growing divisions across the political landscape illuminate the central question of identity posed in this book: to what extent in the second part of the twentieth century can Britain be described as one nation? The most fervent of the British in the United Kingdom would seem to be the Northern Ireland Protestant community – but their very fervour sets them apart. Ultimately their allegiance to Britain, their 'loyalty', is conditional on the union's being maintained unsullied. The Thatcher government's attempts to mediate between the two communities in Northern Ireland through the Anglo-Irish Agreement has placed the British allegiance of the Protestant majority under enormous strain. Their dilemma was articulated by the deputy leader of the Official Unionist Party, Harold McCusker, who served a five-day jail sentence in early 1987 for refusing to pay a fine for the non-payment of his road tax, in protest against the Agreement:

> Feeling British to me is a sense of identification with the institutions, character, and history of the nation to which I belong. I have a son in the British Army, and in every generation of my family that has been the case. The symbols of my national life are Buckingham Palace, Big Ben, Westminster, Windsor Castle. I cannot rid myself of that sense of belonging, but the Anglo-Irish Agreement is trying to push me away from that. People on the mainland, who are never asked to define their Britishness, are now asking Ulstermen to abandon theirs.[12]

When the Anglo-Irish Agreement was signed in November 1985 McCusker was quoted as saying, 'I no longer feel British.' The alternative, and increasingly stronger, identity for Northern Ireland Protestants is allegiance to Ulster.

Though the Scots have a clear sense of Britishness, there is no doubt that they are Scottish first. As the political scientist Anthony Birch expressed it: 'They see themselves as Scottish first and British second, the one referring to their membership of a national society, and the other to their citizenship in a multi-national state.'[13] While Britain's imperial identity and leading position as a world power were not seriously in question the Scots found no difficulty in maintaining this duality. But the decline of Britain, which for Scotland has meant de-industrialization and mass unemployment, has changed the terms of the connection. An immediate focus has been the catastrophic run-down of the Scottish steel industry. The closure of the Gartcosh finishing plant, with the loss of 700 jobs, in March 1986, left the Ravenscraig integrated steel plant – like Gartcosh situated to the south of Glasgow – fatally exposed. Its life, and the 10,000 jobs either directly or indirectly dependent on it, has been guaranteed until the end of the 1980s, but few are sanguine about its chances beyond then. When such economic circumstances are combined with the increasing representation of Labour in Scotland in sharp contrast to its position in southern England, the recipe for instability is clear. There is a Scottish Nationalist edge to Labour's questioning the authenticity of a Conservative mandate in Scotland.

Welsh identity is more uncertain because it is so disputed and under threat. The veteran Welsh Nationalist, Gwynfor Evans, wrote in 1968: 'We Welsh are not just being denied self-expression as a nation today . . . we are fighting in the last ditch for our very identity.'[14] The struggle has produced some victories – most notably the concession of the Welsh-languge television channel, Sianel Pedwar Cymru – but more generally frustration and dissension. Frustration lies behind the campaigns by unknown groups who since 1979 have burnt down more than a hundred holiday homes, mainly in the Welsh-speaking heartlands of Dyfed and Gwynedd. Dissension accompanying an identity in retreat has also been seen in English-speaking Wales. The Welsh coal-mining valleys are arguably among the most British area in the United Kingdom. But here the consequences of the 1984–5 miners' strike are still being worked through. The solidity of the strike in south Wales was related partly to the fact that it achieved a Welsh national dimension, with miners' support groups springing up throughout Wales. However, this came as something of a discovery and was grafted on to a deeper, more traditional sense of class solidarity that is essentially British in its articulation. For the Welsh miners, loyalty to their union, even to a figure like Arthur Scargill himself, is given meaning by the British dimension, mixed in with memories of wars, Empire and depressions. According to the Welsh philosopher J. R. Jones, this duality of identity between Welshness and Britishness:

> . . . has for generations planted in the minds of the majority of people in Wales something which has sometimes been likened to schizophrenia, an uncertainty or ambiguity as to their national identity, as to who exactly, or which People, they are . . .[15]

So, for the Welsh to become aware of their separate identity they first have to come to terms with Britain and Britishness. This does not appear to be the case with the English. As has been argued, for them there is little sense of Britishness being a natural, additional, dimension beyond Englishness. But Englishness as a national identity, as a national*ism*, has traditionally been uneasy in expression. The reasons are complex and reach far back into history. Nationalism as conventionally understood is populist in the sense that it has arisen out of popular revolutions in the period of industrial growth. The classic example is the French Revolution of 1789. England's seventeenth-century revolution predated industrialization; her institutions – most notably Parliament – were in place before the evolution of mass democracy and easily adjusted to their arrival.

The consequence is that patriotism rather than nationalism has characteristically been the emotion most connected with Englishness. Nationalism is more political, associated with the idea of the People as the main constituent of the nation. In England, institutions – the monarchy and Parliament – have traditionally had a prior claim. The English – or, more strictly, Anglo-British – identity tends to be located in the rulers above rather than the People below: constitutionally, after all, there are no British people, only subjects. Moreover, as is explored in Chapter VII, the English – for geographical and historical reasons – lack the strong sense of territory that is one of the main features of conventional nationalism. Instead they tend to have the idea of a Greater England which is, at one and the same time, both narrower and wider than the England that borders on Wales and Scotland. The narrow sense of Greater England is the identity centred on the Home Counties as being quintessentially 'English' and which is discussed in Chapter VI. This is, of course, narrow only in its territorial dimension: otherwise the identity has a global, cosmopolitan reference. At the same time, the wider notion of Greater England elides into that of Britain, not to exist alongside it, but to embrace and absorb it.

Greater England is, in fact, the homeland of the fused Anglo-British identity. A. J. P. Taylor begins his *English History, 1914–1945* with a denial that the term 'British' has any meaning. It is, he says, the name of a Roman province which never included the whole of modern Scotland and which was foisted upon the English by the inhabitants of the northern kingdom as part of the parliamentary union of 1707. This perspective crosses the political spectrum, though it is seldom articulated, being most of the time an unconscious assumption. When it is deployed, its expression often takes the form of half-embarrassed self-discovery, as illustrated by this declaration from Roy Hattersley:

English is what I am . . . What inducements could possibly provoke even the thought of being anything but English? Only when such thoughts are forced into my head do I think of being English. Then I have no doubt where my love and loyalty lie . . . I do mean 'English'. My passport proclaims that I am a citizen of the United Kingdom. But that is a country which I think of as a shape on a map. I know exactly what England is . . . I can think of no other country in which I would want to live. I am simply part of the English family.[16]

One of the hallmarks of Mrs Thatcher is that she displays little reticence when articulating such feelings. A prominent Scottish Tory, once a high office bearer, recalls meeting her in the late

1970s to discuss the party's devolution difficulties in Scotland. 'I'm an English nationalist and never you forget it,' she said[17].

Mrs Thatcher's vision of England is rooted in images from the early part of this century, images that were forever captured by Noel Coward in his 1930s stage and film epic *Cavalcade*. Inspired by Coward's glimpes of an old *Illustrated London News* photograph of a troopship sailing for the Boer War, the play and the film that followed it portray a panorama of England through thirty years from 1900. The plot revolves round the fortunes of the Marryot family and their below-stairs servants – characters that were to be strongly echoed in the television series *Upstairs, Downstairs* more than forty years later. In *Cavalcade* these two families expressed qualities that Coward felt deeply were characteristic of the English – their continuity of personality and nostalgia for the past, and their tight-lipped sense of decency and fair play. Coward's final toast in the production brought all those feelings to the surface:

> Let's drink to the future of England. Let us couple the future of England with the past of England. The glories and victories and triumphs that are over, and the sorrows that are over too. Let's drink to our sons who made part of the pattern, and to our hearts that died with them. Let's drink to the spirit of gallantry and courage that made a strange heaven out of unbelievable hell, and let's drink to the hope that one day this country of ours, which we love so much, will find Dignity and Greatness and Peace again.

So it was highly revealing that this toast was quoted at some length (though not attributed to Coward) by Mrs Thatcher in her television address the night before her election as Prime Minister in 1979. She was, indeed, to pursue this yearning for greatness – so central to the character of the English – to some effect. But Mrs Thatcher was revealing more than she realized in seeing Coward's *Cavalcade* as synonymous with her England. The play was, in fact, bitterly anti-working class, identifying all that is good and patriotic with the upper-class

Marryot family, and all that is suspect and treacherous with their servants. Given this background to Mrs Thatcher's view of the kind of England/Britain she wished to restore to greatness, it was easy for her to find a major obstacle to this progress at the bottom end of society. This was identified early on, in a speech to the 1975 Conservative Party Conference, as the collectivist and corporatist trade unions and their cohorts within the Labour Party, 'that seem anxious not to overcome our economic difficulties, but to exploit them, to destroy the free enterprise society and put a Marxist system in its place'. These were the 'enemies within' which during the 1984–5 coalfields dispute were specifically targeted in the shape of Arthur Scargill and his followers in the National Union of Mineworkers:

> In the Falklands, we had to fight the enemy without. Here the enemy is within, and it is more difficult to fight, and more dangerous to liberty.[18]

The use of this term 'enemy within' which was so resented, and which even alarmed the more traditional elements within the Conservative Party itself, symbolized the divisions that the Thatcher attempt to restore England/Britain to 'greatness' provoked.

The primary focus for the divisions, however, was economic: the recession and continued decline of specific parts of the country. The plight of the inner cities, vividly illustrated by the riots of 1981 and 1985, together with the growing north/south divide – neatly defined by the line from the Wash to the Severn – have accentuated territorial as well as the class divisions of English society. The south-eastern corner of England continues with economic growth to become some kind of super-region which looks increasingly to Europe and decreasingly to the rest of the country, a trend that will be accelerated by the Channel Tunnel. By comparison, northern cities like Newcastle, Sheffield, Leeds, Bradford, Manchester, and above all Liverpool, take on the appearance of belonging to another culture. Neville Scott of the Manchester Chamber of Commerce confessed in March 1986: 'I think some of these regions in the UK do not actually feel part of the UK any more.'[19] Fred Ridley, Professor of Politics at Liverpool University, warned of a 'split kingdom as well as a split society' if the trends continued.

> The simple fact is that Liverpool's economy has collapsed. It is a disaster already and getting worse. The gulf between standards of living and life chances here and the Home Counties is now a gulf between continents . . . So far, riots have been undirected, confined to the streets where the rioters themselves lived: involving no march of destruction on public buildings or large stores in the city centre, for example. Can we be sure that they will remain localized events, hurting no one but local residents and police?[20]

It is in the increasing militarization of the police in the 1980s that the divisions in the Kingdom are most dramatically stated. Northern Ireland, of course, is an ever-present reminder. But the high profile of the police in the riots of the inner cities and their use, army style, to break the year-long miners' strike dispelled comfortable notions of a stable society. Peter Madgwick of the Oxford Polytechnic judged that if there was a constitutional crisis in Britain in the 1980s it was in the change in perception of the police by many from a benign into a hostile force.

> During the year-long miners' strike of 1984–5, the police engaged in pitched battles with strikers. The miners eventually lost, but the police were not perceived as victors. The miners lost the war, but won most of the battles, at least in the sense that they made the cost of keeping the pits open intolerably high. The police could not win, because what they had to do to win was unacceptable in the police tradition of policing.[21]

It is against this background that Anglo-British nationalism, nostalgic for past glories, should be seen. Its heaviest symbolic expression is acted out annually with the last night of the

Promenade Concerts and the singing of such songs as 'Rule Britannia' and 'Land of Hope and Glory'. These aspirations for 'greatness' and for 'a world role', the essence of British identity, still motivate much of British political life. Thus, during the 1983 general election campaign Michael Foot argued that Britain could lead the world to disarmament. In the final Conservative election broadcast, Mrs Thatcher declared: 'If only we have the wisdom and will to grasp the opportunities, Britain can become a world leader once again.' But it was the Alliance that, though in other contexts standing for reforming the constitution and modernizing Britain in a European direction, captured the straining for 'greatness' best of all. Its manifesto stated: 'We yearn for a world role and are qualified by our history and experience to perform one.' Such sentiments placed the Alliance firmly in southern English territory, and made it indistinguishable, to that extent, from the ethos of Conservatism. It helps explain why if any force broke a political mould in the 1980s, it was that of the new Right under Mrs Thatcher.

Understanding the yearning for 'a world role' that underpins the Anglo-British identity requires reference to the institutions that sustain it: primarily the monarchy and its formula of wielding power through Parliament, a formula devised in 1688 that has remained largely intact ever since. Disraeli described the operation as succinctly as has ever been done when, fortified by two bottles of brandy, he addressed the Conservative Association for three and a quarter hours at Manchester's Free Trade Hall in April 1872:

Since the settlement of (the) Constitution, now nearly two centuries ago, England has never experienced a revolution, though there is no country in which there has been so continuous and such considerable change. How is this? Because the wisdom of your forefathers placed the prize of supreme power without the sphere of human passions. Whatever the struggle of the parties, whatever the strife of factions, whatever the excitement and exaltation of the public mind, there has always been something in this country round which all classes and all parties could rally, representing the majesty of the law, the administration of justice, and involving, at the same time, the security of every man's rights and fountain of honour.[22]

It is, of course, a political fiction but nonetheless a fiction, or myth if you like, that has served better and longer than most of the myths that reside at the heart of all national identities. At the end of the twentieth century, however, the myth is looking more than a little threadbare. Reality is threatening, at last, to break through. It is true that the monarchy remains in place, if anything more omnipresent than in Disraeli's day. But virtually everything else has changed beyond recognition. Britain enters the 1990s a modest European power struggling inside the European Community to maintain equal status with France and West Germany, whose economies and standards of living have long surpassed the British level. Confronted by the Divided Kingdom, how long can the one-nation myth of British world power endure?

NOTES

1 For detailed analysis of Britain's decline see Andrew Gamble, *Britain in Decline*, Macmillan, 1985; and Alan Sked, *Britain's Decline*, Basil Blackwell, 1987.
2 Harold Macmillan, *The Blast of War*, Macmillan, 1967, p. xv.
3 Rosalind Brunt, 'Love and Britishness' in *Marxism Today*, June 1986.
4 Robert Rhodes James (ed.), *Churchill Speaks 1897–1963*, Windwood, 1981.
5 Anthony Barnett, *Iron Britannia – Why Parliament Waged its Falklands War*, Alison and Busby, 1982, p. 47.
6 Interview, March 1986.
7 Interview, March 1986.
8 Barnett, op. cit., p. 48.
9 Patrick Wright, *On Living in an Old Country*, Verso, 1985, p. 136.

10 Graham Dawson and Bob West, *National Fictions*, British Film Institute, 1984, p. 13.
11 Christopher Harvie, *Filming Scotland 2000 – A Diary*, unpublished mimeograph, 1987. See also his 'Grasping the Thistle' in Kenneth Cargill (ed.), *Scotland 2000 – Eight views on the State of the Nation*, BBC Scotland, 1987, based on the BBC Scotland TV series of the same name, broadcast in the spring of 1987.
12 *Guardian*, 13 February 1987.
13 Anthony H. Birch, *Political Integration and Disintegration in the British Isles*, Allen and Unwin, 1977, p. 99.
14 Owen Dudley Edwards et al., *Celtic Nationalism*, Routledge and Kegan Paul, 1968, p. 259.
15 J. R. Jones, 'Need The Language Divide us?', 1967 lecture translated from the Welsh in *Planet* No 49/50 January 1980, p. 29.
16 Roy Hattersley, 'My Country Right or Wrong', *Sunday Telegraph*, 4 January 1987.
17 Quoted by the *Guardian*'s political correspondent, James Naughtie (formerly with the *Scotsman*), in 'The View from the Other End of the Telescope' in *Fortnight* magazine, Belfast, November 1986. When Mrs Thatcher became leader of the Conservative Party in 1975 one of her first actions was to countermand her predecessor's commitment to the principle of an elected Assembly for Scotland. A consequence was the resignation of her two Scottish front-bench spokesmen, Alick Buchanan-Smith, the Shadow Secretary of State for Scotland, and his deputy, Malcolm Rifkind.
18 Margaret Thatcher, speech to the Conservative Backbench 1922 Committee, 20 July 1984.
19 *Financial Times*, 22 March 1986.
20 Fred Ridley, 'The Disaster that won't Stop at Liverpool', *Guardian*, 27 September 1985. See also his 'The Government of Divide and Rule', *Guardian*, 22 November 1985.
21 Peter Madgwick, 'The United Kingdom in Face of Regional and Communal Cultures', mimeographed paper, January 1986.
22 Quoted in G. E. Buckle, *The Life of Benjamin Disraeli, Earl of Beaconsfield*, Vol. V, London, John Murray, 1920, p. 187.

—2—

Identity in doubt – the North

During a tour of the North-east in September 1985 Mrs Thatcher gave an impromptu film interview in a windswept shipyard at Wallsend. A local television reporter asked her:

Prime Minister, there is an impression abroad that you don't care about us – indeed you have forgotten about us. People want to know why you're not meeting the unemployed?

Mrs Thatcher gave a deep sigh, wagged her finger, and responded:

Well look, I can't do everything. Isn't it important for me to go around to show the success of the North-east . . . Why don't you, instead of asking me questions, 'Oh, are they going to get any more orders . . . Oh, there are a lot of unemployed here' . . . Why don't you say, 'Look, 80 per cent are in work'? Yes, we have to try to get work for the 20 per cent, but some of the work being done here is fantastically successful.

Don't you think that's the way to persuade more companies to come to this region and get more jobs for the people who are unemployed – not always standing there as moaning minnies? Now stop it![1]

These remarks provoked a furore, with newspaper headlines about the Prime Minister attacking people in the North as 'moaning minnies'. The wider context of her outburst was a plea for the region to present a more positive image: at a private meeting with business and council leaders in Durham she went further and urged the region to present a united front and speak with one voice. Within six months, however, came an announcement of a further 3,000 redundancies in the North-east's shipbuilding industry, virtually bringing it to an end. It was the last of the region's three basic industries to go in a single decade: first steel, then coal, and then shipbuilding. The job losses in these three sectors in the decade to 1986 are worth quoting:

	Number Employed	
	1976	1986
Steel	26,000	7,438
Coal	22,900	13,000
Shipbuilding	31,100	1,200

The catastrophic decline in the North-east's shipbuilding industry was made the more poignant by the boom in pleasure-boat building in southern England. In 1986 there were some 500 yards building pleasure boats – the vast majority in the South – turning out 54,970 craft a year, 25 per cent more than in 1981. No one knows exactly how many people are employed in the industry, but it is at least as many the 90,000 or so who build merchant ships.[2]

Typical is the small Sadler's boatyard at Poole in Dorset. As the owner, Martin Sadler, said, 'A boatyard can be anywhere these days, so long as it is south of Watford.' Fibreglass yachts, like the ones his firm makes, weigh very little, so when they are finished they can be easily trailered down to the nearest marina. During the mid-1980s Sadler's opened a new factory, increased its workforce from sixty to ninety, and boosted production by 60 per cent.

The men were non-unionized – there were no demarcation lines – they worked a great deal of overtime, and took home an average of more than £200 a week. The gulf between the declining shipyards of the North and the booming boatyards of the South serves as a metaphor for industrial history in Britain since World War II: the shift of industry from North to South; the change from basic industries to service and leisure industries; and the replacement of skilled union labour by semi-skilled, highly paid, but highly insecure workers.

In 1985 Newcastle University's Centre for Urban and Regional Studies surveyed the country 'In Search of Britain's Booming Towns'[3]. The study compiled a list of 280 towns, establishing their local economic performance on the basis of unemployment rate; percentage rate of change in employment 1971–81; percentage change population 1971–81; and number of households with two cars. On this basis the top six towns were all in the South-east (indeed, with only Aberdeen being a blip – for oil reasons – at number 19, the first northern town on the list is at number 39, Harrogate):

1 *Winchester*
2 Horsham
3 Bracknell
4 Milton Keynes
5 Maidenhead
6 Basingstoke

And apart from one Scottish entry, all bottom six towns are in the North-east:

275 Sunderland
276 Hartlepool
277 Coatbridge and Airdrie
278 South Shields
279 Mexborough
280 *Consett*

The closure of Consett's steelworks in September 1980, putting 3,700 out of work, thrust the town down to the bottom of the list. By the mid-1980s unemployment there was hovering around 25 per cent with some 6,000 men in the area chasing just a handful of jobs. Only 11 per cent of the town's households had two cars.

In Winchester 25 per cent of the households had two cars and unemployment was the lowest in Britain, at around 5 per cent. There were two jobs for every three people in the city (population 32,000) against a British average of two jobs for five people. The town's chief executive, David Cowan, said they had to fight off development proposals: demand for office space soared in 1985 with the opening of the M3 link to London.

It is, of course, true that the divisions in prosperity are more complicated than that simply defined by a line drawn from the Severn to the Wash. Class divisions between the wealthy and less well-off apply just as vividly in North-west Britain as in the South-east. The briefest of visits to the more affluent suburbs of Newcastle, north Leeds or the Manchester stockbroker belt of north Cheshire would confirm that. Taken overall, however, the economic indicators demonstrate a widening gap between North and South. The clearest and most undeniable evidence is house prices. During the mid-1980s these were rising by some 20 per cent a year in London, 14 per cent in the South-east, but just 6 per cent in the Midlands and only between 1 and 2 per cent in the North of England. The figures illustrate the magnitude of the problem facing workers wishing to move to areas where job prospects are better. The money from selling a large detached house in the North would fall far short of buying even a low-priced terraced home in London. The price gap also hits mobility in the other direction. Many people are reluctant to move North for fear they will not be able to return South at a later date without a sharp drop in their standard of housing.

Unemployment is another sure indicator of relative wealth, and the differences between North and South are again undeniable. A major article in the *Sunday Times* in early 1987 attempted to argue that the line drawn from the Severn to the Wash is 'a false frontier'. It quoted John Hall, director of Newcastle's £180-million Metrocentre, a shopping complex

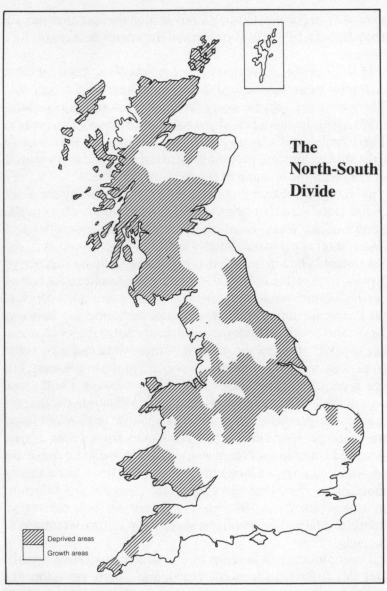

The
North-South
Divide

Deprived areas
Growth areas

The North-South divide, as defined by the Institute for Employment Research at Warwick University. Note that their map does not include Northern Ireland, though undoubtedly this would be classified as 'deprived'.

opened in the mid-1980s and attracting 300,000 customers a week. The North-east, he said, was not a depressed area:

It is one of the old industrial areas. Therefore it has suffered as the heavy, smoke-stack industries like steel, coal and shipbuilding have declined. Yet here, where we are nearing the end of that period of decline, we still have 82 per cent of the population in work. That, I think, is a success story in itself.[4]

The problem with this kind of analysis is that there are few signs of unemployment levels in North-west Britain being reduced, even as the overall economy recovers. New investment more often than not entails fewer jobs. The same article quoted Department of Employment statistics which showed that of the 2 million jobs lost between June 1979 and June 1986, 94 per cent had been in Scotland, the North, the Midlands, Wales and Northern Ireland. What was equally as significant was the experience of the South-east during this six-year period. During the first three years, between 1979 and 1983, the South-east suffered some 30 per cent of the overall job losses, a proportion not far out of line with its relative share of population. However, in the second three-year period, from 1983 to 1986, the region went on to win some 400,000 new jobs, mainly in sectors like banking, finance and tourism. This was a quite disproportionate 78 per cent slice of the job gains made by the whole country during that period.

In early 1988 a report by the Institute for Employment Research at Warwick University predicted that the North/South divide was likely to worsen, since the fastest-growing areas were all in the South-east, around London, with the slowest growing in the North[5]. The report assessed the economic prosperity and dynamism of 280 local labour markets in Britain and found the top performing areas in a crescent around London—Milton Keynes, Newbury, Didcot, Welwyn, Aldershot and Farnborough, Cambridge, Huntingdon, Hertford and Ware, Basingstoke, and Woking and Weybridge. The South-east has become, in fact, a super-region. In an arc curving south-west from Cambridge through Bristol to Southampton have concentrated the newer and expanding industries: electronics, scientific instruments, computer software, and the high technology and information industries generally. Punched through the arc the M4 motorway has created a 'silicon western corridor' along which are dotted prosperous market towns like Newbury, Hungerford, Maidenhead, Wokingham and further west, Swindon and Bristol. Similarly the M3 through Basingstoke and Winchester to Southampton, linking eastwards via the M27 with Portsmouth and Havant, provides another corridor of high technology, mostly defence-related industries.

In sharp contrast to the M4 and M3, the M62 motorway linking Liverpool with Hull – Merseyside to the Humber – has proved to be a ribbon of depression. In one sense the M62 marks the boundary of the North, the towns along its route having Rugby League and unemployment as the main badges of their identity – Oldham, Rochdale and Bolton in Lancashire; Brighouse, Dewsbury and Halifax in Yorkshire. Nick Garnett, Northern Correspondent of the *Financial Times* for most of the 1980s, says that unemployment and decline are giving the North a greater sense of a local identity than of being English:

Among common themes in the North is the way investment in big single projects results in such feeble spin-offs in the local economy. Michael Heseltine pointed out on television how the Government has helped East London pick up its economic bootstraps. But that is where investment capital wants to go. It does not want to go to the North. The Merseyside Development Corporation which Mr Heseltine instigated when Environment Secretary after the 1981 riots, has beavered away for more than four years. A lovely waterfront is in the making but there is little sign that this will provide the economic catalyst for that sad city.

The fine Metro light railway in Newcastle has helped generate a mini boom of shopping and chintzy nightspots in the Tyne city. The regional economy though is so feeble that you can see the lifeblood draining away from its weaker neighbours like North Shields which struggle along the river.[6]

But where exactly is the North? Viewed from London the answer might be, 'Anywhere north of Watford.' And in the recession-hit Britain of the 1980s it does seem the northern boundary is creeping southwards from the line described by the M62 motorway to embrace more and more of the previously prosperous Midlands. A more accurate definition, as stated in Chapter I, would be a boundary stretching from the Severn to the Wash: by 1986 unemployment was 60 per cent higher to the north of this line than to the south.

The North/South Divide along the Severn-Wash axis is underpinned by massive government-led expenditure in Ministry of Defence research establishments and weapons manufacture. This has more than offset regional development policies in the North, which have declined in the 1980s in any event: by 1987 expenditure on regional policy was 50 per cent down on its 1982 level, while Defence expenditure increased by nearly 30 per cent between 1979 and 1986. The equipment budget of the Ministry of Defence alone amounted to some £8.3 billion in 1985–86. And as the table and map on pages 52–3 demonstrate, regional beneficiaries of Defence spending are the South-east and South-west. The Ministry of Defence budget is, in effect, an unofficial regional policy.

Moreover, the operation of this unofficial policy has a crucial spin-off in the research and development field which, again, is concentrated overwhelmingly south of the Severn-Wash line. Government figures show that 55 per cent of government research and development expenditure was devoted in 1987 to Defence. More than half (54 per cent) of government research development establishments are located in the South-east. Where the government goes others follow: the South-east accounts for 45 per cent of private company research and development establishments, 77 per cent of other private research and development establishments, and 43 per cent of

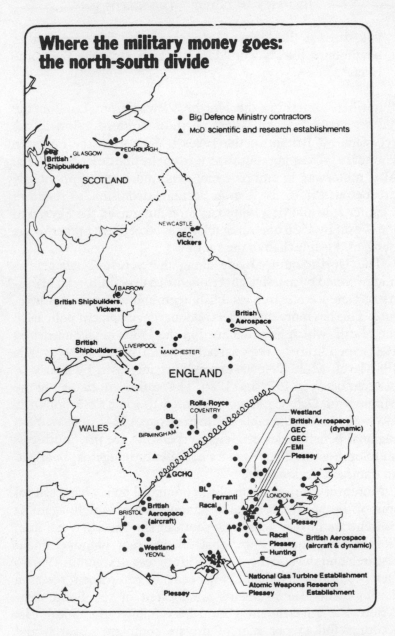

Where the military money goes: the north-south divide

● Big Defence Ministry contractors
▲ MoD scientific and research establishments

GLASGOW EDINBURGH
British Shipbuilders
SCOTLAND

NEWCASTLE
GEC, Vickers

BARROW
British Shipbuilders, Vickers

British Aerospace

British Shipbuilders LIVERPOOL MANCHESTER

ENGLAND

Rolls-Royce
COVENTRY

BL
BIRMINGHAM

WALES

Westland
British Aerospace (dynamic)
GEC
GEC
EMI
Plessey

GCHQ

BL Ferranti

British Aerospace (aircraft) BRISTOL Racal LONDON

Plessey

Racal
Plessey British Aerospace (aircraft & dynamic)
Hunting

Westland
YEOVIL

National Gas Turbine Establishment
Atomic Weapons Research
Plessey Plessey Establishment

From 'The Money Map of Defence' by James Simmie and Nicholas James, *New Society*, 31 January 1986.

Where the military money went 1983/84

	Expenditure (£M)	% total
South-east	3747	54
South-west	763	11
East Anglia	208	3
East Midlands	346	5
West Midlands	278	4
North-west	763	11
Yorks/Humberside	139	2
Northern	139	2
Scotland	416	6
Wales	69	1
Northern Ireland	69	1
	6939	100

the research associations.[7] Hardly surprising, then, that the South-east has an above-average proportion of innovative industry and generally has a greater capacity to generate new firms.

The South-east and its 'sunbelt triangle' pushing out to an apex at Bristol from Cambridge in the north and Southampton in the south, has acquired a huge comparative advantage for advanced technology sectors, particularly in the electronics industry. The South-east alone accounts for more than 50 per cent of UK employment in the electronics industry. There is a sense in which this region is becoming ever more detached from the rest of Britain, operating in world terms as a financial and commercial centre and from the 1990s to be attached to Europe by the umbilical cord of the Channel Tunnel, whose construction will itself generate enormous growth. The Professor of Politics at Liverpool University, Fred Ridley, says that with the Channel Tunnel the day is not too far away when the South-east of England will have more in common with northern France than northern England.

City of London financiers, whose outlook is international, now invest more abroad than at home. The North is not just a foreign country to them socially, but a country of less interest commercially than Europe and the USA.

If prosperity is concentrated in the South-east then economic power is concentrated even more dramatically in London. What is left of Liverpool's manufacturing industry is dominated by companies with headquarters in London or abroad. As the avalanche of take-over bids continues and business becomes ever more concentrated in multi-nationals, decisions about new investment are increasingly taken outside the North – as are decisions about factory closures.

These decisions, called rationalization, are based on international considerations and reflect little concern about the fate of Northern towns, since the decision-makers themselves have no stake in life there. We are as much at the mercy of 'foreigners' in the North as any colonial territory.[8]

A problem the North has in coming to terms with these realities is that its sense of separate identity has rarely been articulated in positive terms. Rather, Northerners have usually defined themselves against the South. This was picked up by Graham Turner in his book *The North Country* (1967):

> North versus South seemed much too simple an antithesis, even if anybody had ever taken the trouble to decide exactly where the Midlands came into it. Yet all over the North, I came across instances of the powerful animus which the South or Southern attitudes provoked. There was this man from Batley who pictured the North as a fat and generous sow lying on her side while the greedy piglets (the South) fed off her. There were novelists like Stan Barstow and Sid Chaplin who told me how much they resented constantly being asked *why* they chose to live in the North, as if they were displaying some deplorable eccentricity. There were the civic dignitaries in the North-east who exploded with passion against the Establishment and all its works and who told me that there would be a 'bloody uprising' if 'they' again left the area helpless under the impact of another slump . . .
>
> Here, plainly, were two separate worlds, two different philosophies of life. This was a place beyond the London–Birmingham axis of prosperity, a place with a keen sense of its own identity and its own unique heritage: a place, too, where the hurts of history still had a sting in them.[9]

This last statement, from the perspective of the late 1980s, had a prophetic as well as an historical edge. The 1984–5 miners' strike and subsequent split within the NUM was to a great extent explainable in North/South terms, and symbolized by Arthur Scargill's withdrawal of the NUM headquarters from London to Sheffield. For most of this century the North Yorkshire and Northumberland and Durham coalfields have had a large number of loss-making pits. In the late 1950s and 1960s the NCB operated a transfer scheme under which miners could move to profitable and expanding coalfields, notably in

Nottinghamshire and elsewhere in the East Midlands. Inevitably, the more enterprising, imaginative and younger miners moved; left behind were those who were less enterprising, less imaginative, and older. This was at least part of the background to the bitterness and tragedy of the 1984–5 mining dispute – a kind of civil war fought across the no-man's-land territory of the Yorkshire-Nottingham boundary, one border between North and South England. Following the strike it was no surprise that the Nottinghamshire miners formed the breakaway Union of Democratic Miners – they had already done something similar with the Spencer Union after 1926.

For the North of England the 1984–5 strike was a pivotal moment. Coming on top of the recession it persuaded the more thoughtful of local leaders that the Northern sense of identity would need to be mobilized more positively if the spiral of decline was to be reversed. Two further developments strengthened this view: the virtual abandonment of traditional regional policy since 1979 and, in 1986, the abolition of the Metropolitan counties which left the North bereft of institutions able to operate and plan at a regional, strategic level.

On regional economic policy the maps on page 57 tell the story. The Assisted Areas taken over by the incoming Conservative government in June 1979 conform almost precisely with upland Britain and take in the whole of the North of England. The erosion of these Areas through 1982 and 1984 was fully reflected in the expenditure figures. Spending on regional aid halved between 1979 and 1986, cut by £1,000 million, and halved again by 1989.

In January 1988 there was a further shake-up in the way regional aid for the Assisted Areas was administered. The Areas themselves remained the same as in 1984, but henceforth development grants awarded in them would not be automatic and be administered according to laid-down criteria. Instead, the grants would be paid out entirely at the discretion of civil servants at the Department of Trade and Industry. This shift towards discretion, really a euphemism for 'picking winners', was likely to dissuade many companies from even considering a

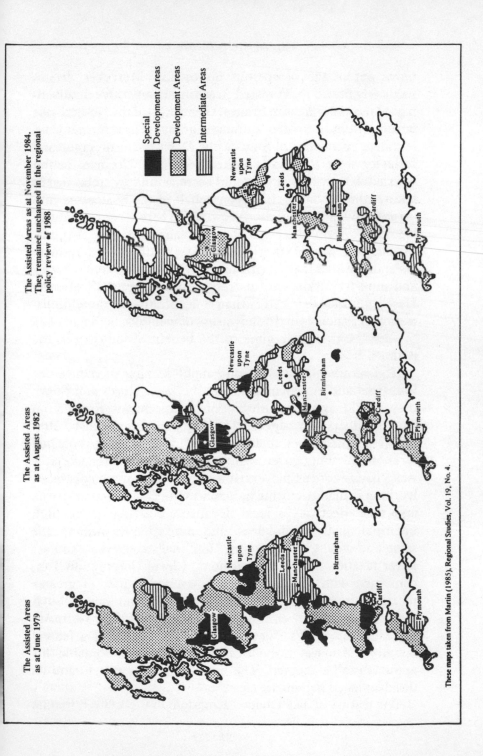

The Assisted Areas
as at June 1979

The Assisted Areas
as at August 1982

The Assisted Areas as at November 1984.
They remained unchanged in the regional
policy review of 1988

Special
Development Areas

Development Areas

Intermediate Areas

Newcastle
upon
Tyne

Glasgow

Leeds

Manchester

Birmingham

Cardiff

Plymouth

These maps taken from Martin (1985), Regional Studies, Vol. 19, No. 4.

move out of the prosperous South-east. Moreover, it immediately placed the Assisted Areas in a competitive disadvantage with similar areas in France, Germany and the Netherlands which continued to offer automatic grants. Three former Conservative Secretaries of State at the Department of Trade and Industry were sceptical about the change. Norman Tebbit worried that civil servants would become 'unduly embroiled in taking commercial decisions on behalf of the businesses concerned'. Leon Brittan observed that, 'There were real advantages in a system whereby a businessman could know that if he satisfied the published criteria he was entitled as of right to assistance rather than having to go cap in hand to civil servants and ministers asking for discretion to be exercised.' Michael Heseltine urged that, rather than concentrating on the administration of regional aid, the government would be better advised to vary the taxation regime to the benefit of industry in the regions.[10]

If governments were serious about seeking to reduce the industrial and employment divide between North and South they would apply non-discretionary incentives focused on labour rather than capital. The Regional Employment Premium, adopted by a Labour government in 1967 but abolished by another Labour government in 1976, was a good example. It was a payment to employers (initially £1.50p per man per week working in manufacturing industry in the Development Areas) and was effectively a local devaluation in regions of high unemployment. A more direct and more effective means to the same end would be to take up Heseltine's suggestion and set lower taxation rates for the regions. Lower Corporation Tax, combined with differential VAT, even the offer of greater mortgage-interest relief, would have a profound impact. Such mechanisms have been used to good effect in West Germany since the late 1940s. West Germany, of course, is a federal country and so has the political mechanisms which enable this approach to be adopted. The implications for Britain and its disadvantaged regions are clear.

One feature of The Divided Kingdom in the 1980s is that its

disadvantaged areas have been increasing. What is highly significant about the November 1984 Assisted Areas map on p. 57 is that for the first time it includes the West Midlands, centring on Birmingham. Until the mid-1970s this was the powerhouse of industrial England, enjoying the highest level of GDP and income per head of any region after London and the South-east. It had experienced thirty years of uninterrupted growth. Then the recession struck. Between 1978 and 1983 Wolverhampton lost 36 per cent of its jobs in metal manufacturing and transport engineering, 29 per cent in construction, 38 per cent in mechanical and instrument engineering, and 59 per cent in electrical engineering. And unemployment climbed remorselessly upwards from 6.8 per cent in 1979 to 18.5 per cent in November 1985. In a forecast commissioned in 1985 by the West Midlands Metropolitan Council, Cambridge Econometrics predicted that while present policies operate, the region will lose another 30 per cent of its manufacturing jobs by the end of the century[11].

Meanwhile, the economy of the South-east continues to be heavily subsidized by public expenditure – the high technology element of Defence spending, government research laboratories, mortgage tax relief, commuter subsidies to British Rail, and the expansion of London's airports, to name the most outstanding. This imbalance between public expenditure and the prosperity of the South and relative decline in public expenditure and the impoverishment in the North suggests that politics rather than economics are at the core of the disparity. The regional problem strikes right at the heart of the way in which Britain is governed.

The fact of the matter is that the old regional economic incentives, designed to attract theoretically footloose industry, are no longer an answer to the North's structural problem of unemployment. The economic activities for which demand is increasing – notably in research and development, business services, high technology – require high educational and professional qualifications: the rate of innovation, and ultimately of economic growth, depends crucially on the presence of such highly qualified manpower. Yet in Britain such highly qualified manpower and technological innovation are both heavily concentrated in an arc extending about 100 miles around London. In the Winchester area, for instance, a quarter of the population have a degree or higher educational qualification – more than double the figure for the North.

This concentration lies at the heart of the emerging regional problem of the 1980s and 1990s. The centrally directed, manufacturing-orientated policies which worked relatively well in the 1960s and early 1970s offer no answer to it. Rather, there is increasing evidence that the problem can only be solved by raising the level of decision-making in the regions where innovation, research and development, and highly-qualified manpower are lacking.

And the obvious way of achieving this is to devolve more central-government functions to the regions. If this were accompanied by devolution of political control as well, then there would be the basis for establishing a counter-weight to the pull of the South. The arguments have been well articulated in a pamphlet published by the North of England Regional Consortium of Local Authorities, written by the Professor of Geography at the University of Manchester, Brian Robson. In it he argues that the social injustice of the North/South divide should be made an all-party priority –

. . . and not a shuttle-cock to be swept to and fro across the net of the Severn-Wash divide by two teams neither of which understands the rules of the game nor has much skill at playing it. The central planning necessary in any policy of positive discrimination should involve a commitment of money over a period of years that cannot be cut back or diverted and a willingness to devolve the administration of such money to those who live and work in the North. A strong regional body allotted a generous sum of money over a period of years would be the first necessity . . .

Now is the opportunity for a firm commitment to regional government, well-funded and independent of London. Let the North be given the opportunity to try to save itself through a positive act of generosity on the part of central government and all those who grow rich and fat in its immediate environs . . .[12]

Viewed from the centre, however, there is a reluctance to perceive the economic disparities between North and South in regional terms, let alone to concede the case for some form of regional government. During the mid 1980s there was a debate within the Conservative government along these lines, with reports that ministers were thinking in terms of establishing development agencies for the English regions. A speech in favour of this policy was made by the former Trade and Industry Minister, Leon Brittan, a Yorkshire MP, in 1986.

I have always believed that the gulf between different parts of the country is unjust and divisive . . . The time has come when we should look urgently at the possibility of setting up development agencies for some of the English regions that would be comparable to the Scottish Development Agency . . .[13]

Whitehall and ministers actually in power invariably see such concessions to the regional lobby as a threat to their centralized power. So instead of development agencies organized along regional lines, the government in 1987, following the general election, redefined the issue as being an inner-city problem. The response was to establish Urban Development Corporations aimed at regenerating relatively small inner-city areas, organizations that by their very nature would not act as a focus for any kind of political mobilization.

At the same time, however, a regional development response was emerging as a result of the initiative of local government in the North: a Northern Development Company in the Northeast was set up by a consortium of local authorities, together with the Northern TUC and CBI, as were regional enterprise boards in Lancashire, Merseyside, West Yorkshire, and the

West Midlands. Chairman of the Yorkshire Enterprise Board is John Gunnell, who led the campaign in the early 1980s against the abolition of the Metropolitan County Councils. He believes their going left a vacuum that eventually will have to be filled by a new tier of regional government, one that will be shaped by the economic demands of the North. In his 1986 annual report he declared:

> We very much need a new regional policy from central government which focuses not only on providing money but on stimulating mechanisms for job creation within the regions . . . Regrettably we still see measures which are effectively creating two nations. New policies must be framed, specifically aimed at eroding that divide.[14]

The West Midlands Enterprise Board was also set up in 1982, and with the same aim of plugging an investment gap in manufacturing industry left vacant by the City of London. The chairman of the Board, Geoff Edge, accuses the established banking system of an investment strike against the regions.

> The merchant banks and the City generally are not interested in unsecured equity finance. They only go into a project if they can see their way out of it within five years. Yet the only way our manufacturing base can be restructured is by the injection of equity capital in return for share issues.
> This is something very difficult to undertake centrally. It requires the detailed knowledge and commitment that can best be mobilized at the regional level. Yet we don't have a significant regional banking sector in Britain. This is the reason why the regional enterprise boards have developed – to provide a framework for the public sector to co-operate with the private sector in investing in locally based companies on commercial terms.[15]

By 1986 the West Midlands Enterprise Board had invested some £9 million in thirty companies, with employees ranging in number from fifty to a thousand, making goods varying from bricks to clothes and engineering products. As well as providing equity capital the Board gives help with marketing, accountancy and stock-taking. The abolition of the West Midlands County Council created a problem of democratic accountability and impetus. Control was transferred to the seven districts that operated within it, and the county and the shire counties surrounding them – Warwickshire, Staffordshire and Shropshire – became involved as well. But Geoff Edge sees this as a temporary phase.

> Joint control causes real political problems. The logical end point is for control to be transferred to an elected regional Assembly, which would also take over responsibility for the health service and strategic economic and environmental planning at the regional level.[16]

The most consciously political of the new bodies, in that it sees itself as an embryonic Development Agency along the lines of the Scottish and Welsh Development Agencies, is the Northern Development Company. But just to make the comparison is to state how far the Northern Development Company is from achieving comparable status. In 1987 its budget, including grants from central government, was £2.2 million; the Scottish Development Agency's budget was more than £100 million. Moreover, the Scottish Development Agency operates in an entirely different context, as is conceded by two commentators in the *Northern Economic Review*:

> The North-east may have the most developed sense of regional identity in England but Scotland is a *nation* . . . Whilst there are different interpretations of Scotland as a political entity, few would question the distinctiveness of Scottish institutions and interest relationships reflecting the sense of national identity. A recent opinion survey found that 70 per cent of the population identified themselves as Scottish before classifying themselves as British . . .

This identity is critically reinforced by a complex of social and political institutions which either do not exist in the English regions, or if they do, lack the same autonomy from the centre. Scotland has its own distinctive educational, legal and religious institutions which not only bind it together as a nation but have consequences in terms of delegated policy making. The North-east, no matter how well developed its sense of identity, cannot lay claim to such a range of institutions.[17]

The primary Scottish institution in this respect is the Scottish Office and its Secretary of State with a seat in the British Cabinet. There is a growing awareness that if the 'North' is to achieve anything like comparable status with Scotland then it must have something similar. Thus, a policy of the Northern Regional Councils' Association, representing twenty-nine local authorities in Cumbria, Northumberland, Tyne and Wear, County Durham and Cleveland, is for the appointment of a Minister for the North, with a seat in the Cabinet. The Association is one of the co-sponsors of the Northern Development Company whose prime moving force was the former chief executive of the Tyne and Wear Metropolitan County (before its abolition), Jim Gardner. He sees the Company as a first step towards the creation of more integrated institutions: 'There will have to be a regional tier of government here within five to ten years,' he said, speaking in early 1986.[18]

In January 1988 the Northern group of Labour MPs, headed by Giles Radice, MP for Durham North, published a Bill in the House of Commons canvassing the need for a Northern Regional Assembly and a Northern Development Agency. This was published at the same time as the Scottish group of Labour MPs presented a Bill for a Scottish Assembly and signalled a new era of co-operation between the two groups. In the 1970s Northern MPs had vigorously opposed Scottish devolution, fearing it would give Scotland an unfair advantage in the distribution of Treasury resources within the United Kingdom.

But in November 1987 the Scottish and Northern Labour groups met at Carlisle and hammered out a joint approach, putting down a marker for future development of policy within the Labour Movement. Between them the two groups had seventy-five MPs following the 1987 general election, making them a powerful bloc within the Labour Parliamentary Party. Jack Thompson, MP for Wansbeck, was quoted after the Carlisle meeting:

> We are supporting the Scots in their devolution bill and they are supporting our calls for regional government. Some years ago it was felt Scottish devolution would be to our disadvantage. Now we are not moving against each other – we are moving in the same direction. Scottish devolution with some sort of regional government in the North would be like for like. We want more than a Development Agency for the North, though that is important. We need a democratic forum as well.[19]

Such statements of aspiration are a first step, but there are formidable difficulties. The Northern Group of Labour MPs represent constituencies in the North-east, Northumberland and Durham. If their plans were to approach political reality, other areas in northern England would undoubtedly demand equality of treatment, and no doubt attempt to block proposals that were just for the North-east in the same way that North-eastern MPs frustrated Scottish plans in the 1970s. It raises the question, 'Where is the North?' During the 1970s there existed, briefly, an organization called the Campaign for the North, an all-party grouping of mainly Liberal and Labour politicians. It was designed as a pressure group rather than a political party, but nevertheless its primary focus was an attempt at political and cultural mobilization. Its failure to take root and continue to exist in the 1980s reflected the lack of a coherent cultural, let alone political, basis for a Northern identity, even of an oppositional kind. One element was the Campaign for the North's failure to define where the North began and ended, whether it should be regarded as a single entity or whether it should be divided into three – the North-east and Cumbria, Yorkshire and Humberside, Manchester and Merseyside. And what about the Midlands?

A second obstacle was the very decline of the North's industrial infrastructure. What still gives the North its self-image is the kind of sturdy self-reliance that comes from making a living from farming, fishing, coal-ming, steel-making and shipbuilding. With so much of Northern identification dependent on a work culture that is fast disappearing, what is there left to hang on to? The manufacturing assembly plants, often foreign-owned, that have to some extent compensated for job-losses in the older industries do not offer an easy answer. Writing about the experience of making three television films about Komatsu, one of seventeen Japanese firms that have put down roots in the North-east (with more on the way), Debbie Christie, a BBC producer, observed:

The Japanese speak of the local workforce with some warmth, but they also use a vocabulary that uncannily echoes British colonialism. They describe British companies as 'primitive', and they are baffled by what they see as sloppy attitudes . . .

One year into the new venture, there are obvious signs of the Japanese ideology in practice in Komatsu's factory. Every morning all the employees line up in rows to exercise for five minutes, unpaid, before works starts. Workers and managers all wear identical blue 'equal status' uniforms. Suggestion groups and consultation are encouraged at all levels. But the Geordies are having to look very closely at exactly what they are being offered. The conflict-free approach is centred on an advisory council that meets once a month. It is the only forum for grumbles and complaints, and managers and elected representatives of the workers sit round a circular table to talk through a wide-ranging agenda. But at a moment when a discussion over tea-breaks turns into an argument, managers and workers slip back into their traditional roles, and it is at that point that the workforce realize that while this forum might give them some influence, it certainly doesn't give them the power or protection of a trade union.[20]

There are more signs of a colonized culture in the significant number of men from the North-east – skilled, for the most part, steel erectors, electricians and fitters – who now earn a living as migrant workers. These men, often made redundant as a result of steel or mine closures, sell their skills in southern England, most commonly in the construction industry, and increasingly across Europe and beyond. This development in the history of the region is caught in the shift of television serials about the area from *The Likely Lads* to *Whatever Happened to the Likely Lads* to *Auf Wiedersehen, Pet*. The most pervasive television image of Northern identity, however, is the long-running soap opera *Coronation Street*. Like its main competing, and southern, serial *EastEnders*, *Coronation Street* is about working-class culture and is also marked by the presence of strong and positive female characters. But there the similarities end. *Coronation Street* is devoid of substantive political or even social issues, and, moreover, there is an almost total absence of a sense of work or the workplace as a background. Instead, there is an almost total concentration on relationships in the home and community life of the working class. In a kind of reflection of the North and Northern identity, *Coronation Street* represents a depoliticization of its culture.

Image in a more general sense is a problem the North has when projecting itself to the South of England, let alone the rest of the world, in its efforts to promote capital investment. An acutely embarrassing instance was the resignation of the chief executive of the Northern Development Company, Martin Easteal, after only five months in post in 1987. His family had been unable to settle in the North-east from Harlow in the South-east. The affair produced damaging headlines such as 'Mr North fails to persuade Mrs South'. The Northern Development Company's response was to make declarations about the possibilities of the North acting more autonomously and in a European context. Dr Andrew Robinson, the Company's head of corporate affairs, remarked:

Our model is the Scottish Development Agency and certain European regions such as Grenoble, Turin, Catalonia, Baden-Wurttemberg – all areas of potential and growth we can learn from. We have been taking a lead in conceptualising where we should be going. Most European countries are organised on regional lines, and the regions compete against each other. They can teach us a lot.[21]

However, the key images of the North – industrialization, a municipal culture, Nonconformist religion, and radical, mainly Liberal, politics – still belong to a past era, to the late nineteenth century when Northern England attempted a self-generated bourgeois revolution that ultimately failed. It could not compete with the hegemony of the South, based around the financial centre of the City of London and its imperial legacy of world connections. The divergence between the interests of the North and South was dramatically demonstrated by the first action of the incoming Conservative government in 1979: the abolition of exchange controls in the interests of the City's overseas investment strategies. This led to a haemorrhage of national resources, largely at the expense of sorely needed investment in Northern manufacturing industry.

The North of England does not have the same cultural and institutional framework of identity as Scotland, Wales, or Northern Ireland. But it does have a shared sense of values that, taken together, denote a separate Northernness, a common experience of work and leisure. Northern people do recognize each other in what they would regard often as uncomfortable company, with people from 'down south', people who 'talk posh'. To that extent the North is a coded term for a working-class, deferential sensibility: its people have a subordinate, defensive sense of awareness. On some occasions 'the North' is a kind of substitute for class consciousness, class looked at through a prism. The Northern crisis of self-doubt arises from the sudden catastrophic decline of the heavy manual industries – coal-mining, steel-making, shipbuilding, farming and fishing – that provided communities with a culture of collective skills and communal interdependence.

But there is a sense of Northernness, too, in the reaction to the decline. There is a healthy anger when Northern people set the affluence and growth in the South against their own decline, and feel a sense of neglect and a denial of their own contribution.

In the absence of a coherent cultural and political base for the Northern regions of England to mobilize upon, economic necessity seems logically the place to start a fight-back. And the growth of the Enterprise Board movement in the North does hold out some prospect for regenerating cultural identity and self-respect for the outlying areas of England.[22] In the long run this will prove the most effective counter-balance to the pull of the South-east. Scotland is likely to respond by demanding some form of self-determination; southern England will continue its development as a super-region, linked via the Channel Tunnel to the affluent heart of the European Community. For the North the choice will be between cultural and political mobilization in its own interest, starting with economic initiatives, or continued, disastrous, decline. The development of regionally based Enterprise Boards in the North is an indication that this message is being taken to heart. If the identity of the North is in doubt, there are at least signs of a growing self-awareness, and out of that a growing self-confidence that should flow from the process of self-discovery that is under way.

NOTES

1 Quoted in the *Guardian*, North-East supplement, 30 May 1986.
2 Martyn Harris, 'While Poole rides High', *New Society*, 23 May 1986.
3 Tony Champion and Anne Green, *In Search of Britain's Booming*

Towns, Centre for Urban and Regional Development Studies, University of Newcastle, 1985.
4 *Sunday Times*, 11 January 1987.
5 Tony Champion and Anne Green, *Local Prosperity and the North-South Divide*, Institute for Employment Research, University of Warwick, January 1988.
6 *Financial Times*, 22 March 1986.
7 R. Rothwell, 'The Role of Technology in Industrial Change: Implication for Regional Policy', *Regional Studies*, Vol. 6(5), 1982.
8 Fred Ridley, 'Splitting Image', *Liverpool Daily Post*, 14 January 1986.
9 Graham Turner, *The North Country*, Eyre and Spottiswoode, 1967.
10 *Financial Times*, 13 January 1988.
11 Simon Head, 'Outgrowths of decay in the heart of England' and 'Steady drift to disaster' in the *New Statesmen*, 25 April 1986 and 2 May 1986.
12 Brian Robson, *Where is the North?*, North of England Regional Consortium, Manchester, 1985.
13 *The Times*, 9 June 1986.
14 Yorkshire Enterprise Board, Annual Report, September 1986.
15 Interview, September 1986.
16 Ibid.
17 Chris Moore and Simon Booth, *Regional Economic Development in the North-East – Critical Lessons from Scotland*, in the *Northern Economic Review*, University of Newcastle, Winter 1986/7, p. 3.
18 Interview, April 1986.
19 'Labour MPs back devolution', *Newcastle Journal*, 16 November 1987.
20 Debbie Christie, 'Japanese Industry with a Geordie Accent', *Listener*, 23 July 1987.
21 *Financial Times*, 30 November 1987.
22 See *Enterprise Boards – Their Contribution to Economic Development and Investment*, Centre for Local Economic Strategies, Manchester, November 1987.

—3—

Identity in the balance – Scotland

The pivotal moment in the life of contemporary Scotland, illuminating its identity and relationship with the rest of the United Kingdom, was the devolution referendum of March 1979. It is often (conveniently) forgotten that the result was a majority in favour of establishing a legislative Assembly in Edinburgh. The majority, however, was small: 52 per cent of those voting. This figure only represented 32.9 per cent of those entitled to vote, well short of the 40 per cent target set by the Westminster legislation which would have allowed the Assembly to be established.

The impact on Scottish political and cultural – and, many would argue, economic – life in the 1980s was profound. The movement towards greater Scottish autonomy that had gathered momentum in the 1960s and 1970s came to a shuddering halt. The Scottish Nationalists, who had appeared to dictate events during the 1970s, drifted into decline and division. Scotland's major political force, the Labour Party, was powerless in the face of southern-English Conservative domination. Even by the mid-1980s the note was one of continuing despair. The Glaswegian novelist, William McIlvanney, was driven to remark:

> For me '79 was so bad, it was such a retreat from potential, from possibilities that maybe the only optimism is that we get our fill of living with Maggie Thatcher. But I'm not exactly

full of rosy-eyed certainties about it. The thing that depresses you for ever is that in Scotland we keep voting Labour and getting a Tory government.[1]

Fatally exposed by the referendum experience was the bundle of contradictions and antagonisms which had hitherto been assumed to combine into a cohesive Scottish identity: Highland and Lowland, Gaelic and English-speaking, a Scots-speaking working class and a highly anglicized middle class, Catholic and Protestant, and two cities so geographically close yet different in character as Glasgow and Edinburgh. Enveloping the whole were the paralysing twin exterior emblems of Scottishness, Tartanry and the Kailyard. Tartanry, associated with mythical memories of the 1745 Jacobite rebellion, is made up of Highland images concerned with epic endeavour and physical grandeur in an irrecoverable past. Kailyard, emanating initially from the work of J. M. Barrie in the 1880s, is a Lowland phenomenon concerned with sentimental characters mentally bounded by their own 'cabbage patch' – the Lowland Scots meaning of 'kailyard'. As Cairns Craig has put it, Tartanry and Kailyard became the foundation of myths of national identity in a country whose individuality had been swamped by its incorporation into the United Kingdom.

By concentrating its focus on the 1745 Rebellion, [Tartanry] had inscribed upon it the inevitable historical defeat of the identity which it offered for the Scots. It was not an identity existing beyond history which could find its application at any particular moment and through any specific contemporary situation: it was an identity lost and irrecoverable . . .

. . . Kailyard has haunted twentieth-century Scottish writers because its phenomenal international success established an image of Scotland as parochial and narrow-minded from which it has been hard to escape . . . What Kailyard did was to turn the language of Lowland Scots into a medium necessarily identified with a couthy, domestic, sentimental

world. After Kailyard it becomes impossible to give expression to a vernacular working-class environment in Scotland
without provoking these connotations.[2]

If the 1979 referendum had the effect of bringing devolution to
an at least temporary impasse, it also had the simultaneous
effect of opening up a line of critical inquiry around the
influence of Tartanry and Kailyard which informed Scottish
cultural development throughout the 1980s. A notable starting
point was an exhibition, 'Scotch Myths', mounted by film-
makers Barbara and Murray Grigor in St Andrews and
Edinburgh during 1981. That event – a massive exposure and
deconstruction of Tartanry and Kailyard as manifested in
postcards, whisky-bottle labels, shortbread tins, tea-cloths and
music-hall songs – stimulated wide-ranging inquiries into the
spread of the virus throughout Scottish popular culture,
particularly film and television.

During the 1980s Scottish intellectuals set about dismember-
ing the outworn and static representations of Scottishness
provided by Tartanry and Kailyard. In their place they sought a
more authentic engagement with the realities of Scottish life.
It can be argued that Scotland saw something of a literary
renaissance during the decade, marked by the best-seller status
of Alastair Gray's *Lanark* (its completion after years of gestation
was stimulated by the referendum result); the founding of the
Scottish Poetry Library; and extensive debates on the introduction of specifically Scottish studies into the secondary-school
curriculum. Economically, the Highlands began to reverse
more than a century of population loss while Glasgow, after
enduring a decade of devastating decline in older manufacturing industries, found a renewed confidence as a cultural and
tourist centre, being declared Europe's Cultural Capital for
1990. Meanwhile, despite the vicissitudes of the rise and fall of
oil prices, the East Coast maintained its 1970s revival based on
the oil and electronics industries, with Edinburgh remaining a
major financial centre, second in the United Kingdom only to
London itself.

Yet, despite all this, the identity of Scotland in the 1980s was in the balance. The basis of a Scottish sensibility has been sustained by the survival of separate civil institutions of law, education and Kirk since the Union of 1707. The 1979 referendum result focused the question how much longer could these institutions survive without a political, democratic expression of Scottishness. There was a growing awareness too, of the economic and political divide between Labour-dominated Scotland and the Conservative-dominated south of England. Even the most centralist and British-minded Scottish Labour politicians began to harbour doubts and to change their minds on the devolution question during the 1980s. Perhaps the most notable was the MP for Livingston, Robin Cook, an arch-opponent of an Assembly in the 1970s who quickly revised his position in the wake of the 1983 general election.

The time has now come when one has got to recognize the reality of the divergence of the political pattern of the south of England from Scotland and therefore I think that should be recognized by some different form of constitutional settlement which allows the Scots to take their own decisions concerning domestic issues which can be settled by a state within a federal system.[3]

The whole-heartedness of such declarations and changes of mind within the Labour Party which, because of its dominance in 1980s Scotland, took on the character of *the* national party, was suspect, however. Everything, it seemed, would depend as before on the outcome of electoral contests in Britain as a whole. And it is hard not to find at least part of the explanation in the continuing influence of the Kailyard and Tartanry on the Scottish cultural psyche. It is probably still the case that the majority of Scots are eager consumers of the artefacts and images whose influence outside Scotland many would claim to deplore. The popularity of such films as *The Maggie*, *Brigadoon* and, more recently, *Local Hero*, in the Highlands themselves, makes the point. As does the continuing success of such weekly publications as the *Sunday Post* which sells a mixture of folksy news and features to around a million of Scotland's 5,250,000 people. This newspaper has been described as the most successful in the world, coming closest to saturation circulation and earning Tom Nairn's celebrated accolade, 'Scotland will be reborn the day the last minister is strangled with the last copy of the *Sunday Post*.'[4] Meanwhile the baleful influence continues, as summarized in the mid-1890s by Colin McArthur in his essay on *The Cinema Image of Scotland*.

> Through the international success and influence of work constructed within Tartanry and Kailyard, these discourses now provide the 'commonsense' images of Scotland throughout the world, an armature of images, jokes, stories, motifs by which Scotland and Scottishness are immediately invoked. This means that the disabling process whereby images of Scotland and the Scots are produced outside of Scotland (as in Hollywood movies with a Scottish setting) is continued but, even more chillingly, because of the historical dominance of these images, Scots themselves have to hand no alternative images of their land and people. The dire outcome is that, when Scots set out to produce images of their own country, Tartanry and Kailyard exercise a magnetic pull on them, irrespective of what they may wish to do or what they think they are doing. The most notorious recent example of this is the film *Local Hero*.[5]

The durability of Tartanry and Kailyard suggests that their influence penetrates deep into Scottish history and culture and, indeed, provides a vital key to Scottish identity. In a note in the pamphlet accompanying the 1981 exhibition 'Scotch Myths' Duncan Macmillan recalled:

> My father used to tell how my grandmother once executed a chicken by the English royal method of block and axe. Stimulated by the honour the headless corpse flew over the house. The brain died immediately but the body went on flapping. The social and economic changes of the late nineteenth and early twentieth century left Scottish culture

brutally split. Is what we have here then the mindless corpse of a once whole creature, decapitated but still twitching? Or worse still, a MacChicken gutless, trussed, frozen, and in tartan polythene? Or is what we see just the grotesque attitude of a still functioning creature, an ostrich with its head in the sand?[6]

A reading of Scottish history over the past 250 years reveals a psychological underpinning of the commonly understood dual nationality – Scottish and British – by a deeper personality split. This seems more keenly felt by the Scottish than the Welsh who embrace a British identity more intimately. The Welsh live easily with the mythology of Britain being somehow a wider Wales, of Henry VII and later Lloyd George somehow recovering lost territory. In contemporary times the acceptance is perhaps related to the proximity of Wales to England, and the melting-pot industrial history of the southern Welsh valleys. For the Scots, however, the grafting of 'British' on to their native identity was, and continues to be, a more painful experience. It is a recurring theme in Scottish literature, perhaps the most famous example being Robert Louis Stevenson's *The Strange Case of Dr Jekyll and Mr Hyde*. Written in 1886, when the British imperial adventure was reaching its height, the character of Dr Jekyll has come to represent, at least in retrospect, the dilemma of the Scottish people – torn between British stability and Scottish adventure; British ideas of pragmatic responsibility and Scottish notions of freedom. In his *Scottish Literature: Character and Influence* (1919) G. Gregory Smith described this condition as the 'Caledonian Antisyzygy' – the latter being Greek for 'union of opposites', literally the 'yoking together' of opposites. Smith diagnosed the disease as a racial propensity to alternate between dour matter-of-fact realism and unrestrained fantasy: 'It goes better with our knowledge of Scottish character and history to accept the antagonism as real and necessary.' This analysis has been explored in different ways by Scottish writers ever since, from Hugh MacDiarmid and Edwin Muir through to Tom Nairn in the contemporary period. There is a sense, however, in which the 'Caledonian Antisyzygy' was rent asunder by the experience of the referendum in 1979. This particular Scottish balancing act could be sustained no longer. Politics and culture during the 1980s were, in their various forms, about recognizing and coming to terms with this situation. Scottishness and Britishness no longer resided easily with one another, and not even uneasily in the old suppressed, hidden form of the internalized Antisyzygy. The 1980s and 1990s are likely to prove to be a period that will resolve this central issue for Scottish identity which is, indeed, in the balance. And for this reason Scotland is the fulcrum of the Divided Kingdom.

These are broad, sweeping statements and need to be placed in perspective by a brief survey of Scottish history: from the heroic period of the Wars of Independence during the 300 years following 1286, through the experience of Union around 1707 and the nineteenth-century imperial adventure, to the twentieth-century conflicts and dilemmas of the recovery of Scottish consciousness against a background of Britain in decline.

Scottish national identity was forged during the Wars of Independence beginning with Edward I's incursions and the resistance mounted by Wallace and Bruce. Scotland remained independent but, especially towards the end of the period, much eroded by the struggle. The main inheritance, however, has been an exalted sense of heroic nationalism built on military tradition, and this remains a central nerve for present-day Scottish Nationalists. In particular, an extremely early statement of the nationalist ethic, often thought to have originated in the French Revolution and Rousseau's ideas of the sovereignty of the people, comes from the Scotland of this period. The Declaration of Arbroath of 1320, a diplomatic despatch to Rome containing the news of Robert the Bruce's assumption of the Scottish crown, contains the following famous qualification:

Yet if he should give up what he has begun, and agree to make us or our kingdom subject to the King of England or the

English, we should exert ourselves at once to drive him out as our enemy and a subverter of his own rights and ours, and make some other man who was well able to defend us our King; for, as long as but a hundred of us remain alive, never will we on any conditions be brought under English rule. It is in truth not for glory, nor riches, nor honours that we are fighting, but for freedom – for that alone, which no honest man gives up but with life itself.[7]

The succession of a Scottish king, James VI, to the English throne in 1603 was the consequence of the marriage of the daughter of Henry VII of England to James IV of Scotland. When this was under discussion in the English court, some of Henry's advisers pointed to the risk that it might bring England under the rule of a Scottish prince. Henry replied that if that happened it would mean the accession, not of England to Scotland, but of Scotland to England, since 'the greater would always draw the less, as England had drawn Normandy under her sway.'[8] This prediction proved to be the case. The union of the Crowns and of the Parliaments a century later stripped Scotland of her executive and legislature. The politically and socially ambitious elements in Scottish society – the 'natural leaders' – followed King and Parliament to London. Their children were educated increasingly in England, from whose schools and universities the English State had drawn its servants as the British State would now continue to do. By residence (in London 'townhouses'), by social contact, by education, and by participation in public life, the aristocracy and gentry of Scotland became indistinguishable from those of England.

Hence the first great split occurred in Scottish life. But, though the Unions of 1603 and 1707 stripped Scotland of her head, as it were – her political, state institutions – the settlements left three great civil institutions of the nation intact. Indeed, it guaranteed them. The law of Scotland was permitted to continue, as was the Presbyterian system of church government. In addition, the Scottish educational provision survived, there being no national English system to which it could be subordinated. These surviving institutions also provided the means whereby a new leadership could be produced. So in the 1980s it was no accident that the leaders of every political party in Scotland were lawyers, trained within the separate Scottish legal system.

But though a distinctive Scottish identity persisted within the interstices of Scotland's remaining civil institutions, there was no incentive during the eighteenth and nineteenth centuries to integrate them with any recovered political organization. Rather, the emerging British industrial revolution and Empire provided wider pastures for Scotland's intelligentsia and entrepreneurs to exploit than could have been foreseen when the Union took place. As Tom Nairn has put it:

> Scottish civil society advanced much farther than had been imagined possible under its foreign monarchy and State. Its dominant class had sacrificed statehood for participation in the English and colonial 'common market' of the day, trusting that this would aid the diffusion of Polite Society in their tenebrous land. In fact, society 'took off' beneath their feet, towards a revolutionary condition of industrialization. Within the larger economic area they had entered, they had created an autonomous sub-system – in effect, an epicentre now borne along upon the grander tide of English imperial expansion. They had entered its flow at a moment when, still in formation, it could tolerate the existence of such a subsystem. Hence, they were neither crushed by it, nor compelled into nationalist reaction against it – the standard fates which, one can be certain, they would not have escaped if Union had been delayed until the end of the eighteenth century.[9]

Moreover, and in keeping with the heroic past, Scotland's contribution to the British endeavour was most vivid in the military field. Indeed, never before had the prospects seemed better for Scots soldiers. Their endeavours also united Highlands and Lowlands, for after 1745 and Culloden Gaelic divisions joined the British army. As the historian William Ferguson has recorded:

> After 1800 all the Scottish regiments, Lowland and High-land, were established, and by the end of the Napoleonic Wars each had an established reputation and a jealously guarded tradition. Quite apart from their exploits in the field these military units played a large part in Scottish life . . . They contributed to the maintenance of national sentiment, and the use by the Highland regiments of the 'garb of old Gaul' actually gave a new and unexpected impetus to that sentiment. The Gaels, from being viewed as barbarous nuisances, became regarded as in some ways the very em-bodiment of Scotland. The kilt and the bagpipes acquired popularity where hitherto they had enjoyed none. The new cult was mawkish and often at variance with the facts of Scottish life . . .[10]

Thus early on in the experience of the Union, elements of what later in the literary context became known as Kailyard set in. In other fields, however, the accent was far from parochial – for instance, medicine, engineering and the natural sciences. But, as Ferguson again comments:

> The reputation won by Scotsmen in science . . . did little to enhance the culture of their country. This is far from being a singular case, for science stands independent of national contexts . . .[11]

The same may be said of emigration, another great activity of nineteenth-century Scotland. The legacy is large enclaves of émigré 'Scottish' communities dotted round the globe which still exert undue influence on Scottish identity at home. The fact was celebrated in an exhibition of 'The Enterprising Scot' by the National Museums of Scotland during 1986. Its accom-panying brochure inquired: 'Why did hundreds of thousands of Scots emigrate? Why are expatriate Scots so proud of their heritage? Why is it that every part of the world has a Burns Supper celebration? Why do clan societies flourish from as far afield as North America and Australia?' They left to take advantage of the opportunities overseas and because there were few countervailing attractions at home. But they took with them romantic notions of Scottishness and sentimental memories to which the Kailyard made an instant appeal and which to a large extent it was created to satisfy. As Cairns Craig has commented, the Kailyard is

> exploitation of Scottish lower-class life by exiled Scots for a public largely made up of exiles who want to remember, nostalgically, the land they have left behind, but also want to be convinced that they were right to leave it behind.[12]

Alongside the emigration was an intellectual evacuation from Scotland during the nineteenth century. Of the leading British intellectuals of the day an extraordinary number were of Scottish extraction – John Stuart Mill, Macaulay, Carlyle, Ruskin and Gladstone, to name the most prominent. The consequences for Scotland have been summarized by Tom Nairn in the following terms:

> Whether as the pawky simplicities of village life, or as swaggering through the heather claymore in hand, 'Scotland' in the sub-romantic sense was largely defined by émigrés. The Kailyard was – and still is – very much the reverse of the coin of emigration. Its lack of 'human and political dignity' does not express some collective fault in the Scots psyche, but the 'historical fact' of the relationship between the intelligentsia and the people. This relationship was determined by the fact that the Scottish bourgeoisie did not face the need to form *its own* 'national community', through the mediation of a more rooted intellectual class and a more complex and sophisticated national culture (i.e. more 'mature, all-round', and so on) . . .

Rendered jobless in these circumstances – without a

middle-class sufficiently exercised over the usual national problems, without a national capital city of the kind which had become indispensable – what could the intelligentsia do? Its natural posture became to seek work outside, but at the same time (aware of its distinct origins and history) to look constantly backwards and inwards, in a typical vein of deforming nostalgia – constantly confirming a false, 'infantile' image of the country quite divorced from its real problems.[13]

It took the collapse of the Empire following World War I, and the emergence of a handful of intellectuals in the 1920s and 1930s who conjured a literary renaissance out of the air, to cut across the dilemma described here. The outstanding figure was Hugh MacDiarmid who, virtually single-handed in the 1920s, took a stand against Tartanry and the Kailyard in favour of a diamond-hard, uncompromising coming-to-terms with the duality and divisions of Scottish identity. Adopting Gregory Smith's Antisyzygy, he projected an idea of Scottishness as a combination of opposites, in Smith's words 'dominated by the conception of infinity, of the unattainable, and hence ever questioning, never satisfied, rationalistic in religion and politics, romantic in art and literature.'[14] MacDiarmid's outstanding work, the long poem *A Drunk Man Looks at the Thistle*, was produced in 1926 and remains a kind of liturgy for an emerging Scottish identity of the late twentieth century. Its central image of the thistle is presented as a deeply ambivalent symbol – representing some ideal beauty or fulfilment by its purple flower (the thistle's 'rose') but conjuring up sterility, failure and pain in its ugly stalks and spikes. As though in a rare moment of clarity in a drunken drifting haze, MacDiarmid recognizes that the Scot is destined to be caught between the two: 'Man torn in twa / And glorious in the lift and grisly on the sod'.

The poem rejects nineteenth-century notions of Scottishness defined in terms of romantic sentimentality. The outstanding declaration, cut into MacDiarmid's tombstone at Langholm, asserts:

> I'll hae nae hauf-way hoose, but aye be whaur
> Extremes meet – it's the only way I ken
> To dodge the curst conceit o' bein' right
> That damns the vast majority o' men.

For MacDiarmid the local need not be parochial. He stressed the view that true internationalism cannot exist without the contribution of small nations each having a unique role, and with Scotland deserving a place amongst them. To achieve this, however, it needed to come to terms with the divisions in its identity and recover a political dimension for the civil society and institutions that existed. In this enterprise the key link is between culture and politics. But which comes first? In a number of articles in the 1920s MacDiarmid confronted this question head on. Thus, writing in the *Scottish Educational Journal* in August 1925 he asked how a Scottish school of fiction was to emerge, in the sense in which one could speak of an English or an American or a Russian school of fiction.

> A year ago I would have been emphatically of the opinion that a pre-requisite to the emergence of anything of the kind would be the establishment of a Scottish Parliament in Edinburgh, with powers no less than those of the Free State Government in Ireland. Only such a political development, I would have said, can carry in its train that reorientation of journalism and book publication and that separation of interests tending cumulatively to create a public with a different response to the English public for which such a school will naturally cater. Now I am not so sure. It may be that effective cultural devolution will precede rather than follow political devolution . . .[15]

It can be argued that it took the experience of the 1979 referendum before this insight penetrated to a significant number of Scottish intellectuals. Certainly, the renewed emphasis on analysis of the influence of Tartanry and Kailyard on

Scottish identity in the years immediately following 1979 indicated as much. For example, in an article in 1981 reviewing the
'Scotch Myths' exhibition referred to earlier, Lindsay Paterson
concluded that Tartanry continued to define Scottish culture in
the eyes of most Scots and the rest of the world. And he attacked
those who either dismissed the phenomenon as irrelevant or
even as the basis from which a new identity might emerge.

For to build here a genuinely decentralized democracy will
require much more than the provision of the appropriate
social institutions – much more than the issuing of a general
invitation to participate. It will require also a readiness to
take part, a popular enthusiasm for helping to shape the
future of society. And such a project in turn requires a
national self-image that might inspire social change rather
than offer escape from its urgent necessity. It requires a
national ideology – a view of Scotland – that engages with
social reality, rather than with a fabulous Highland fairytale.
It requires a vision of what Scottish people are and could be
that goes beyond the pawky smutty postcards, the comic-
strip caricatures, and the wife-beating buffoons. And it
requires a national movement that has its roots not in the
cheap distortions of the tartan myths (part of which is the
xenophobia of the kailyard), but rather in a positive aspiration to a self-confident, realistic, national awareness.

Only on such a basis could we begin to get rid of that
endemic self-deprecation which baulks (as in the referendum
for instance) at any suggestion of radical change. Tartan's
principal legacy is, in other words, a cancerous national
inferiority complex: the quite unmistakable psychological
end-product of two centuries of tawdry palliatives – of
escaping from social problems into wishful fantasy. It is the
result of being told, and telling ourselves, that adventure is a
thing only of the distant romantic past – now safely tamed on
to postcards, on to football grounds, into bagpipes in the
mists of wee bit hills and glens, or into impotent nostalgia for
past glories (and that includes nostalgia for bygone days of

Red Socialism). And it is the result of believing that we are a community of pawky inadequates: staunch, kindly, and occasionally mischievous no doubt – rising even, at times, to some ephemeral protest – but always in the end laughable, blindly loyal (now to a lethargic Labour establishment), and certainly not really up to running our own affairs . . .[16]

What indications are there, as the twenty-first century draws near, of any renewal in Scottish self-confidence that is the pre-requisite for, as Paterson puts it, Scotland running its own affairs? The answer is that there are broad economic and cultural undercurrents where Scots are getting to grips with urgent problems and issues, and finding increasing frustration in their efforts to do so. This frustration, more and more, is being directed at political structures south of the border which are seen as out of sympathy and having neither the time nor the inclination to focus on Scottish affairs.

In the Highlands there is both a sense of renewal and a sense of pessimism about future prospects while agricultural priorities are determined outside the country. With a geographical area of half of Scotland it has a population of only 340,000. But that figure shows that the population of the Highlands and Islands is rising again after a hundred years of catastrophic decline which reached its nadir in the 1960s when the population dropped below 300,000. The oil industry has brought new activity and people, and accelerated infrastructure projects such as the dual carriageway from Edinburgh through Perth to the Highland capital, Inverness. Underpinning the Highland revival, however, is the fresh lease of life that has been given to crofting, the region's unique part-time method of farming. Crofters have had EEC agricultural support, but mostly have revived through their own efforts. In 1986 they formed themselves into their first all-Highland Union, with some 3,000 members. Their director, James Hunter, says that more than any other form of economic activity, crofting guarantees the maintenance of viable communities in places that would otherwise be deserted: 'Compare the north end of Skye, where the big farms formed during the Clearances were given back to crofters, with the many places in the Highlands and Islands where that did not happen.'[17] The crofting revival is also the foundation for the beginning of a growth in Gaelic speaking and a renewed pride in the Gaelic culture and heritage.

Against this there are worries about the area's lack of influence. In the case of crofting, changes in the EEC's quota production system may well have serious knock-on effects. For example, if farmers in East Anglia were to start to rear sheep intensively on land where they used to grow barley, Highland farmers' extensive sheep-farming operations would be at risk. Speaking of Skye, where he is based, James Hunter observed:

> The island is remote from the centres of British life. Its influence on government, as only a small part of one of over 600 British parliamentary constituencies, is virtually nil.[18]

In the Lowlands the Scottish economy has been undergoing a painful transformation. Since the mid-1970s more than 250,000 jobs have been shed in Scotland's heavy manufacturing industries – steel, shipbuilding and engineering. However, output of the electronics industry, based to a significant extent on foreign companies, has doubled, and many new jobs have been created in services. The electronics industry employs more than 41,000 people in around 300 companies. And Scotland has a high proportion of Europe's personal computer and integrated circuit manufacturing, each sector employing some 5,000 people.

Much of the credit for attracting the new industry must go to the Scottish Development Agency, set up in 1975 as part of the move towards devolution. Its chief executive in the mid-1980s, George Matthewson, stated that much of its success was due to factors peculiar to Scotland.

> We are a tightly-knit organization operating in a small country with a limited élite of business, financial and political leaders who know each other extremely well. The Scottish Office concentrates a considerable number of functions for

the administration of Scotland under virtually one roof. And national consciousness means local authorities and lesser development agencies are often prepared to put Scotland first.[19]

But though there have been undoubted successes in restructuring the economy and attracting new industry, the scale of the recession and the speed of the run-down of older industries in the early 1980s left yawning gaps. Unemployment remained high, in the mid-teens, throughout the 1980s and the differential compared with the figures in southern Britain widened. Many of the new high-tech industries constituted little more than a branch economy, while the fall in the price of oil during 1986 meant the loss of more than 10,000 jobs. Little wonder therefore that the majority of Scots still believed that real jobs meant manufacturing jobs, preferably in heavy industry. This last was demonstrated by the near-unanimous campaign to keep the Ravenscraig steel plant open following the closure of the nearby Gartcosh finishing mill with the loss of 700 jobs in March 1986. The knock-on effect of closing Ravenscraig would be 10,000 or more redundancies which, as the *Glasgow Herald* declared, would be an 'economic catastrophe for Scotland':

> – the greatest collapse of them all, one which would probably not be forgiven for a generation. Virtually the entire steel industry would go in one moment. The question must be asked: why us? Why not Wales or England where there are other integrated plants? You can close an integrated plant in Wales and there will still be a Welsh steel industry. The same goes for England, but not here . . .[20]

Economic logic, however, pointed to closure, with only immediate electoral considerations standing in the way. Ravenscraig's production could much more efficiently be concentrated in south Wales, at Llanwern and Port Talbot. As it was, following the closure of Gartcosh, Ravenscraig's fishing mill switched to Shotton in north Wales. The major steel users in

Scotland – the Linwood car plant, the Bathgate truck plant, and most of the Clyde shipbuilding works – all closed in the early 1980s. Despite these economic arguments, Ravenscraig presented a political dilemma for all British parties operating in Scotland, a dilemma articulated most succinctly by the Labour MP for Motherwell South, Jeremy Bray. Writing of the 'ghost that haunts my colleagues in all parties in Parliament' he observed:

> We all fear a Westminster Government which pushes Scotland too far. If a wave of nationalist resentment, precipitated by some disaster like a decision to close Ravenscraig, drove Scotland to independence, the first act of an independent Scotland would be to go ahead and close Ravenscraig.
>
> Bereft of its finishing mill (Gartcosh), its markets, and its quotas (from the EEC), the Government would have no alternative. Independence offers no way of saving Ravenscraig. But it could be the consequence of failing to act on Ravenscraig . . . [21]

Both the relative success of the Scottish Development Agency and the underlying precariousness of the Scottish economy pointed to greater autonomy for Scotland. Certainly this was the view of the Scottish TUC which throughout the 1980s put its weight behind the all-party Campaign for a Scottish Assembly. Campbell Christie, formerly deputy general secretary of the Society of Civil and Public Servants in London, returned to Scotland in 1986 to become General Secretary of the Scottish TUC, with the objective of an Assembly very much in mind. He believes the greater economic clout an Assembly would put behind the Scottish Development Agency would be vital for protecting and creating jobs.[22] And so far as one can tell from opinion polls, these were seen as priorities by a large majority of the Scottish people: consistently through the 1980s the polls showed around 30 per cent favouring independence and a further 40 per cent devolution. These levels were higher than in the mid-1970s, when self-government had last been at a high tide*. Paradoxically, however, it was now Labour rather than the SNP that was benefiting most – attracting around 50 per cent of support compared with 15–20 per cent for the SNP. It seemed as though the conditions necessary for 'the next advance to Scottish self-government', specified by Neal Ascherson in the wake of the 1979 referendum, still persisted in the late 1980s:

> First, the tacit admission that Labour are still the critical operational force. Secondly, Labour's decision that an Assembly can protect Scotland against Toryism, and Labour's sense that Mrs Thatcher is not mandated to govern Scotland. Thirdly, public pressure which is not guided by the SNP. Fourthly, an SNP too weak to frighten Labour into paralysis but strong enough to make them press ahead with devolution as a means of self-preservation. Fifthly, trade-union pressure for self-government which can, if necessary, find allies beyond the Labour Party.[23]

The outcome of the general election in June 1987 fully confirmed all these points. The most immediate impression was one of disaster for the Conservatives. An Anti-Tory swing, complemented by tactical voting, cost them eleven seats. This left them with just ten of the seventy-two Scottish seats in the House of Commons and 24 per cent of the Scottish vote. Labour, on the other hand, took 42 per cent and gained nine seats, having fifty Scottish MPs in all. The result immediately highlighted the question of the Conservatives' Scottish mandate: quite apart from the election statistics, they had hardly enough MPs to form an effective administration at the Scottish Office, and in January 1988 they chose to wind up the Scottish

* As the 1980s drew to a close the trend in the polls shifted towards independence. A MORI opinion poll in the *Scotsman* on 30 April 1988 put support for an independent Scotland at 35 per cent – 6 per cent up on a year previously – while another 42 per cent backed a Scottish assembly within the UK. Only 20 per cent supported the status quo – 5 per cent below the figure for a year earlier.

Select Committee in the House of Commons rather than face the humiliation of propping up their majority on it with MPs from English constituencies. More importantly, the general election in Scotland had been fought with these prospects very much in mind. Common currency in the campaign was 'the Doomsday scenario', a phrase invented by the magazine *Radical Scotland* which focused the question of what would happen in the event of another enormous Labour majority in Scotland frustrated by a Conservative victory south of the Border. The response of the Conservative Secretary of State for Scotland, Malcolm Rifkind, was to argue that the election was about a British mandate, not a Scottish one, so the question did not arise.

> I don't believe that in a democracy government can govern without the general consent of the public. If you are implying that if the government of the United Kingdom does not have a majority in Scotland or in England at any given time, then there is not consent, that implies a nationalist view of life. If you are a Scottish Nationalist, and you believe that Scotland should be a separate state, then clearly a government that does not reflect the wishes of the Scottish public on a range of issues cannot have legitimacy. Eighty-five per cent of the Scottish public do not vote for the Nationalist party. They vote for Unionist parties and for others including the Labour Party and the Liberals and Social Democrats as well as the Conservatives, who believe in a United Kingdom and a United Kingdom government. Therefore, the only constitutional mandate, whether in Scotland or in England, is that of a democratically elected British Parliament.[24]

In a strict constitutional sense Rifkind is, of course, correct. But it is a high-risk political argument for the Conservatives to deploy, being an open invitation to Scots who want change to vote Nationalist: on this basis elections in Scotland would be converted into a running plebiscite for the Union. It also sidesteps the question of the legitimacy of the devolved administration Scotland already has, in the shape of the Scottish Office and its steadily widening range of powers over all aspects of Scottish society. More fundamentally, however, the 'no mandate' argument is not one about constitutional law; it is an argument to encourage people to reject the *democratic* legitimacy of the British system in ruling Scotland. This is precisely what the Labour Party in Scotland began to do with some enthusiasm in the wake of the 1987 general election. Most notably, Brian Wilson, formerly chairman of the 'Labour Vote No' campaign in the 1979 devolution referendum and a member of the 1970s 'Scotland is British' committee, now the newly elected MP for Cunninghame North, announced his conversion to the Assembly cause. Writing in the *Guardian* he explained:

> Touring my new constituency on Saturday, I stopped for a pint in Ardrossan, a town that has never previously had a Labour MP. The goodwill towards me could not have been greater, the bitterness over Mrs Thatcher's national triumph more intense, or the sense of expectation more apparent.
>
> 'You've got to do something for us,' I was told repeatedly. It was a plea from friends which only a fool would disregard or misinterpret. By 'you' they meant the Labour in which they had just invested such a massive vote of confidence. By 'us' they meant Scotland, which had declared near-total rejection of the Thatcherite evil.[25]

The dilemma for the Labour Party in Scotland, however, is that the more it questions the right of a government for which Scotland did not vote to impose policies on Scotland, the more it accepts the case for Scottish independence. Thus, in the wake of the election Robin Cook — again an anti-devolutionist in the 1970s — argued that if Scotland had an Assembly, Labour should accept that Scots MPs at Westminster should not vote on domestic English affairs and that it should even consider a reduction in the number of Scottish MPs sitting there.[26] This was but a short step away from renouncing Labour's all-British aspirations altogether: Labour depends on its weight of Scottish (and Welsh) MPs to stand any chance of forming a majority at Westminster. The Labour Party in Scotland is slowly being forced to confront its British/Scottish identity and question whether a dual position can be sustained in the face of Labour's collapse in southern England.

In coming to terms with its dilemma, and whether it faces up to the democratic imperative the Scottish people are thrusting upon it, Labour cannot remain unaffected by the changes in the cultural climate of Scotland described earlier in this chapter. It was notable, for example, that in a Festival for Scottish Democracy organized by the Scottish TUC in Glasgow in September 1987, part of its campaign for an Assembly, much energy was expended by the artists present in debunking the Tartan myth in favour of a more autonomous, authentic and modern idea of Scotland related to equality and social justice. The relationship of culture and politics in any society is complex, however, and as MacDiarmid indicated in the 1920s, it is not always easy to judge which is dependent on the other. In the Scottish case, there is no doubt that the central issue is the country's involvement with England and the split that has occurred between culture and politics as a result. As has been argued, this has further led to most Scots feeling a dual identity too easily defined as Scottish and British because of the complex interlocking value systems of both sides of the coin. Part cause of this and part effect was the massive emigration of Scots to England and the Empire, and the production of pathological images of the homeland in the shape of Tartanry and the Kailyard. MacDiarmid contrived to resolve the dilemma by exposing and celebrating the split as the 'Caledonian Anti-syzygy'. The demands of politics are more straightforward, however. It can be argued that the politics of devolution, beginning in the 1960s and continuing through the 1980s, are about confronting the Scots with their essential duality and forcing a choice. In this light the outcome of the 1979 referendum appears quite comprehensible – a clear, though split, result. As the Scottish political scientist, James Kellas, put it:

. . . there was a sense of truth about what happened which makes the event a critical one and not a deviant happening; that is, it was not something that should not have happened in the circumstances. What the Scots and the politicians did in early 1979 was to expose the essential ambiguity of the United Kingdom: its multi-national yet homogeneous nature, its conflicts based on nation as well as class; and its balance between élite and mass initiatives in politics.[27]

But what the referendum and the events that led up to it also demonstrated was the political potential long latent in the separate Scottish civil institutions and administration as well as in a distinct economy and culture. What the referendum provoked as well was a crisis for Scottish culture. It is one thing to recognize the regressive and deformed characteristics of Tartanry and the Kailyard; it is quite another to find more authentic and representative images. However, appreciation of reality must come first. In 1980s Scotland this has been reinforced by the impact of the recession, and by the growing disparities between northern and southern Britain, both economically and politically. One resource that has been tapped to great effect during the 1980s has been the history of Scottish working-class resistance and struggle, exemplified by Red Clydeside, the Crofters' Wars and the Lanarkshire weavers. These experiences have been relayed to a wide audience by John McGrath's 7:84 Theatre Company and its offshoot, Wildcat. McGrath's *The Cheviot, The Stag and the Black, Black Oil*, for instance, cuts through conventional accounts of Scottish history by suggesting connections between three distinct moments in the experience of the Highlands: the Clearances in which crofting people were removed to make way for sheep; the development of game parks; and the exploitation of off-shore oil. Wildcat is a professional music theatre group which tours Scotland purveying an irreverent mix of humour and socialist politics resonant with the issues of identity discussed here. In an interview with one of the company's players, David Anderson, in early 1986 the magazine *Radical Scotland* posed the following question:

You say the Scots have an identity. I think that the English have a secure identity and that perhaps the Scots don't have that security. A theatre that appeals to being Scottish runs the risk of chauvinistic nationalism, Romanticism, Harry Lauder's picture-postcard image of Scotland. Presumably that's not reflected in the theatre you're involved in?

DA: We've got to stay away from Harry Lauderism – and McGrath, very early on, did a whole spoof on Harry Lauder and *that* Scottish identity. The Scottish identity has to be very different from that. Interestingly, over the last couple of years the audiences we've had have been getting far more politically nationalist. Certainly we've talked more about MacLean's ideas and found the response to be very positive and increasingly so. Also the audiences are getting more politically pissed off. The last show was a review; there were all kinds of things but the stuff that was criticizing this particular government was what went down best. The audience is more up front than we are at the moment. I think it's quite a positive argument that a national Scottish government – that is not to say a Scottish National government – is a desirable thing and the sooner the better. I believe that most of our audience – which I think is a decent cross-section of the working-class and some middle-class folk – I think that's how they feel too. I don't think they need us to say that at all. Don't you feel that people are becoming more interested in a more urgent, practical way of getting out of the clutches of the Tories?[28]

If this assessment of the mood of Scotland is broadly accurate it raises key questions about Scottish politics in the 1990s assuming, as seems likely, the country continues to vote heavily Labour while seeing a Tory government returned at Westminster. In these circumstances Scotland, more than any other element in the diversity of politics and culture that makes up the United Kingdom, will project its divisions to the fore – even more than Northern Ireland, part of whose tragedy is that her people are seen, by the English, as ultimately peripheral. Not so with Scotland whose identity and politics influence the heart of British culture. One example of the contrast makes the point: from the foundation of Stormont in 1920 until its demise in 1972, the twelve Ulster MPs at Westminster voted on United Kingdom matters over which Parliament itself had no say in Ulster. This anomaly continued without problem, partly because, though the Ulster MPs invariably voted with the Conservatives, they were not elected on the basis of the mainland's left-right political divide, and in any event their numbers were relatively small; but more fundamentally because their presence did not force any questions of identity in the British Parliament. None of these factors would obtain if the Stormont situation were applied to Scotland. The anomalous position of the seventy-two Scottish MPs at Westminster would be bound to cause profound changes in the government of England; in effect, English MPs in the House of Commons would become an English Assembly by default.

The re-emergence of Scottish politics in the latter half of the twentieth century is at the heart of the issues besetting the Divided Kingdom. As events continue to unfold they are revealing aspects of Scottish and English identity central to understanding what sustains and divides British political culture.

NOTES

1 William McIlvanney, 'Inhabiting the Paradox' in *Radical Scotland*, No. 11, Oct./Nov. 1984, p. 27.
2 Cairns Craig, 'Myths Against History: Tartanry and Kailyard in Nineteenth-century Scottish Literature', in Colin McArthur (ed.), *Scotch Reels*, BFI Publishing, 1982, p. 10–11.
3 Robin Cook, 'Recipes for Socialism' in *Radical Scotland*, No. 4, Aug./Sept. 1983, p. 11.
4 Used on the cover of *Radical Scotland*, No. 1, Feb./March 1983.
5 Colin McArthur, *The Cinema Image of Scotland*, published by the Tate Gallery to accompany a Scottish film season during the autumn of 1986 at the gallery, p. 8.

6 *Scotch Myths: An exploration of Scotchness*, ISBN 0906272 05X, Edinburgh International Festival, 1981.

7 *The Declaration of Arbroath*, ed. Sir James Fergusson, Edinburgh 1970, p. 9.

8 Quoted in R. L. Mackie, *King James IV of Scotland*, Edinburgh, 1958, p. 93.

9 Tom Nairn, 'Old and New Scottish Nationalism' in his *The Break-Up of Britain*, Verso edition, 1981, p. 139.

10 William Ferguson, *Scotland: 1689 to the Present* (Vol. IV of the *Edinburgh History of Scotland*, 1968), p. 265.

11 Ferguson, ibid., p. 319.

12 Craig, op. cit., p. 11.

13 Nairn, op. cit., p. 160–1.

14 Quoted by Roderick Watson, *The Literature of Scotland*, Macmillan, 1984, p. 351.

15 Quoted by Edwin Morgan in 'The Future of the Antisyzygy' in *The Bulletin of Scottish Politics*, No. 1, Autumn 1980 (Scottish International Institute, Edinburgh).

16 Lindsay Paterson, *Scotch Myths*, in the *Bulletin of Scottish Politics*, No. 2, Spring 1981, p. 71.

17 James Hunter (with Cailean Maclean), *Skye – The Island*, Mainstream (Edinburgh), 1986, p. 180.

18 Ibid., p. 184.

19 *Financial Times*, 14 October 1986.

20 *Glasgow Herald*, 31 October 1985.

21 *Glasgow Herald*, 12 February 1986.

22 *Radical Scotland* profile, 'Man with a Mission', No. 15 June/July 1985, p. 11.

23 Neal Ascherson, 'After Devolution' in *Bulletin of Scottish Politics*, No. 1, Autumn 1980.

24 Quoted by Christopher Harvie, 'Grasping The Thistle' in Kenneth Cargill (ed.), *Scotland 2000 – Eight views on the State of the Nation*, BBC Scotland, 1987, p. 5–6.

25 *Guardian*, 15 June 1987.

26 *Glasgow Herald*, 3 September 1987.

27 James Kellas, 'On to an Assembly?' in John Bochel et al. (eds), *The Referendum Experience – Scotland 1979*, Aberdeen University Press, 1981, p. 152.

28 'Wildnights and after', *Radical Scotland*, Feb./March 1986, p. 31.

—4—

Clash of identities – Ulster

The Lyric Players Theatre is set in the suburban University area of South Belfast. In the 1980s it has been the unlikely focus of an effort to create a united, self-sustained and Ulster cultural identity in Northern Ireland: unlikely, because it has been seen, in the past at any rate, as very much a middle-class institution, catering for what has been a middle-class and essentially minority theatrical taste.

Yet in the 1980s there has been an upsurge of new theatre-writing in Northern Ireland, most of it emerging out of working-class experience and, because of that, appealing to a working-class audience as well as communicating something of the reality of working-class life to middle-class people. During the 1980s some fifty different writers were involved in making more than a hundred plays, which were all either produced in the theatre or broadcast on radio and television.[1]

Many of these new plays had their first airing at the Lyric. Perhaps the theatre's greatest success in this period was its appeal to a mixed Catholic and Protestant, though mainly middle-class, audience. To achieve this it had to persuade people to come to it from all over Belfast, to travel across town and through unfamiliar territory. The Lyric's two most influential playwrights in the 1980s, coming from different sides of the sectarian divide, were part of the reason for what has happened. Both Graham Reid and Martin Lynch – Protestant and Catholic writers respectively – grew up in working-class areas of Belfast and, though separated by religious affiliation, nevertheless went through remarkably similar experiences. These are reflected in their plays.

Graham Reid was brought up in the Donegall Road area of Belfast, narrow terraced streets built for workers in the linen industry and one of the oldest working-class areas in the city. Much of the area has now been redeveloped but still in the summer marching season its paving stones are painted red, white and blue and bunting stretches from window to window across the street.

Reid left school at the age of fifteen – his first job was as a lamplighter. By the time he was twenty he was married with two children and still living in the area where he was brought up. Work consisted of odd jobs such as portering, interspersed with periods of unemployment. This was the early 1970s when sectarian strife in Belfast was at its height. Though Reid did not play a leading role, like most other men in the area he was involved in forming street vigilante groups organized by the Ulster Defence Association.

It was at this time that he made perhaps the most significant step in his career when he decided to attend the Belfast College of Business Studies as a mature student. After graduating in 1977 he taught history at the Gransha Boys' High School, Bangor, but gave this up in 1980 to concentrate on full-time writing, encouraged by an Arts Council grant.

Martin Lynch was brought up in the Turf Lodge estate, an area populated by Catholic dockers who included his father. Like Reid he left school at fifteen, though he took some O Levels when he was twenty-seven (after studying, co-incidentally, at the College of Business Studies). He regards his real education, however, as having been achieved in the Republican Movement through the 1970s.

After leaving school he took a job as a cloth-cutter, fully expecting that he would in time follow the other men in his family into the docks. He remained in this job until the summer of 1969, just before the Unity Flats riots. He had been in-terested in politics since childhood – his father's Republicanism was part of everyday life at home. But his own involvement with political struggle did not start until 1969: 'at the outbreak of actual violence and deaths'. And this was intensified with the start of internment in 1971. He was involved as an organizer for the Republican clubs movement, their main liaison officer in Turf Lodge. Later he became a key activist in the Workers' Party. In this period, however, his main preoccupation was community action, organizing young people in the Catholic Church's Turf Lodge Youth Club and forming a Socialist Fellowship there. In the late 1970s he began organizing youth drama, writing some of the material himself. This began in 1975 when friends suggested he went to the Lyric Theatre to see Patrick Galvin's *We Do It For Love*. The experience was a revelation.

> Terrific. My culture had been pubs and discos and TV and movies and things like that, and this was the first time at live theatre and BAM! Caught by the goolies. But I remember at the end of the play saying, 'Jeez, that was dead on. I think I could write like that. I know I could say more than that . . .'[2]

He began writing for the Turf Lodge Fellowship drama group with the plays *We want work, we want bread* and *Is there life before death?* (the latter provided the main theme of a BBC Northern Ireland documentary in the late 1970s, and was transmitted again by BBC 2 in the autumn of 1982 as an Open Door programme). By 1980 the Lyric Theatre had noticed Lynch's writing and invited him to join them as resident playwright, his first paid job in eight years.

Because of their backgrounds, and the period through which they grew up, both Reid and Lynch continually reflect violence and sectarian conflict in their work. In an essay on the new Ulster writing, evocatively entitled *Evacuating the Museum*, Philomena Muinzer has reflected on the identity crisis afflicting those who attempt to explore relationships in contemporary Ulster. Its inhabitants live as a double minority, Catholics in the North, Protestants in the larger land-mass; the former lacking a

State, the latter a nation. Inevitably they strive to discover, even create, a new reality, a new context in which stability and a secure sense of place can be felt. But the starting point is conflict.

All around them these Ulster writers see the facts of war primitively expressed. In the Ulster landscape archaic signs are also contemporary and provocative: cromlechs and Norman keeps bitterly remind them of modern graves, modern occupation. Over the city of Belfast hangs Cavehill, a constant monument to the United Irishmen who met there in 1795, and it has the great profile of a man, whom Seamus Heaney describes as a terrorist being questioned:

> 'Gunfire barks its questions off Cavehill and the profiled basalt maintains its stare South: proud, protestant and northern, and male.'[3]

The conflict has been personally felt by both Martin Lynch and Graham Reid. Lynch was arrested with monotonous regularity during the 1970s, about thirty times – mostly for four-hour screenings. On five occasions he was taken in for three days, three times to Castlereagh. These experiences provided firsthand research for the first of his plays performed at the Lyric Theatre, *The Interrogation of Ambrose Fogarty*. His article in the Belfast-based magazine *Fortnight* in September 1984, entitled 'A Black Footpath in Turf Lodge', provides eloquent testimony of the impact made on him by the violence.

> The short stretch of footpath between the top of the Whiterock Road and Turf Lodge hardly qualifies as one of the beauties of Belfast but in these troubled times it's as representative of our city as the Crown Bar or the Cavehill . . .

At this spot he witnessed first the explosion of a 'Loyalist murder bomb', secondly the Provisional IRA shooting a man dead, which is when he saw 'a pool of dark red, almost black, blood form a solid halo. I turned away at the sight of the man's brains as the army arrived.' And, finally, the location was the spot where that same army shot another man. When he arrived at the scene: 'A woman asked for something steel to press open his teeth. I gave her my front door key. He died three or four minutes later.'

For Reid the experience of violence has been less direct and public; more internalized and private. When he was two years old his parents separated; when he was fifteen his father committed suicide. This appears to have been the start of an on-going concern with death which is born of that primary insight into the ease which life can be extinguished.

At one very real level, of course, the material used by both Reid and Lynch in their plays presents a stereotyped image of life in Northern Ireland – an image reinforced by the regular news reports of bombings and sectarian killings. The areas where these events take place as a general rule are small, with strictly delineated boundaries. It is possible in Northern Ireland to live in localities where the walls are not daubed with political slogans, where British soldiers do not patrol, and where, by and large, life closely resembles that led by the inhabitants of any other provincial city or small town on mainland Britain. Indeed, the majority of middle-class people in Northern Ireland, whether Catholic or Protestant, lead just such a lifestyle. Direct experience of the conflict is normally confined to the working class and the areas in which they live. And the work of writers like Reid and Lynch only reaches the mass of these people when transferred to television.

However, if there is one factor that differentiates the whole of Northern Ireland from the British mainland it is the degree to which myth and stereotyped images condition attitudes and influence behaviour. The continuing institutional separation of Catholics from Protestants, most notably in their different churches and schools, is of crucial importance. So, too, is the ownership of land, with Protestant farmers invariably occupying the more fertile lowland areas and Catholics the more marginal hill farms. Social clubs tend to recruit exclusively from one 'side' or the other, particularly in the case of Protestant working men's clubs and, of course, the Protestant Orange orders. On the Catholic side there are organizations intended to uphold 'Irish culture', including Irish dance, traditional music, and the games of hurling and Gaelic football. The separation of the two cultures means each side has clearly contrasting images of itself and the other:

> Protestants contrast their industriousness, cleanliness, loyalty to the state and freedom of religious expression with Catholic laziness, scruffiness, treachery, clannishness and priest domination. Catholics contrast Protestant bigotry, narrow-mindedness, discrimination and money-centredness with their own tolerance, openness and interest in 'culture'.[4]

The myths most jealously harboured and most potent in their impact on contemporary events derive from the separate Catholic and Protestant views of history. The central events of the Catholic/Nationalist view arise out of English incursions into Ireland, most of which were unsuccessful until Cromwell's sortie in the seventeenth century. The main effect then was to replace Irish land ownership with English and Scots. The rights of tenants were removed, Irish trade and industry were undermined, and legal restrictions were placed on Catholics. Irish culture declined and general injustices continued into the nineteenth century. The solution was independence, but even this was spoiled by the partition of Ireland and by the discriminatory laws and practices of the artificially created 'majority' in the North. A specialist in the myths of Northern-Ireland, Anthony Buckley of the Ulster Folk and Transport Museum, put it this way:

> Irish nationalist history contains a catalogue of grievances whose rhetorical force lies in the reciprocity principle. Since the British (or 'planters') stole the land of their Irish forefathers; since they destroyed Ireland's trade, despoiled its culture and suppressed its religion, then Irish people have at

least the right to claim their land back, to press for the reunification of their island and to claim fair and equal treatment. In short, Irish history contains so many injustices perpetrated against native Irishmen by successive generations of British governments and planters, that the nationalists who are their heirs can lay claim to the rhetorical high ground of moral advantage against the putative descendants of their oppressors.[5]

Just as the seventeenth century is important for the Nationalist/ Catholic view of Irish history, so also is it to the Unionist/ Protestant cause. This is largely because the celebration of its events provides them with their most politically charged folk festivals. The best known is that on 12 July, when the Protestant Orange Order celebrates the defeat of the Catholic James II at the hands of William III. On 13 July, the County Armagh Royal Black Institution, whose members are drawn from the Orange Order, hold a well-attended 'Sham Fight' in which, with much shotgun fire and mock sword-fightings, James II is similarly 'defeated'. And in August and December, the 'Apprentice Boys of Derry' celebrate the relief of the Siege of Derry by marching round the city's walls. The siege occurred when, in the face of indecision by Lundy, the city governor, apprentice boys shut the gates against the advancing James. Lundy escaped by stealth, in consequence of which his huge sixteen-foot effigy is burned as part of the celebrations each December.

Of all these events, the Siege of Derry has the most important symbolic significance for Protestants since it evokes for them the idea of wicked, uncivilized, tyrannical people outside the walls confronting civilized, freedom-loving and 'religious' people within. These views reflect the Protestant stereotypes which categorize Catholics as superstitious, untidy and feckless in comparison with the Protestants' rationality, tidiness and hard work. Looking back tempts Protestants to compare Ulster with America and say, 'Nobody expects that it should be given back to the Indians' (or, for that matter, Australia to the

Aborigines). The Siege of Derry is also the source of the abidingly popular Protestant slogans 'No Surrender' and 'Not an Inch'. But as Anthony Buckley points out, in their mobilization of myth, Protestants tend to emphasize more recent history, since partition and the creation of Northern Ireland.

> They argue that since the 1920s Catholics have failed to accept the democratic will of the majority, and have instead subverted the state, using even violent means. Thus Protestants too have a catalogue of grievances against nationalists, some of them deeply felt, but the list which they nowadays use tends to start in the 1920s.[6]

The separated cultures of Protestant and Catholic in Northern Ireland, together with radically contrasting perspectives on their shared history, have combined to produce the stereotyped images each has of the other, images that are continually reinforced by the succession of atrocities perpetrated on both sides. Events in the mid-1980s forced a clear break in this process, however. The moves towards greater co-operation between the governments of Britain and the Irish Republic, which culminated in the Anglo-Irish Agreement in 1985, sent a shock wave through the Protestant community. Like the Scots and the Welsh, Protestants in Northern Ireland have a dual identity related to Ulster and to Britain. Their sense of Britishness, however, while often displayed more fervently is more conditional. This point was underlined in the wake of the Anglo-Irish Agreement by two Ulster-based academics, Roy Wallis and Steve Bruce:

> Ulster's Protestants see themselves as owing allegiance to Britain only so long as Britain supports their determination not to become incorporated into, or dominated by, the Republic of Ireland. Although their fathers did not seek a separate, semi-autonomous state at the time of partition, they soon began to see this as the surest safeguard of their freedom. Since the prorogation of the Stormont Parliament

and the assumption of responsibility for Northern Ireland by the Westminster government in 1972, some Protestant leaders have at times advocated the total integration of Ulster with mainland Britain on the same basis as Scotland or Wales. But the idea has less appeal than being able to determine their own affairs directly; and in the face of any greater control over the affairs of Northern Ireland, many Protestants would prefer that Ulster become entirely independent of the United Kingdom. Thus, the identity of Northern Ireland's Loyalists as 'British' is inevitably subordinated to their identity as Ulster Protestants . . .

The Protestants of Northern Ireland are well aware that the British public is largely indifferent to their troubles, sometimes contemptuous of their endeavours to preserve themselves and often uncomprehending of their attitudes and culture. Moreover, they know that the British want to avoid further ravages as a result of Irish politics, and to escape the cost – in money, lives and bad international relations – entailed by maintaining the right of the Loyalist majority to determine their fate. Although forced to rely on British support, Ulster Loyalists know that, at the end of the day, a substantial proportion of the British do not want them*, at least not at this high cost. Being British is not a viable identity when the British do not much want Ulster and when some future British government might seek to cut its losses by handing it over to the Irish Republic . . .[7]

It is against this background that the significance of the new generation of writers in Northern Ireland, represented here by Graham Reid and Martin Lynch, should be judged. An examination of their work reveals a sustained effort to explore the common experiences of both Protestant and Catholic in North-

---

* In a Gallup poll commissioned by the BBC's *Brass Tacks* programme (broadcast on 29 May 1986) 35 per cent of 1,060 people interviewed in mainland Britain wanted to see Ulster independent; 24 per cent wanted to see it become part of the Republic; and only 26 per cent wanted it to stay in the United Kingdom.

ern Ireland, especially where violence is concerned. There is a sense that in the commonality can be found a shared knowledge that contains within it the potential for supplanting Catholic and Protestant polarities. And it has remained the case, throughout 'The Troubles', that Catholics and Protestants in Northern Ireland have considered that they have more in common with each other than with people outside the Province – a factor which has continued to surprise, even at times mystify, outside observers.

Thus, for instance, in Graham Reid's *The Hidden Curriculum*, the first of his plays performed at the Lyric Theatre, in 1982, he set out to show that working-class Protestants, just as much as working-class Catholics, suffer from social deprivation. One of the characters in the play, Tom Allen, reflects bitterly:

> They don't know about us in the *Guardian* or the *Sunday Times*. They don't want to know . . . we're just loyalist extremists. We're never reasonable and we're never recognized. We're just a mass of extremists from West Belfast and they think that stretches from the Mourne Mountains to the Giant's Causeway. They think there's a million of us swarming all over the place, smothering all the wee innocent Catholics. But there aren't. There's a handful of us and we're just fighting to survive . . .
>
> Look at me, do I look like a rich, influential member of the Protestant ascendancy? I've got nothing . . . I live in a slum . . . I can't get a job . . . my ma ran off with her fancyman . . . my sister got knocked up the shoot by a Brit . . . my brother's in jail . . . and my da's dying in agony. (Pause) Now you go out on to the Falls Road and see how many of the poor underprivileged minority want to change places with me.

The Hidden Curriculum, drawing on Reid's own experience as a teacher in Northern Ireland, articulates his disillusion with an educational system that churns out sixteen-year-olds equipped for jobs that do not exist and who are semi-illiterate. As he told the *Guardian* in November 1985:

The tragedy of Northern Ireland is that kids who felt they couldn't make it legitimately felt they could make it illegitimately by joining the paramilitaries; they could become Mr Big very quickly.[8]

In his play *Remembrance*, premièred at the Lyric Theatre in 1984, Reid explores both sides of the sectarian divide. Its theme is love, which ironically grows in the sterile surroundings of a cemetery between a widower and widow – Protestant and Catholic respectively. Both have sons who were killed by sectarian violence, yet in spite of this division a relationship develops. The play is an expression of a conviction that despite the violence and intolerance, communication is still possible between the two communities in Northern Ireland. This is not to say, of course, that darker forces do not lurk in the background. As the widow's daughter says:

Ma, we live in Northern Ireland. My children won't have their own minds when they're old enough.

In Martin Lynch's first professional play, *Dockers*, performed at the Lyric in January 1981, the plot follows one man's struggle to get better wages and conditions for the dockers. The hero, John Graham, argues with a fellow dockworker that logic demands that Catholics and Protestants should work together:

GRAHAM . . . any trade unionist can see that the present situation whereby the employers can play the work off two unions wouldn't arise if we were one strong union. Catholic dockers and Protestant dockers. That's common sense . . . How it ever got to the stage of two unions I'll never know.
MCKIBBEN Because they're Protestants and we're Catholics.
GRAHAM But we're all dockers.
MCKIBBEN That's got nothin' to do with it.

In the play the opponents of a single union resort to intimidation, and ultimately to violence, to prevent its coming about. As Graham complains:

They'd rather march in their hundreds on St Patrick's Day commemoratin' a frigging myth, than march as part of the working-class movement through the streets of their own city. It's the same old story in Ireland. Socialism versus the Saints. And here we are, the only Third World country in Western Europe, and the Saints is winnin' hands down.

In his later play *My Minstrel Boy* (November 1985), set during the hunger strikes in 1981, Lynch attacks the inevitable connection of religion with politics in Northern Ireland. One of the boys (called Liverpool) remarks that when they are in London 'the Shankill Road men and the Falls men get on great'. But when they're back home religion takes over as a trigger for violence.

LIVERPOOL Maybe there something in the air here, which drives us all mad.
CHEESY There is – it's called horseshit – otherwise known as religion.

But at the very moment this attempt at expressing unity across the religious divide was being enacted on the stage at the Lyric Theatre, an event was taking place that seemed calculated to drive both sides into their religious bunkers. It is difficult to convey the sense of insecurity, anger and betrayal provoked in the Protestant community of Northern Ireland by the signing of the Anglo-Irish Agreement at Hillsborough in November 1985. It prompted the Protestant historian A. T. Q. Stewart to warn that the Ulster Protestants' sense of Britishness was being put on trial and should not be taken for granted. It was not something in the gift of Westminster.

It is by no means the same thing as Englishness. Nothing irritates an Ulsterman more than the assumption that the United Kingdom exists simply for the comfort and security of England and the English.
That is why it is often said that Belfast is pro-British and

anti-English, whereas Dublin is pro-English and anti-British. The Hillsborough agreement is living proof of this. English people who approve of the treaty should be in no doubt about the anti-Britishness of their new ally, a country and a nation which ostentatiously sympathized with Mussolini and Hitler, and much more recently gave enthusiastic support to Argentina during the Falklands War. This is not enough, however, to overcome the deep English racialist dislike of the Ulster Protestants, as the overwhelming support for the agreement in the House of Commons would tend to indicate . . .

. . . For Ulster Protestants, all was changed utterly on 15 November 1985. A terrible, unwished-for duty was born. Overnight the bickering between Unionists ceased. One no longer spoke of Unionists, but only of Protestants. Twenty years ago they had a parliament, a government and a state (of sorts) within the United Kingdom. The Troubles (more accurately, the English response to the Troubles, and basic misinterpretation of their real cause) deprived them of their government. In 1972 Edward Heath deprived them of their parliament. And now Mrs Thatcher has in effect deprived them of their homeland, or at least the right to have any say in how it is to be governed . . .[9]

The signing of the Hillsborough agreement quickened the efforts of a few within the Protestant community who for some years had been attempting to create a new focus for an identity in Northern Ireland to which both Protestants and Catholics could give their allegiance. It has been argued that, in the field of writing and the theatre, something similar was happening spontaneously in the 1980s: what the critic Lynda Henderson called 'a growing cultural self-respect',[10] which is the primary basis for any coherent and cohesive sense of identity. At the same time moves were under way to rediscover Ulster history and to work out constitutional mechanisms for Ulster independence. The fact that these efforts were carried out by the so-called 'New Ulster Movement', a small group associated with the Ulster Defence Association, seemed at first to serve only to marginalize the initiatives. But the Hillsborough accord in November 1985 suddenly gave a new relevance to what was being said. In early 1986 Michael Hall, a Belfast social worker who has contacts with extremists on both sides of the religious divide, published a popular, graphically illustrated new history of the Province entitled *Ulster: The Hidden History*. He explained that Ulster Protestants needed to re-examine their past in order to understand the confusion they felt about the present.

> With an amazing inability to see how their own activities and attitudes paved the way for the present 'troubles', they have watched successive British governments retreat, as they see it, in the face of Republican pressure. 'Our' Government, they lament, is giving in to 'them'. What price loyalty if their heritage and freedom (neatly ignoring their bigotry and injustice) was being sold down the river?
>
> But while most Protestants began to march yet again along the old paths of 'Not an Inch!' and 'No Surrender!', others, albeit a minority, were realizing that things couldn't go on as before. Change of some sort was necessary, not just in the social and political realities, but in the whole question of identity. The frequent crises were only proving what a sham the cherished British connection was, when it was only too apparent that the two sides distrusted and disliked each other intensely.
>
> Paradoxically, it was to be in their history, within which the Protestants had seemingly been trapped, that they were to find a way forward . . .[11]

Hall's 'hidden history' was based on the work of Ian Adamson, a Belfast doctor who had previously published two books *The Cruthin* (1974) and *The Identity of Ulster* (1982).[12] Adamson argues that the earliest inhabitants of Ireland were not the Gaels but the Cruthin who had lived there for at least 6,000 years before the Gaels invaded. These pre-Gaelic inhabitants, whose stronghold was in the north of Ireland, fought the encroachment of the Gaels tooth and nail. It was only in the fifth and sixth centuries that successive defeats resulted in the gradual emigration of the Cruthin across the narrow waters of the North Channel into Lowland Scotland.

Regardless of the historical authenticity of these assertions, here is further Irish mythology in the making, and all the more striking because of its explicit relation to modern political issues. In his work Adamson makes a number of bold claims. First, he challenges the assumption that all ancient Irish culture is Gaelic. He suggests, for example, that the Book of Kells is 'Pictish' or 'Scottish Irish'. Moreover, he appropriates Cú Chulainn, hero of the (Gaelic language) epic *Táin Bó Cuailgne*, for the Cruthin. Cú Chulainn's statue stands in Dublin's Central Post Office as a memorial to the nationalist dead of 1916, whose actions precipitated Irish independence. Placed in Adamson's context, however, Cú Chulainn represents the struggle of Ulster against the invading Gael. But, most powerfully of all, Adamson's account of Ulster's history enables him to claim that when the Plantation of Ulster began in the seventeenth century, the Scots who came over from the Lowlands were in fact descendants of the Cruthin race returning to the land of their birthright. As Anthony Buckley has it, the Cruthin argument addresses directly the rhetorical challenge of Irish nationalist history:

> It makes the claim that Ulster Protestants, and particularly those who emigrated from Scotland, have at least as much right to live in Ireland as do Irish Catholics. Second, it takes from the nationalist heritage many of its most treasured cultural traits by arguing their Cruthinic rather than Gaelic origins. And finally, the historical lynchpin of Irish nationalism, the Plantation of Ireland, is transformed from a conquest by an oppressive people into a reconquest by a people who had been forcefully expelled.[13]

The historical accuracy or, indeed, the real meaning for present-day Ireland of all this is secondary to the fact that these ideas have been taken up with enthusiasm by extreme elements within the Protestant community, elements that are increasingly giving precedence to the Ulster rather than British dimension of their identity. When he wrote his first book Adamson lectured to various groups including members of the paramilitary organization, the Ulster Defence Association. The second printing of the book had an introductory preface by Glen Barr, then an officer with the UDA, who became leader of the Ulster Workers' Council which co-ordinated the Loyalist general strike that destroyed the 'power-sharing executive' in 1974. In the late 1970s Barr was the leading figure in the UDA's New Ulster Political Research Group which began making tentative steps towards formulating a consciousness of a separate Ulster, separate, that is, from both London and Dublin, and one in which Catholics and Protestants could discover a commonality of interest. In its pamphlet *Beyond the Religious Divide* the Group put forward detailed proposals for an independent Ulster within the EEC, including a Bill of Rights and arrangements for Britain to continue a financial commitment for not less than twenty-five years. Only within such a negotiated framework could there be the evolution of 'proper', that is conventional, politics in the Province. The search group examined all the options that had been put forward to provide a solution to the conflict – from total integration with the rest of the United Kingdom through the return of a Stormont-type Northern Ireland government, to a federal or united Ireland – and found them all wanting:

It is sufficient to say that principally we found that any proposal which involved London would be rejected by the minority community and any proposal which involved Dublin would be rejected by the majority community.

This being the case the New Ulster Political Research Group had to search for an answer which removes both Britain and Southern Ireland from the situation and gives Northern Irish people prime negotiating rights about their future.

We believe there is one proposal which does offer peace, stability and reconciliation. It is the only proposal which does not have a victor and a loser. It will encourage the development of a common identity between the two communities, regardless of religion. It offers first-class Ulster-citizenship to all our people, because like it or not, the Protestant of Northern Ireland is looked upon as a second-class British citizen in Britain, and the Roman Catholic of Northern Ireland as a second-class Irish citizen in Southern Ireland.

Negotiated independence for Northern Ireland is the only hope of achieving a united Northern Ireland.[14]

Nearly a decade later, under pressure from the continuing conflict and the attempt by the London and Dublin governments to bypass the wishes of the Protestant population of Northern Ireland through the Anglo-Irish Agreement, the Ulster Political Research Group modified this stance. In a pamphlet entitled *Common Sense*, issued in mid-1987, it called for a constitutional settlement in which Ulster Protestants would 'no longer feel compelled to defend the frontier' and which would allow Ulster Catholics 'to play a full role in society'. There were four main recommendations:

1) A devolved legislative government for Northern Ireland and a written constitution, ratified by the people of Ulster in a referendum.
2) A modern democratic political structure based on consensus government, proportional representation and shared responsibility.
3) A Bill of Rights.
4) A supreme court charged with the responsibility of upholding constitutional law and safeguarding the rights of the individual as represented in the Bill of Rights.

The pamphlet recognized, if tacitly, that such fundamental changes to the framework of the British State, embracing sovereignty of the people rather than the Crown in Parliament, would in itself serve to push Ulster towards independence. The pamphlet also drew attention to the little recognized reality of Ulster political life that serves most to separate it from mainland British political culture: the fact that the main British political parties, Conservative, Labour and Democrats, refuse to organize in Northern Ireland. As the pamphlet stated, 'Ulster people may well find it strange that British political parties suggest that we turn away from "sectarianism", yet refused to provide organized alternatives for the Northern Ireland electorate.'[15] During the mid-1980s a Campaign for Equal Citizenship was initiated in Northern Ireland to persuade the British parties to put up candidates in the Province. Its leader, Belfast lawyer Robert McCartney, claimed lineage from Edward Carson, Ulster's champion against British-imposed Home Rule in the first decades of the century. In a speech to a closed session of the Official Unionists' conference in November 1986, McCartney quoted Carson's 1912 words: 'We ask for no special rights but we claim the same rights from the same government as every other part of the United Kingdom.'[16]

This was a critical conference for the integrationists' cause within Northern Ireland Protestant politics. McCartney failed to persuade the Official Unionists to adopt a policy calling for complete integration of Ulster with Britain – implying the eventual abandonment of the Unionist party in favour of the British mainland parties – by forty votes. Soon afterwards he was expelled from the Official Unionist party altogether. The then leader of the Ulster Defence Association, Andy Tyrie, one of the authors of the pamphlet *Common Sense*, caught the mood of the Protestant community when he said, in early 1988, 'We must take back the Ulster problem to ourselves. We must replace British nationalism and Irish nationalism with an Ulster nationalism.'[17]

Though the voices calling for a separate Ulster identity have, until the mid-1980s at any rate, been in the minority and easily marginalized because of their para-military connections, there are signs that deeper cultural movements in the community are providing support for the idea. Certainly this is one conclusion that can be drawn from an examination of the upsurge in new writing in Ulster in the 1980s, as exemplified by Martin Lynch and Graham Reid. Despite his coming from a Catholic culture, Lynch's plays treat people as people regardless of creed or nationality, and have succeeded in drawing a culturally mixed audience. He remains committed to articulating this message within the context of Northern Ireland and is looking for new institutions and structures to pursue it.

> What I would really like to see come about in Belfast is the setting up, for want of a better name, of a cultural centre that would house facilities for theatre, music and all other art forms, a place where the family could come along and take part, a centre accessible to all. Such a place would encourage everyone to express themselves in some form or other. I'd like to see people come from Cregagh and Divis and Turf Lodge and Sandy Row. I think that a lot of working-class people feel a lack of confidence in themselves . . . such a centre would be just the place to show them that their voices can be heard.[18]

The experience of writing in the early 1980s, and the success that has resulted from it, have distanced Graham Reid, unlike Martin Lynch, from his community. In these years he first moved from the location of his roots in working-class central Belfast to the suburban middle-class outskirts of County Down and, finally, to exile in London. Part of this process was the success and subsequent television filming of his trio of Billy plays which give an accurate portrait of working-class Protestant family life in Northern Ireland. What had happened was that he had grown through the old divisions between Catholic and Protestant, and no longer identified with them. The experience was accompanied by a curious sense of deflation. After the filming of the last Billy play, *A Coming to Terms for Billy*, Reid described his feelings. It would be, he wrote:

> . . . the last time I'd be in Coolderry Street for a long time; perhaps for ever . . . It had once been a street where every

face was a familiar face. Now it looked small, most of the people were strangers . . .[19]

As a result of the television plays, and the changes of fortune they had brought him, he was no longer part of the Belfast community. But in a sense what that community had been, with its divisions and suffering, was in the past as well:

They smile and congratulate me; they say I've put Coolderry Street on the map. Do they know why I've put Coolderry Street on the map – do they see what I see, hear what I hear, when I watch my 'Play for Today' . . . that are all about yesterday?[20]

The decisive defeat of the divorce referendum in the Republic of Ireland in early July 1986 reinforced the external pressures that are pushing Ulster along the road to some form of independence. It was a signal that neither mainland Britain nor the Republic identified with the Province; not only Northern Ireland was saying 'No' to Irish unity, but the Republic also. The New Ireland Forum report, that came out of Dublin in 1984 – signed by all the democratic political parties in the Republic – had spelled out the kind of society that it considered the only feasible basis for Irish unity:

It must be a society within which . . . all cultural, political and religious belief can be freely expressed and practised. Fundamental to such a society are freedom of conscience . . . reconciliation and the cherishing of the diversity of all traditions. Public legislation must have regard for the conscientious beliefs of different minority groups . . .[21]

The message for the people of Northern Ireland arising out of the heavy defeat for the divorce proposals in the referendum in the South, was that if they wished to pursue the ideals outlined in the New Forum report they had little option but to attempt to do so within the framework of Ulster alone. In this project the attitudes of the Protestant majority will, inevitably, prove decisive. And here the main point was established early on in the present Troubles, in 1971, by an American political scientist who has adopted Scotland as his home, Richard Rose:

> An Ulster Protestant may describe himself as British, but doing this does not necessarily mean he thinks as English, Scottish and Welsh people do when they identify themselves thus. For the residents of Great Britain, this label *supplements* their primary nationality. For the Ulsterman, it is a *substitute* for it [my emphasis].[22]

Ulster Loyalism is in some ways like the surrogate identity found in Scotland's phoney Gaelic or Tartan culture. There the 'impossible' substitute is also a way of keeping something – in this case English domination – at arm's length. Both were founded on specifically political weakness, the absence of belief in a community's ability and need to manage a separate destiny. But while Scottish Tartan-Gaelicism is at least an insistence upon a distinct identity, Ulster Loyalism is the nominal dissolution of all distinctions: the only proclamation, in fact, of pure 'Britishness' to be found anywhere within the Divided Kingdom.

One solution for this identity – if it were supremely confident in itself – would be to simply re-draw its boundaries to exclude the more Catholic areas and create a more confined, more completely Protestant community. To state this option is to highlight the practical difficulties and its ultimate illogicality. In practical terms there is no straightforward way of dividing the Catholic and Protestant communities from one another in Northern Ireland and allowing heavily Catholic areas to join the Republic – at least, not without envisaging a scale of violence reminiscent of the partition of India from Pakistan in 1948. The more fundamental objection, however, is that the Ulster Protestant 'Loyalist' is not primarily British in identification and, ultimately, is not perceived as such by the peoples of mainland Britain, certainly not by the English. Herein lies the illogicality of integration as a solution to the Northern Ireland problem. Integration, as demanded by some prominent Northern Ireland politicians in the 1970s and 1980s, would require the British political parties to operate within Northern Ireland. This they will not do.

As the twenty-first century draws near Northern Ireland's Protestants are discovering that they are not really 'British' at all, certainly not in any sense that can be shared with the rest of the United Kingdom as part of a unitary political system. The complex reality facing Ulster's Protestants was summarized by the poet, the late John Hewitt, a product of the Ulster dissenting tradition, when he wrote:

> I am an Ulsterman. I was born in the island of Ireland, before the partition of the island. So legally and emotionally too, I am an Irishman. My native language is English; my literary loyalties and political enthusiasms are English. Therefore, I am Ulster, Irish, British. And, in that I live in a region of an island in an archipelago off the shores of Europe, I am European.[23]

Note that Hewitt, who gave these matters more thought than most, elided English into British in this statement. Nonetheless, this sense that there are layers of interacting identities to be thought through and accommodated is something shared by all the peoples of Northern Ireland. The signs are that in the process they are discovering, indeed recovering, a distinctive Ulster awareness that will prove their bedrock in the future.

NOTES

1 Lynda Henderson, 'A Wealth of New Ulster Writing', *Fortnight*, No. 201, February 1984, p. 28–30.
2 Susan Triesman, 'Caught by the Goolies' in *Platform*, Spring 1983.
3 Philomena Muinzer, 'Evacuating the Museum' in *New Theatre Quarterly*, February 1987.

4 H. Donnan and G. MacFarlane, '"You get on better with your own": social continuity and change in rural Northern Ireland', in P. Clancy, S. Drury, K. Lynch and L. O'Dowd, *Ireland: A Sociological Profile*, Dublin: Institute of Public Administration, 1986.

5 Anthony D. Buckley, '"We're trying to find our identity" – Uses of history among Ulster Protestants', unpublished paper presented to a 'History and Ethnicity' Conference of the History Association, Norwich, 1987.

6 Ibid.

7 Roy Wallis and Steve Bruce, 'Ian Paisley: Defender of the Faith' in *Social Studies Review*, Vol. 1, No. 4, March 1986, p. 13.

8 Hugh Herbert, 'The Mask of Violence', *Guardian*, 12 November 1985.

9 A. T. Q. Stewart, 'The Siege of Ulster', *Spectator*, 11 January 1986.

10 Lynda Henderson, op. cit.

11 Michael Hall, *Protestant Conceptions of National Identity – An Overview*, mimeographed paper, January 1986.

12 Michael Hall *Ulster: The Hidden History*, Pretani Press, Belfast, 1986. Ian Adamson: *The Cruthin: The Ancient Kindred*, Donard, Belfast, 1974; and *The Identity of Ulster: the land, the language and the people*, Petani Press, Belfast, 1982.

13 Anthony D. Buckley, op. cit.

14 Ulster Defence Association, *Beyond the Religious Divide*, March, 1979.

15 Ulster Political Research Group, *Common Sense*, 1987, p. 7.

16 Carson's first speech at Craigavon, near Belfast, 23 September 1911; quoted in Marjoribanks and Colvin, *The Life of Lord Carson*, Vol. 2, p. 78, 1932. The circumstances of the speech are explained in A. T. Q. Stewart, *The Ulster Crisis*, Faber, 1967, p. 47–8.

17 Quoted in 'Ulster's Long Goodbye' by John Lloyd, *Financial Times*, 20 February 1988.

18 *Belfast Telegraph*, 'The Voice of the Dispossessed', 26 March 1984.

19 Graham Reid, 'Another Ulster' in *Fortnight*, No. 202, March 1984, p. 29.

20 Ibid.

21 Quoted by Tom Hadden and Kevin Boyle, 'When New Ireland is Divorced from Reality', *Guardian*, 7 July 1986.

22 Richard Rose, *Governing Without Consensus: An Irish Perspective*, Faber, 1971, p. 206.
23 John Hewitt, 'A Question of Identity' in *Papers from a weekend workshop at Corrymeela – a critical look at independence*, unpublished mimeograph, 1976 (available from the Linen Hall Library, Belfast).

5

Identity in retreat – Wales

For much of the twentieth century Wales has been a nation in retreat. Its identity has been defined largely in terms of economic reliance on farming, coal-mining and steel-making, Nonconformism in religion and, above all, a distinctive language. All have been in decline during the century, and sharpened decline since the 1960s. Yet cultures in decline characteristically display remarkable bursts of energy and creativity, rather like the final burst of a firework before its extinction. This is certainly true of Wales, and these last decades of the twentieth century are helping decide whether the political renaissance that attempted a flowering during the 1960s and 1970s will flourish or just fade away.

Since World War II employment in farming has slumped to about 2 per cent of those at work. In the 1950s 130,000 were still employed in the South Wales coalfield; when the miners struck in 1984 the numbers were down to 21,500, and soon after the end of the strike, a year later, were down again to 13,500. By the end of the 1980s, following further closures, fewer than 8,000 miners were working in the coalfield and British Coal had downgraded its separate-area status.

Steel industry employment in Wales peaked at 72,000 in 1970. By the end of the 1980s, with steel-making at East Moors (Cardiff), Ebbw Vale and Shotton ended, and the workforces at Llanwern and Port Talbot halved, the industry employed fewer than 20,000 men.

Empty and decaying chapels across Wales testify to the secularization of the culture, while the language has continued a catastrophic slump throughout the century, from 37 per cent of the population speaking Welsh in 1921 to 19 per cent in 1981 – that is, 503,549 people out of a total population of 2,645,114. In his 1962 lecture on *The Fate of the Language* Saunders Lewis predicted that 'Welsh will end as a living language, should the present trend continue, about the beginning of the twenty-first century . . . Nothing can change that except determination, will power, struggle, sacrifice and endeavour.'[1]

There is no doubt that in Welsh culture and politics the 'fate of the language' is something of an obsession among both Welsh and non-Welsh speakers. The reason why this is so says a great deal about Welsh identity. As Ned Thomas has put it:

. . . by its existence, the language tells us that we are Welsh. All the feeling of nationality that is supported for the Englishman by the Queen, the Houses of Parliament, the London policeman, the bewigged judges, the customs officers at Dover and a whole range of political, cultural and popular institutions, rests for the Welshman on the language and literature, and on a few cultural phenomena such as the Eisteddfod which are closely linked with the language. For centuries the Welsh identity has not been political or institutional but linguistic and literary . . .[2]

It is for this reason that in Wales the language carries a symbolic charge out of all proportion to that which one expects to find in every language alongside its function as a tool of communication:

There is something ultimately mysterious, because unconscious, in this clinging to the language. It is a question of holding on to an identity, and if this identity were able to flower in other ways, say through political control of our own future, the language would probably not continue to carry the high symbolic charge it carries now.[3]

This is not just an issue for Welsh-speakers in Wales. English-speaking Welsh people are deeply involved as well, and not least because most of them have or have had relatives who speak the language.

> There is a full range of emotional attitudes among those who speak no Welsh, ranging from fierce resolve to learn it, through ambivalence, to contempt and hostility. Neutrality of attitude towards Welsh often betokens a recent English immigrant. Emotional attitudes of one kind or another are a sure sign of Welshness.
> This introduces a dynamic instability into the language structure and indeed into the politics of Wales. While the Welsh language maintains a certain strength and liveliness it will always have the capacity in certain circumstances to attach to itself the loyalties of some English-speaking Welsh people. But in other circumstances, as has happened in the past, these same people may look towards a British or even English identity.[4]

Though it is far from being the case that the identity of the Welsh – whether Welsh-speaking or not – is entirely related to language, the final point in the above quotation does highlight the essential duality of the people's self-perception. Welshness is so interfused with Britishness that at times it seems more accurate to speak of a merged rather than dual identity. In this the Welsh are to be distinguished from the Scots, Northern Irish and the English. A simple explanation for the difference is the physical closeness and continual historical interaction between the Welsh and the English. Historically, the connection has taken the form of a movement out of Wales into England, accompanied by strong influences flowing the other way. So it was as the leader of a largely Welsh-speaking army that Henry VII picked up Richard III's fallen crown from Bosworth field in 1485. In fulfilment of the long-promised legend, Henry named his first son Arthur, and the Welsh gentry, the Uchelwyr, flocked to London to become British. The phrase 'British

Empire' was invented in 1580 by a Welshman, Dr John Dee, mathematician and chief scientific adviser to Elizabeth I. It was in 1536, of course, that Henry VII's Act of 'Union' incorporated Wales into England, proscribing the Welsh language in the process. Yet, before the century was out Elizabeth I had authorized the translation of the Bible into Welsh; this was accomplished in 1588, and it was through this medium that Nonconformist religion was imported into Wales from England in the following centuries.

Also imported into Wales, with a kind of explosion from the end of the eighteenth century onwards, was industrial capitalism. Until this period the Welsh numbered no more than 400,000, often less. But by the early 1900s, the height of the Welsh industrial revolution, the number had increased fivefold. What these statistics mean is that modern Wales is largely a creation of the industrial revolution concentrated between the years 1870 and 1911. In 1851 Wales had a population of slightly over one million, with two-thirds living in the countryside. Just sixty years later this population had doubled and two-thirds of it was now concentrated in urban areas. The pell-mell expansion of coal-mining in the southern valleys brought a migration of some 400,000 people out of rural into urban Wales. These people, incidentally, were overwhelmingly Welsh-speaking, so that until the 1920s Welsh was the majority language in large areas of industrial Wales. This migration was quickly followed by an influx from outside Wales. In the decade 1901–11 the South Wales coalfield attracted 129,000 people, most of whom came from England. In this period Wales was drawing immigrants at a rate almost as high as that of the United States – an annual rate of 4.5 per 1,000, against the USA's 6.3 per 1,000[5].

If the prevailing social and economic movement of this period was from England into Wales, politically the influence was the other way around. The old Liberal Party dominated British politics, and it, in turn, was strongly influenced by Welsh elements, most notably Lloyd George. As Chancellor of the Exchequer in 1909 he laid the foundation for the welfare state and then went on, during World War I, to become the most

powerful Prime Minister Britain would ever have. Lloyd
George's career retains an immense psychological significance
in Welsh politics because of the way in which he fused Welsh
and British aspirations. He had been, of course, a leader of the
Cymru Fydd (Young Wales) movement of the 1880s and 1890s.
But, though it was a forerunner of modern Welsh nationalism,
there is no doubt that the aim of Cymru Fydd was simply to
promote equal participation for the Welsh in the British political system. As another leader of Cymru Fydd, T. E. Ellis, the
member for Meirionnydd, put it in 1892, speaking at the British
Empire Club in London: 'The more Wales has the power of
initiative and decision in her own affairs, the more closely will
she be bound to the very texture of the imperial fabric.'[6]

It was World War I that saw, in the most horrific way
possible, the fullest participation of Wales in British affairs.
With Lloyd George in the lead at the apex of British imperial
power, Welshmen enlisted in their thousands – 280,000, two-
thirds of the country's male population between twenty and
forty years of age. The experience marked the end of
nineteenth-century Wales and the certainties that went with it.
It marked the end of Cymru Fydd nationalism, defined as
collaborating Liberalism in league with suffocating Nonconformism. And it provided the opening for the politics of hard
nationalism: the founding of Plaid Cymru in 1925 and the
confrontation with the British State that ensued.

But it was many years before this opening could be exploited
to any great degree. The haemorrhage caused by World War I
was equalled in its impact on Welsh society by the devastation
wrought by the depression of the 1920s and 1930s. Welsh
industry was based too narrowly on the primary production of
coal and steel. Coal production – much of it for the world's fleet
of steam-powered ships – was geared almost entirely to the
export sector of the British economy. And when Wales's main
markets in Europe and North America were lost in the years
after the war, not least because of the general and rapid change
to oil from coal-generated steam-power for ships, that dependence proved fatal. Welsh unemployment reached 38 per cent

in 1932, forcing mass emigration from both rural and industrial parts of the country. Wales lost 450,000 people in this way between 1921 and 1939, most of them going to England.

At the very time of this enforced move into England, a political current of socialist ideology was flowing the other way. Although it was given a distinctly Welsh flavour, most notably by personalities such as James Griffiths and Aneurin Bevan, socialist ideology – certainly the State Centralist variety of the Webbs – was imported into Wales from England. Early on, there were attempts to counter this brand of socialism with more decentralist forms in line with what can be termed the radical/nationalist tradition. Leaders such as Keir Hardie (MP for Merthyr, 1900–15) and Arthur Henderson, Labour's general secretary who in 1918 pledged the party to the 'widest and generous measure of Home Rule' for Wales, found no problem in accepting it. But as soon as Labour became regarded as a party of government, after 1923, such commitments and ideas rapidly lost ground. The attractions of parliamentary power politics, and the centralized control of the party machine at the all-British level which that entailed, proved overwhelming. In the 1931 general election, Labour was almost wiped out in England; in Wales it lost only one seat. This was a lesson which the party has never forgotten – it accounted for much of the Labour opposition to the proposed Welsh Assembly wielded so effectively in the 1979 referendum. For the Assembly implied in the long run a smaller number of Welsh Labour MPs, thus reducing the party's chances of forming a government at Westminster. After all, but for Wales there would have been no Labour government in 1950 (majority seven) or in 1964 (majority five). And without Welsh support there would not have been even a minority government after February 1974.

The success of a dissident minority of Welsh MPs in mobilizing a greater part of their party against their own government's Assembly proposals was an episode of immense significance. It demonstrated that, for the established parliamentary and local government power centres of the party at least, Welshness and Welsh politics were of secondary account when British interests were at stake, as the 'Labour No Assembly' manifesto, published in Wales during the referendum campaign, made clear:

> We believe that the conquest of the economic and social wrongs in our system can best be secured by maximizing the strength of our movement through the democratic power of a majority Labour government ruling through Parliament.[7]

Yet underpinning such arguments is an ambivalence about identity that runs like a fault line through Welsh society. The nerve was touched starkly by Enoch Powell during a 'No Assembly' campaign rally.

> Whatever may be true of Scotland, at no time in the last thousand years – and maybe longer still – has it been possible to draw a line on the map along Offa's Dyke, and pointing to the west of it, to say 'that is Wales'. The whole history of England, so long as it has been a nation, has been penetrated and interfused with Wales and the Welsh . . . the heritage and achievement of the Welsh people is nothing less than the heritage of Britain itself.[8]

However, Powell's use of the terms 'English' and 'British' as interchangeable reveals the fundamental flaw in the concept of Britishness. For although the idea has specific meaning within Wales – and in Scotland and Northern Ireland – in England it is hard to define except in relation to Englishness.

An intriguing attempt to argue that in the concept of Britain there is something more than being Welsh, English or Scottish has been made by the expatriate Welshman, Daniel Jenkins, in his book *The British, Their Identity and Their Religion*, published in 1975 as the devolution debate was gathering pace. His central assertion was that 'intelligent Scotsmen and Welshmen find it easy to be good Scotsmen and good Welshmen and at the same time to participate fully in the wider life of Britain.'[9] But when he comes to specify those elements that characterize

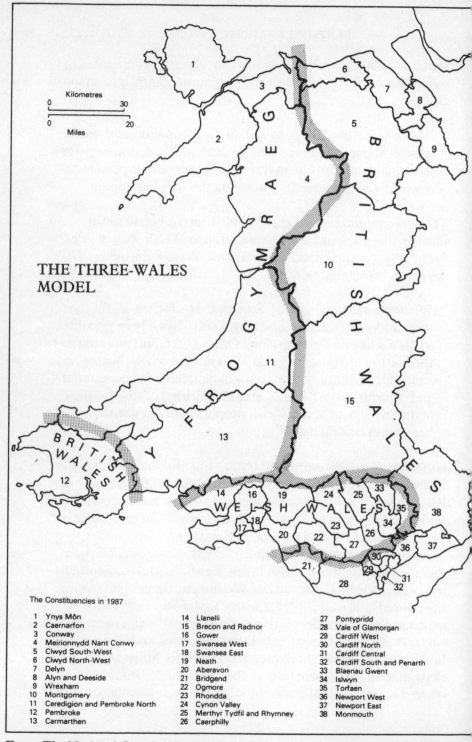

THE THREE-WALES MODEL

Kilometres
0 ———————— 30

Miles
0 ———————— 20

Y FROG YMRAEG

BRITISH WALES

WELSH WALES

The Constituencies in 1987

1 Ynys Môn
2 Caernarfon
3 Conway
4 Meirionnydd Nant Conwy
5 Clwyd South-West
6 Clwyd North-West
7 Delyn
8 Alyn and Deeside
9 Wrexham
10 Montgomery
11 Ceredigion and Pembroke North
12 Pembroke
13 Carmarthen

14 Llanelli
15 Brecon and Radnor
16 Gower
17 Swansea West
18 Swansea East
19 Neath
20 Aberavon
21 Bridgend
22 Ogmore
23 Rhondda
24 Cynon Valley
25 Merthyr Tydfil and Rhymney
26 Caerphilly

27 Pontypridd
28 Vale of Glamorgan
29 Cardiff West
30 Cardiff North
31 Cardiff Central
32 Cardiff South and Penarth
33 Blaenau Gwent
34 Islwyn
35 Torfaen
36 Newport West
37 Newport East
38 Monmouth

From *The National Question Again*, ed. by John Osmond, Gomer Press, 1985 (D. Balsom's model)

British, as opposed to Scottish or Welsh, identity he can only list moral qualities that are the essence of English romanticism: reserve, respect for privacy, the ideal of the 'gentleman', modesty, fair play, and the social style that derives from them.

The historical inter-penetration of Wales and England has combined with economic disruption during the twentieth century – the decline of farming, coal and steel and their replacement in the main by assembly and service industries – to produce a fractured and fragmented Wales, split into three distinct political areas.[10] The first, 'Y Fro Gymraeg' – the Welsh-speaking heartland – covers north-west and west central Wales, that is, most of Gwynedd, Dyfed, and parts of Clwyd and Powys. Here the language is still strong, a great many people identify themselves as Welsh; and Welsh issues, and to a large extent, nationalist issues, set the political agenda.

Second, is 'Welsh Wales', made up of the southern industrial valleys of West and Mid Glamorgan and Gwent. This is Labour's electoral stronghold, from which it spread out to dominate Welsh politics for much of this century and into which it had, by the early 1980s, retreated. The 1984–5 miners' strike reactivated some of the radical traditions of this area, traditions which both present themselves as distinctively Welsh and insist on a British political context. One could perhaps say that 'Welsh Wales' tends to define itself as a radical area within Britain, overlapping in its culture with areas of similar heavy industry in Scotland and northern England.

The third area is 'British Wales', the indistinct remainder of the country – the south Wales and north-east coastal belts, southern Pembrokeshire, and the regions bordering England. Here those who think of themselves as Welsh are barely half the population and the Conservatives have emerged as an important political force.

The focus of Welsh identity and separateness is concentrated in 'Y Fro Gymraeg' and 'Welsh Wales' and in their interaction with 'British Wales', and particularly with the administrative capital, Cardiff, the headquarters of a growing network of Welsh-based institutions centred on the Welsh Office. As Denis

Balsom, the originator of the three-Wales model (based on the 1979 Welsh Election Study) described here and shown on p. 128, has remarked:

> In one field only does the Welsh dimension loom large in *British Wales*; the growth of the government bureaucratic machine in Cardiff. Herein lies the greatest paradox. The institutions that were created in response to particular Welsh demands now largely supervise and oversee the demise of much of the particular character of Wales. Wales, however, remains the rationale of the bureaucratic machine and, what is more, continues to acquire power and influence rather than to wither like its host.[11]

The erosion of the particular character of 'Y Fro Gymraeg' and 'Welsh Wales' has been accompanied, however, by vivid campaigns of defence, campaigns that more than once in the past twenty years have thrust Wales into the forefront of British politics and questioned the unity of the United Kingdom. Two personalities, Dafydd Iwan and Kim Howells, between them express much of the force and vitality of the identity that still exists in these areas. Though neither is an elected politician, both became effective spokesmen for their respective communities in the 1980s. And both in their present activities are confronting dilemmas that clearly reflect the ambiguities inherent in the Welsh sense of identity and its precarious future.

During the 1984–5 miners' strike Kim Howells, research officer with the South Wales NUM, achieved a sudden prominence in Wales and beyond. He emerged, in fact, as one of the most effective spokesmen for the miners' cause throughout Britain. He conveyed within Wales, and to the world outside, a reasoned resolution rather different in style from Arthur Scargill's rhetoric. Indeed, towards the end of the strike there was confrontation between the two when Howells articulated South Wales's criticisms of Scargill's handling of the dispute and for a short while was silenced as an official spokeman at

Scargill's insistence. However, in his personality and his projection of the dispute, Howells spoke for the Welsh miners and personified the reasons why the area was the most united of all the coalfields in the dispute, and why it was the area that led the return to work.

The mobilization of the Welsh coalfield in the early months of the dispute was extraordinary. Welsh pickets were operating throughout the English coalfields and camped twenty-four hours a day, seven days a week outside twenty-two power stations. As Howells himself wrote afterwards:

> The cost was astronomic and the effort enormous. For month after month, the coalfield despatched an average of four to five thousand pickets to these various targets. South Wales coach hire companies had never experienced anything like it. Men whose previous expertise had revolved around supporting roofs or ripping roadways forward suddenly found themselves becoming experts at interpreting Ordnance Survey maps or organizing transport or dishing out legal advice or sniffing out likely sources of accommodation or food and funds. Others rapidly became accomplished speakers, organizers and fund-raisers.[12]

With South Wales the first NUM area hit by the government's new sequestration laws – a tribute to the extent of its picketing involvement – the need for funds rapidly became a priority. Feeding up to 20,000 families each week, as well as paying the huge costs of picketing, was made possible only by creating what Howells described as an alternative welfare state inside Wales:

> The people of the coalfields had no choice but to create new defences and in building them they rediscovered old socialist and collectivist truths. They realized that by uniting and sharing all that they had, they could survive and overcome the worst that the present State apparatus could throw at them.

In South Wales we also rediscovered something else: that we are part of a real nation which extends northwards beyond the coalfield, into the mountains of Powys, Dyfed and Gwynedd. For the first time since the industrial revolution in Wales, the two halves of the nation came together in mutual support. Pickets from the south travelled to the nuclear and hydro-stations in the north. Support groups in the north brought food, money and clothes to the south. Friendships and alliances flourished; old differences of attitude and accent withered and out of it all grew the most important, 'formal' political organization to emerge during the course of the strike – the Wales Congress in Support of Mining Communities.[13]

However, Howells does not have any sentimental vision of his Valleys 'Welsh Wales' community and is well aware of the dangers inherent in the homegrown tendency to sentimentalize and thereby trivialize it. He is well-known for attacking kitsch images of Welshness based on rugby, leeks and male-voice choirs. All these were brought together in the 1970s in the person of the Valleys entertainer Max Boyce who drew from Howells a scornful diatribe. The Welsh, he wrote:

. . . appear content to stand by and watch as Boyce and his equivalents in the media strain from the public image of South Wales those very ingredients which have set it apart from so many other centres of industrial production: its socialism, its reputation for trade-union solidarity and its internationalism.

In Leisure Centres throughout Wales, Boyce's audiences sit and snicker at his portrayal of their own idiosyncrasies. But they do not laugh at themselves – not all of them anyway. They laugh at an *externally manufactured* image of themselves and one, moreover, which emphasizes those characteristics which are least offensive and troublesome to those who govern us – like newspaper proprietors and television controllers.

And they laugh because they are confused by the junk peddled by those journalists, 'commentators', clerics, vocal expatriates and rootless 'Professional Welshmen' who pass themselves off as the arbiters of taste and national identity in this media-stricken principality . . .[14]

There is a clear analogy here with the Tartanry and Kailyard images of Scottish identity and their debilitating and undermining impact on any autonomous political expression. In Wales, however, the position is more complex. It is not just a question of clearing away this undergrowth of false representation and allowing more authentic and democratic forms to flourish. Among a minority of the Welsh these have been protected by the barrier of the Welsh language. So the majority English-speaking Welsh have the double dilemma of an 'externally manufactured' image on one side and an internal but inaccessible sensibility on the other.

The origins of Howells' consciousness of both the virtues and the faults of his south Wales Valley culture lie in his upbringing in the Cynon Valley, which he revealed in an interview shortly after the end of the 1984–5 strike.

All my family, all my father's side are from Trecynon, but I'm from Penywaun which is a council estate a mile and a half up the valley – a very different place of course. Penywaun was part of the Bevanite housing policy – we were all very proud to grow up there. Now it's appallingly run down and it distresses me every time I go back there to see my mother and father. In a sense it chronicles the story of post-war south Wales. It was raised as a shining marvellous place for kids to grow up in, and now it has fallen apart. There's seven or eight houses in my mother's street boarded up. And yet once everyone wanted to go and live there.

I was brought up in a really revolutionary household. Bevan was no hero in our house. We didn't listen to Welsh choirs, we listened to jazz, modern jazz. Brought up on Charlie Parker, I was, and Welsh choirs were anathema to us;

they were a bunch of men singing hymns dressed in penguin suits, aping the bourgeoisie. We were taught from an early age that we were hamstrung by an atrophied culture, and yet whenever the Welsh choirs came on the wireless my mother and father would burst into tears of emotion. I remember sitting in the Palladium in Aberdare in the late 'sixties watching a re-run of *How Green was My Valley* and I remember thinking for the first time, this is a film extolling the virtues of scabs, full of Welshmen with Irish accents, and it's absolute nonsense; yet I looked around and the entire audience had their eyes filled with tears . . . in one of the most left-wing constituencies in Britain. It's a very curious culture, isn't it?[15]

Ambiguity and ambivalence are contained within Kim Howells himself. Though he clearly recognizes a Welsh dimension as something beyond the Valleys of 'Welsh Wales', there is no certainty about what it means, for instance for political action. Howells is very much tied into the British dimension via Labour movement politics. And he is curiously neutral about the Welsh language: both his parents and his wife are Welsh-speaking, but his children are not.

There is no ambiguity in the life and political activity of Dafydd Iwan on these questions. A dedicated language activist – he was chairman of Cymdeithas yr Iaith Gymraeg (the Welsh Language Society) from 1968 to 1971 and remains a member of its organizing Senedd – he is also a leading Plaid Cymru politician. He has been active in most of Cymdeithas yr Iaith's key campaigns – on bilingual road signs, on a separate Welsh-language television channel, and the problem of holiday homes in the rural Welsh-speaking heartlands. A decisive moment was the 1971 Swansea conspiracy trial when Iwan, along with six other Cymdeithas yr Iaith activists faced charges arising out of the road-signs campaign. Iwan was sentenced to twelve months, suspended for three years. In the trial he conducted the defence case with a finesse that brought him national attention. In his final speech he declared that the young people of Wales had a battle to fight, a battle which lent meaning and purpose to their lives.

It is a battle to restore our heritage: our language and culture, our religion and song, our land and our people. We must restore them to their old greatness and inherent dignity. The wonderful thing about this battle is that it is not fought with arms of war, but the arms of justice and the rights of man.[16]

But it is as a singer that Dafydd Iwan has become most widely known, a writer and singer of songs about the Welsh language and culture and the campaigns to restore them, and the politics of Wales. One of his best songs 'Pam Fod Eira Yn Wyn?' (why is the snow white?) originated from his speech at the Swansea trial. It was a rhetorical question aimed at those who doubt the legitimacy and sacrifice of Cymdeithas yr Iaith's direct-action strategy to thrust the language on to the political agenda. The combination of words, melody and timbre of voice give Iwan's songs their peculiar charisma. As Ned Thomas remarks:

The note of tragedy, the note of passion, of conviction, of scorn, in the words he sings, touch all strings and bring out all the reverberations in the highly politicized modern Welsh culture.[17]

An early favourite was called simply 'Can Yr Ysgol' (the school song). The lyrics refer to a past age when Welsh was banned in the schools of Wales. A small boy speaks of his home life, which is lived in the Welsh language – using the emotive symbols of mother, small bed, mealtimes – and contrasts this with his life at school where he has 'lessons geography, lessons history' and so on. In the final verse, he speaks of Sundays when in Sunday School he finds that Jesus Christ still speaks Welsh. This division between the emotional and official spheres of life is made real even for today's youth, who have experienced far more subtle forms of alienation from their mother tongue.

Iwan's material has often caused controversy – songs like

'Carlo' satirizing the investiture of Prince Charles in 1969, and 'Magi Thatcher' which was banned by the BBC in December 1980. But some of the best songs are political in a more oblique way. 'Gad Fi'n Llonydd' (leave me alone) satirizes those who want to go on with their comfortable lives and keep out of politics. 'The Big Shot' (on the other side of the 'Carlo' record) satirizes the provincial boss who exists in many parts of Wales, thriving on nepotism and political patronage.

> I've been on the education committe since 1933,
> I know every headmaster in the country, or rather
> > they know me.

In 'Peidiwch Gofyn imi Ddangos Fy Ochr' (don't ask me to take sides) Iwan touches the same nerve as Kim Howells in his parody of the stage Welshman.

> I love to see Wales playing rugby
> 'Bread of 'Eaven' and 'I Bob Un'
> And if I've had a pint or two
> I'll even boo 'God Save the Queen'.

The tone of the songs reflects the political mood of the times. Thus in the early 1970s when Welsh aspirations were upbeat, with Welsh language campaigns gathering momentum and the prospect of devolution in the air, Iwan's keynote song was 'I'r Gad' (to battle), a call to political action.

> We're fed up with empty talking,
> Safe committees by the score,
> No more gutless shilly-shallying,
> We're smashing signs and we'll smash more.

In the early 1980s when defeat was the prevalent mood, with the 1979 referendum result still fresh in the mind and pit and steel closures accelerating, Iwan's songs stressed survival and the durability of Welsh nationhood. 'Yma o Hyd' (we're still here) emphasizes the length of life of Wales as a nation. It was written for a tour Iwan undertook during 1983 with the folk group Ar Log (For Hire) to commemorate the 1,500th anniversary of the supposed emergence of Wales as a nation, when the Roman leader Magnus Maximus departed from Wales. The rousing chorus line in the song declares: 'Despite everybody and everything, We're still here!'

In the 1980s, when the campaign over Welsh-language broadcasting was largely achieved with the establishment of Sianel Pedwar Cymru, the overriding preoccupation of the language campaigners was the influx of outside, usually English, people into Gwynedd and Dyfed. This has been happening on such a scale over the past twenty years that it is in the process of changing the human ecological balance of the Welsh-speaking heartland. For example, according to the Anglesey Structure Plan published in 1982, very little 'natural' increase in the population was anticipated in the rest of the decade. Yet there were at that time valid planning permissions in the pipeline to build 1,800 new homes on the island. Between 1971 and 1977 some 12,000 newcomers moved to live on Anglesey, with about 8,400 of them from outside Wales. The Structure Plan estimated that more than 75,000 additional immigrants will have moved to the island by the year 2011.

As Cymdeithas yr Iaith's 1982 Manifesto put it, the Welsh language is literally losing ground:

. . . the actual geographical SIZE of the Welsh-speaking areas is being reduced from year to year . . . there is a growing process of thinning afoot WITHIN these areas, a process which is gradually displacing the language even from its traditional strongholds.

These features are all sure signs of the inevitable death of the Welsh language, for linguists believe that a language cannot continue as a spoken language without its own exclusive territory, and without that territory having a certain degree of geographical unity.[18]

This is leading to the most difficult, complex and potentially explosive confrontation between Welsh nationalists and the British State. For what is being demanded is the introduction of linguistic and community considerations into the property market – demands which offend against the fundamental principles of a government committed to an individualistic free economy. These are the frustrations lying behind the campaigns by unknown groups that since 1979 have burnt down more than a hundred holiday homes, mainly in Dyfed and Gwynedd. Dafydd Iwan, who is a founder of Cymdeithas Tai Gwynedd, a housing association dedicated to providing homes and work for native Welsh people, is fearful that the demographic trends could eventually split Plaid Cymru itself, with a minority breaking away to focus its efforts on Gwynedd and Dyfed and abandoning the notion of an all-Wales political dimension so far as nationalist politics is concerned.

These pressures are only serving to highlight a dilemma that has always been at the centre of the aspirations of Welsh nationalists. A politics of identity is inevitably exclusive, but one that rests on a language only spoken by the minority in a community is even more so. In this respect Welsh nationalists have a far more difficult task than their counterparts in Scotland where the nationalist message does not, by its nature, exclude very many people living there. Moreover, as Peter Madgwick has pointed out, in Wales political nationalism is outweighed by a strong tradition of anti- (Welsh)-nationalism.

This is quite precise and intense among a small proportion of the electorate, so that intense nationalism is balanced by intense anti-nationalism. At the same time, and more significantly, hostility to nationalism is institutionalized in the Welsh Labour Party, in which leaders like Neil Kinnock follow in the London-orientated tradition of Aneurin Bevan.[19]

But if this is a dilemma for Dafydd Iwan and other nationalist leaders in Y Fro Gymraeg it poses equal problems for the aspirations of Kim Howells' 'Welsh Wales'. Here, what happened to the Wales Congress in Support of Mining Communities in the wake of the 1984–5 strike is a case in point. While the strike was still under way the Congress received public backing and often active support from a number of Welsh Labour MPs and other leading Labour figures, especially in the Wales TUC. Even so, from the start the majority of the foot-soldiers of the Congress, apart from the miners themselves and particularly their wives, were activists from Plaid Cymru, Cymdeithas yr Iaith, and the Euro-Communist wing of the Welsh Communist Party. As Kim Howells wrote, as the strike was coming to an end, the Congress

> . . . forced people out of their political trenches and provided a forum for debate and action of the kind sadly missing, not merely in Wales but throughout these islands. It has opened up the possibility of mutual action to defend and strengthen communities, whether their lifeblood is coal or farming or engineering or oil-refining. Its existence has given certain established politicians nightmares; it has perplexed others and given a new lease of life to still more. Its potential has hardly been realized . . .[20]

But so far as the mainstream Welsh Labour Party was concerned, the role of the Welsh Congress finished when the strike ended. The Labour MP most identified with the Congress (she was its Treasurer), Aberdare Member Ann Clwyd, remarked that it is political parties not movements that fight for political change in Britain. The Welsh Labour Executive resolved to continue its connection with the Congress, but only so long as it kept to its original aims of supporting mining communities; there should be no attempt to use it as a platform for wider debate and activity.[21] These reactions point to the fact that the interests of Wales have a low priority in Labour's overriding aim of achieving power at Westminster. As Peter Madgwick put it:

Labour Members of Parliament from Wales indulge the rhetoric, support the miners, but otherwise lean to the centre and right of the party. The party leadership, for good electoral reasons, shows signs of pitching its appeal to the depressed inner cities of the English metropolitan areas – Toxteth, not Tonypandy, Lambeth not Llanelli.[22]

The circumstances of identity in retreat are forcing Y Fro Gymraeg and 'Welsh Wales' to forge a new relationship with one another, an uneasy kind of alliance. Writing in 1970 the late J. R. Jones reflected:

It is said of one experience that it is one of the most agonizing possible . . . that of having to leave the soil of your own country forever, of turning your back on your heritage, being torn away from the roots of your familiar land. I have not suffered that experience. But I know of an experience equally agonizing and more irreversible (for you could return to your home), and that is the experience of knowing, not that you are leaving your country, but that your country is leaving you, is ceasing to exist under your very feet, being sucked away from you, as it were by a consuming, swallowing wind, into the hands and the possession of another country and civilization.[23]

Now something of the same kind of experience is afflicting the valleys of 'Welsh Wales'. Rapid deindustrialization since the late 1970s has taken away from this community the vital base and confident protesting style which it took as its birthright. This crisis has been articulated by the historian Gwyn A. Williams, who observed, towards the end of his history of Wales, that the 1983 general election (confirmed by the 1987 results) exposed the myth that South Wales was still a Labour heartland. Of the fifteen seats which embrace 'Welsh Wales' (see map on p. 128) only seven remain which give Labour more than 50 per cent of the vote. The rest registered anti-Labour pluralities.

Of the old 20,000-majority familiars, only a traditional three remain: Rhondda, Merthyr Tydfil and what used to be Ebbw Vale (Blaenau Gwent). They stand like Aneurin Bevan's memorial stones on the Pound above Tredegar and they are beginning to look like the Stonehenge of Welsh politics.[24]

Pondering the future, Williams gloomily acknowledges that 'some human society will obviously survive'. But:

> What seems to be clear is that a majority of the inhabitants of Wales are choosing a British identity which seems to require the elimination of a Welsh one. There is an irony here since the reconstruction of the British economy and society is no less clearly getting rid of Britain as we have known it. Britain as we have known it appears to have started its own long march out of history. This history of the Welsh may close then with the intriguing thought that the Welsh, First of the British, look like being the Last.[25]

The increasing fragmentation of Welsh culture and society evident from this chapter should be explanation enough of the heavy four-to-one defeat of the Welsh Assembly proposals in the 1979 referendum. And yet, the picture is not that clear. Referendums tend to reflect the particular circumstances in which they are held. There was evidence after nearly a decade of recessionary blows to the economy and, still for most of Wales, alien Conservative rule, that a majority might be found for a fresh devolutionary advance. An opinion poll by HTV Wales in June 1987 showed 52 per cent in favour of an Assembly, 36 per cent against, with 12 per cent 'don't know' – a higher level of support than was registered at any time during the 1970s. The Yes figure rose to 60 per cent when respondents were asked what their attitude on the question would be if a Scottish Assembly were in place.

Part of the reason why devolution continues to be at least an underlying issue in Welsh politics is the continuing growth of a network of Welsh-based institutions that has taken Welsh identity beyond reliance upon language and religion. Foremost amongst these is the Welsh Office which, though only established in 1964, has since grown rapidly in size and influence. The original handful of civil servants had increased to 1,210 within ten years, and to 2,206 by 1984. In the early 1980s they moved into an opulent £23m extension in Cardiff's Cathay's Park – a Welsh Whitehall – and by the end of the 1980s spending within the responsibility of the Secretary of State for Wales (who has a seat in the Cabinet) had grown to more than £3.5 billion a year. This figure represented some 80 per cent of public expenditure in Wales.

In 1973 the Wales TUC was set up, against the opposition of the trade-union establishment in London, and provided a new focus for consultation and pressure. It was the Welsh Office that had, in fact, provided much of the impetus behind the Wales TUC, as one of its early chairmen, D. Ivor Davies, explained.

> The establishment of the Secretary of State for Wales and the Welsh Office symbolized a developing awareness of nationhood amongst the people. In this situation the trade-union movement was at a disadvantage.[26]

Administrative developments had now acquired a ratchet effect that would ensure continued momentum in the 1980s, the result of the 1979 referendum notwithstanding. Thus in 1981 the Welsh Office gained its most important power since industrial development functions were devolved in 1975: direct negotiations with the Treasury for its funding, rather than operating through other departments. This change had a number of important consequences. First, like his counterpart in Scotland, the Secretary of State was given the politically sensitive task of arguing in Cabinet for a total sum for Wales each year and, secondly, responsibility for deciding expenditure priorities within it. The Welsh Office was now responsible for distributing the rate support grant – amounting to £1,256m in 1988–89 – to the eight Welsh counties and thirty-seven districts.

In the absence of a democratic forum at the Welsh level, little of the negotiations and political manoeuvring central to this new relationship between the Treasury and the Welsh Office on the one hand, and between the Welsh Office and the Welsh local authorities on the other, is visible to the Welsh public. Nevertheless, they are of immense consequence – the essence of what politics is about and the heart of the devolution legislation of the 1970s. The fact that these transactions are now firmly implanted into a Welsh context, albeit administratively, is an important new baseline for any future constitutional development.

At the same time, the developing institutional structure is reinforcing a sense of unity in the Welsh economy, a key area where in the past unity has generally been lacking. Economically it has been all too easy to divide Wales into at least three distinct regions – north Wales linked to Liverpool and Merseyside; mid-Wales linked to Birmingham and the Midlands; and south Wales linked to Bristol and Severnside. By the 1980s economic recession had lessened the pull of both Merseyside and the West Midlands while, despite its proximity, there has never been much community of interest between Bristol and south Wales. But quite apart from these factors a network of economic institutions now treats Wales as a single unit. For instance, there are at least eight different agencies charged with the development of employment opportunities in Wales: the Welsh Office; the Welsh Development Agency; Mid Wales Development; the Welsh arm of the Manpower Services Commission; the Land Authority for Wales; the Welsh local authorities; BSC (Industry) Ltd and NCB (Enterprises) Ltd, set up to promote industrial development in the steel and coal rundown areas; and the EEC, operating mainly through the Regional and Social Funds. However, though there is a distinctive administrative and policy-making network in Wales, this cannot yet be described as an autonomous political system – a fact demonstrated by the 1979 referendum.

The point can be further made by contrasting Wales with Scotland. Much of Scottish national consciousness is based on the survival, since 1707, of an interlocking institutional framework, in particular the separate Scottish legal and educational systems and Kirk. Moreover, institutions such as the Scottish Office and Scottish TUC have a longer history than their counterparts in Wales which have been created only relatively recently. As a result, loyalties tend to be more regional within Wales than is the case in Scotland. In turn, this has limited the development of a sense of Welsh citizenship – a concept very much bound up with institutions – and the sense of responsibility that goes with it. The idea of Scottish citizenship, however, is meaningful, and arguably accounted by itself for the narrow majority in favour achieved in the Scottish devolution referendum.

It is not difficult to point to an essential condition for the development of a sense of Welsh citizenship comparable with that in Scotland, and that is an equivalent communications network. The importance of this was symbolized by the struggles necessary to secure Sianel Pedwar Cymru, the Welsh fourth television channel, between the 1979 general election and the autumn of 1982 when it finally reached the airwaves. The success of S4C holds out the potential, nothing more, for the creation of a more comprehensive and integrated English-language service for the large majority of the Welsh people. As the resolution approved by a national broadcasting conference held in Aberystwyth in late 1979 put it:

We refuse to live in a mass society forced to accept messages produced by someone else, in a direct language or culture belonging to someone else. We declare once more that the campaign for a Welsh and Welsh-language television service is part of a wider popular fight for the right to communicate with each other on the mass media.

English-speaking Welsh people are caught in a special dilemma in this respect. On one side of them is a surging mass of American/English culture channelled overwhelmingly through London-based television; on the other is a Welsh-language culture becoming aggressive in fighting back. English-speaking Welsh people tend to be caught in the middle. On the one hand they feel a need to discover some home territory on which to build an authentic expression of their own identity. At the same time they cannot relate to the vivid expression of Welsh-language culture which is doing this. The result tends to be a retreat into the dependency of an 'Anglo–Welsh' culture combined with a denial that English is a Welsh language. The English-speaking Welsh then vote with their television aerials, turning them away from Wales towards transmitting stations in England.

The position is further compounded by the centralized character of the British media which inevitably leads to distortions and warped perceptions of identity. Plaid Cymru has always been acutely aware of the negative impact of this on its own fortunes. In early 1982 it commissioned a survey by the Department of Communication Studies at the Polytechnic of Wales of a hundred hours of television news and current affairs programmes broadcast out of Cardiff and London. This concluded that while the London-based news had little difficulty in identifying a distinctive Welsh linguistic and cultural tradition, it failed to recognize any political or economic distinctiveness:

In particular, there is an entire submerged Wales of protest; a political history quite unlike the land of song, chapel and rugby stereotypes that serve to identify it within and beyond the news. Recent examples of protests that have national implications are the continuing battle between the State and the language; the peace campaign (the women who marched to Greenham Common started from Cardiff, whilst others marched to Brawdy), and protests against unemployment, attacks on civil liberties etc. The submerged Wales is invisible in the news from London not because news is uninterested in protest, but because it simply doesn't have an available notion of Welsh identity within which such protests make sense as being, amongst other things, Welsh . . . The London news media are actively promoting stereotypes and excluding other identities that are just as Welsh. This makes it hard for people in Wales to watch the news and feel themselves to be Welsh at the same time.[27]

In the absence of a cohesive internal-communication network, whether of the media or of the economy generally, it is little wonder that the innate Welsh tendency to tribalism and fragmentation based on locality has flourished at the expense of any all-Wales consciousness, let alone any sense of Welsh citizenship of the kind that is more developed in Scotland.

It can be argued that with the development of Radio Cymru in the late 1970s and now Sianel Pedwar Cymru in the 1980s, the Welsh language community has the basis of a fully integrated communications network. The same cannot be said of English-speaking Wales. But the momentum provided by Welsh-language broadcasting may well have an impact on English-language broadcasting in Wales, both in terms of the structure of its operation and its content. The creation of Radio Wales alongside Radio Cymru, the former broadcasting on medium-wave and the latter on VHF, set a precedent and an immediate example for S4C to follow. The presence and success of S4C will act as a continual measure against which the English-language output of BBC Wales and HTV Wales will be gauged – both starting from a position of being overwhelmingly dominated by the schedules of the London network.

It can therefore be seen that, as has already been argued, built into Wales's present administrative and communication structures is the potential and momentum for further growth. The kind of arguments being put for the further extension of Welsh institutional autonomy were those heard at the 1986 conference of the Wales TUC. This saw the launching of a campaign to loosen the ties of the Wales from the British TUC, and to bring the Welsh organization into line with the greater freedom enjoyed by the Scottish TUC. The Welsh secretary of the Transport and General Workers' Union, George Wright (actually an Englishman from Birmingham), argued that at the very time the Wales TUC should be increasing its autonomy so as to defend a deprived community more effectively, it was in fact being run down to the level of a regional council in England.

We've lost our effectiveness, are unable to campaign in ways that we would wish, to assist our affiliates who are in dispute in Wales, because of central control. We're not to the fore in the eyes of the media, as the strong independent imaginative voice of the workers of Wales, and our international links are extremely limited. Our right to resolve our own problems is almost non-existent, and our future looks in doubt.

We must be big enough to think for ourselves here in Wales, we must believe in ourselves. No one in London, New York or Tokyo, or Bonn or Washington or Moscow is going to resolve the problems that face the Welsh people. Only we are going to do that by exercising the right degree of self-determination.[28]

So far as the Welsh language is concerned the undoubted retreat in the west and north has, to some extent, been counterbalanced by a small growth in the south and east. The 1981 census showed a small increase in the numbers of children speaking Welsh and this undoubtedly reflected the extraordinary growth of Welsh-medium primary and secondary schools in anglicized Wales. Between 1970 and 1984, the number of primary school children being taught through the medium of Welsh rose from 6,243 a year to 10,412, and secondary school children from 2,017 to 8,933.[29] This growth continued through the latter half of the 1980s. Moreover, there has been an extraordinary increase since the mid-1960s in the numbers of adults learning Welsh. Throughout Wales, but mainly in the south, a complex network of evening and other classes testifies to a surge of interest. Of special note are the intensive Ulpan courses, used in Israel since 1948 to teach Hebrew and taken up in Wales for the Welsh language in the early 1970s. These courses, conducted in the early morning as well as the evening and regulated by the extra-mural departments of the University of Wales, involve students attending five times a week for periods of up to a year.

By the mid-1980s there were, on average, 500 once- or twice-weekly classes, sixty Ulpan courses, and eighteen summer and residential schools being offered by various bodies and movements in Wales every year, and about 6,000 students learning Welsh.

What is the motivation behind this burst of activity and commitment on behalf of the language? No doubt, if the 6,000 adults learning the language at any one time were questioned as to their reasons, there would be 6,000 individual responses. Mixed motives, too, unquestionably accompany the decision of many English-speaking parents to send their children to Welsh-medium schools. For some it is the fact that in some counties children attending Welsh-medium primary schools can begin their education a year early. For others, there is the belief that the Welsh-medium schools are simply better, with better examination results at the end. Then again, within Wales increasing numbers of jobs have a Welsh-speaking qualification attached to them. But underlying all these decisions, a gesture is being made by English-speakers which is hard not to relate to the question of identity.

The connection was made in the 1960s by the philosopher J. R. Jones in his lecture 'Need the language divide us?' He pointed out that if language was regarded as a purely functional means of communication, then there was no task left that the Welsh language could perform better than English:

You can look at the whole range of public life today in Wales at the functional level without finding a single special and unique task which Welsh could perform. They are all performed already by English. So what is the point? . . . The conclusion to be drawn is that we must start looking for the *special* task of the Welsh language in a completely different direction – a direction in which we do not often look when enquiring about the usefulness of a language. My message is that there is such a definite and inalienable task for the Welsh language in the second half of the twentieth century – a task which nothing else in the world could perform – the

structural task of being the *only means of saving the separate
identity of the Welsh people* . . .

The task of Welsh in the days of the religious revivals was
that of saving the souls of the Welsh as individuals. Its only
possible special task now is the structural one of saving the
separate identity of the Welsh *as a People*.[30]

The central problem and challenge of this vision is how the
badge of identity it prescribes can be affixed to the large
majority of Welsh people – somewhere to one side of 80 per cent
– who do not speak the language. One advantage, as indicated
earlier, is that very few are neutral on this issue. Many, of
course, are actively hostile, often through feelings of suppressed guilt at having some first-hand personal or family
experience of language loss. The late Gwyn Thomas who
scorned linguistic and political nationalism, but who yet
seemed to personify the complexity and ambiguity of Welshness, wrote in 1979:

My father and mother were Welsh-speaking, yet I did not
exchange a word in that language with them. The death of
Welsh ran through our family of twelve like a geological fault.
Places like the Rhondda were parts of America that never
managed to get to the boat.[31]

In the 1980s, as the language continues to make itself felt even
in the most anglicized regions of Wales – most notably through
the Welsh-language media – the English-speaking Welsh are
being coaxed to some kind of accommodation. This can only
be helped by the process of Welsh self-identification that is
accompanying the growth of Welsh institutions generally, a
growth that is steadily increasing the forums and places
where English-speaking Welsh speak to each other as Welsh
people. Out of this it should be possible, to pursue J. R.
Jones's argument, for those who do not know the language
'functionally', that is, as a means of communication:

. . . to come to see it as the language of their separate identity – the language which built for them the only structure they have as a separate People. They will respect it when they see that without it they are not a People at all. The slogan which I should like to see plastered over the walls and bridges of Wales is – 'Remember Cornwall'.[32]

The increasing numbers choosing Welsh-medium education and learning Welsh in the 1980s suggest that J. R. Jones's exhortation of the 1960s is being taken to heart. It still remains the case, however, as the 1979 referendum demonstrated, that the Welsh do seem to recoil instinctively whenever there is a public opportunity to assert their identity. It is as though Wales has lived far too long in the shadow of a powerful English presence to risk brash adventure: much better to make progress quietly, by stealth. But while such caution may have paid dividends in the past, contemporary circumstances present a changed environment. In the Wales of the 1980s and 1990s more than a century of single-party politics is being transformed into a far more fluid multi-party system with the promise of a Labour government in London more questionable than in the past. The British nation-state is being challenged in Brussels and Belfast. Scottish politics remain an uncertain but potentially influential focus for change; and, as has been described above, a variety of institutional and administrative expressions of Welsh identity continue to evolve. There should not be too much surprise if the Welsh discover, some time in the 1990s, that the kind of modest political arrangements envisaged in the 1978 Wales Act that would have established a Welsh Assembly, would be the most natural way to accommodate themselves to the changing patterns of the last part of the twentieth century.

NOTES

1 Saunders Lewis, *The Fate of the Language*, reproduced in English in *Presenting Saunders Lewis*, University of Wales Press, 1973.

2 Ned Thomas, *The Welsh Extremist*, Lolfa, 1973, p. 30–31.
3 Ibid., p. 37.
4 Ned Thomas, *Wales in the Balance*, Aberystwyth, mimeographed paper, 1986.
5 See Brinley Thomas, 'Wales and the Atlantic Economy' in *The Welsh Economy – Studies in Expansion*, ed. Brinley Thomas, University of Wales Press, 1962.
6 Quoted by David Smith in 'Wales Through the Looking Glass' in David Smith (ed.), *A People and a Proletariat*, Pluto Press, 1980, p. 222.
7 'Labour No Assembly' manifesto, 'Facts to Beat Fantasies', Blackwood, Gwent, February 1979, p. 1.
8 Enoch Powell, speech at the Temple of Peace, Cardiff, 2 February 1979.
9 Daniel Jenkins, *The British, Their Identity and Their Religion*, SCM Press, 1975, p. 132.
10 See Denis Balsom, 'The Three-Wales Model' in John Osmond (ed.), *The National Question Again – Welsh Political Identity in the 1980s*, Gomer, 1985.
11 Ibid., p. 16.
12 Kim Howells, 'Stopping Out – The Birth of a New Kind of Politics' in Huw Beynon (ed.), *Digging Deeper*, Verso, 1985, p. 141–2.
13 Ibid., p. 147.
14 Kim Howells, 'Plastic Max' in ARCADE-*Wales Fortnightly*, No. 2, November 1980.
15 Interview in *Planet*, No. 51, Aberystwyth, June 1985, p. 9–10.
16 *Western Mail*, 15 May 1971.
17 Ned Thomas, *The Welsh Extremist*, op. cit. p. 92.
18 Cymdeithas yr Iaith Gymraeg, *Manifesto 1982*, Aberystwyth, p. 60.
19 Peter Madgwick, *Wales 1966–1985, From Carmarthen to Brecon and Radnor*, UK Politics Workgroup mimeographed paper, 1985, p. 7.
20 Kim Howells, 'Stopping Out', op.cit., p. 147.
21 John Osmond, 'The future of the Wales Congress' in *Planet*, No. 51, p. 119–124.
22 Madgwick, op.cit., p. 2.
23 J. R. Jones, *Gwaedd yng Nghymru* (A Cry from Wales), Cyhoeddiadau Modern, 1970.

24 Gwyn A. Williams, *When Was Wales?* Penguin, 1985, p. 303.
25 Ibid., p. 303.
26 Private interview, October 1976.
27 Trevor Wright and John Hartley, 'Representations for the people – Television news, Plaid Cymru and Wales', Plaid Cymru, Cardiff, 1983.
28 Quoted in *Planet*, No. 57, Aberystwyth, June 1986, p. 119.
29 Figures from the Welsh Joint Education Committee research department, Cardiff.
30 J. R. Jones, 'Need the Language Divide Us?' 1967 lecture, translated from the Welsh in *Planet*, No. 49/50, January 1980, p. 28.
31 Quoted by Dai Smith in his *Wales! Wales?*, George Allen and Unwin, 1984, p. 152.
32 J. R. Jones, op.cit., p. 29–30.

6

Identity ascendant – the 'Home Counties'

Questions of identity are invariably highlighted and articulated at moments of crisis, both in personal and national experience. For the English the key moment of crisis in the twentieth century was the summer of 1940 when, in the wake of Dunkirk, the country was faced with imminent invasion. The two voices which between them captured the twin poles of the English character – certainly as the English perceive it themselves – were Winston Churchill and J. B. Priestley.

Churchill's wartime broadcasts, drawing on majestic imagery and the language of an heroic past, caused the weekly magazine *Time and Tide* to describe him (June 22, 1940) as 'the essential Englishman, the descendant of Marlborough, the shaggy lion that never admits defeat'. At the same time, in 1940 and 1941, J. B. Priestley's broadcast postscripts to the BBC's Sunday evening news bulletins focused on the ordinary people, their sense of community and the qualities sustaining it, their kindness, humour and courage. The responses of Churchill and Priestley to Dunkirk emphasized the contrast between them. Where Churchill spoke in ringing heroic terms of the abstract qualities Dunkirk demonstrated – 'valour, perseverance, perfect discipline, faultless service, resource, skill and unconquerable fidelity' – Priestley eulogized the little seaside pleasure-steamers pressed into service for the evacuation, and evoked the world they represented, the world of 'pierrots and piers, ham and egg teas, palmists, automatic machines and crowded, sweating promenades'.

It was more than just a difference in style, it was a significantly different view of why the war was being fought. For Churchill it was simple: 'We have to gain the victory. That is our task;' beyond the victory, he relied on the vague generalized statement that the world would move forward into 'broad sunlit uplands'. But for Priestley it was what came after the war that was vitally important. England was fighting, he said, 'not so that we can go back to anything. There's nothing that really worked that we can go back to.' The aim must be 'new and better homes, real homes, a decent chance at last – new life'. He had detected the radical shift in the national mood which the war had triggered:

> The war because it demands a huge collective effort, is compelling us to change not only our ordinary, social and economic habits but also our habits of thought. We've actually changed over from the property view to the sense of community, which simply means that we realize we're all in the same boat.[1]

Two reactions to the Churchill and Priestley broadcasts at the time summarize the different aspects of the English character they epitomized. In his book *Britain's Wartime Revolution* (1944) the left-wing journalist Hamilton Fyfe quoted his diary entry for February 1941:

> Churchill gave another of his really stirring radio talks this evening, stressing especially the probability of invasion. Richard Acland was right when he said in the House not long ago, 'we literally love the Premier'. It is odd that one who is half-American – and that the better half – should so completely embody that John Bullishness which the English like to consider their main characteristic. Baldwin tried to act the part and failed. Churchill does it instinctively. When he calls Mussolini 'a crafty, cold-blooded, black-hearted Italian', and

Hitler 'that wicked man whose crime-stained system is now at bay', the phrases come from his inmost being. When he tells how he gave Wavell the word 'Go' in the language of the Gospel according to St Matthew: 'Ask and it shall be given, seek and ye shall find, knock and it shall be opened unto you', and then exclaims triumphantly: 'The Army of the Nile has asked and it was given. They sought and they have found. They knocked and it has been opened unto them', he hits exactly that mixture of piety and profanity which the English learn from their earliest years.

In its 12 October 1940 issue, *Time and Tide* spoke of the impact of the Priestley talks – the BBC credited him with 'the biggest listening audience in the war', 30 per cent of the regular listeners (BBC *Year Book*, 1946) – and commented that they reflected a new spirit in the country:

> Somehow J. B. Priestley has succeeded in evoking for us – for almost all of us – the very spirit of the age we want to live in. A world of kindness, equality, justice, simplicity and fellowship. There are, of course, still a few people who mistrust the spirit of the Priestley broadcasts, people who have no wish whatever to listen to forecasts of a more just and equal society where their privileges will mean nothing and their chances be the same as those of their fellows . . . Over the country as a whole the Priestley broadcasts have been accepted by the vast majority of the well-to-do and the badly-to-do, as the expression of their own desire for a new order of a very different stamp from the old order . . . the foundations of the new England must be laid to provide for immense improvements in such directions as housing, health and education.

There is no doubt that during the early part of World War II both Churchill and Priestley gave voice to keenly felt English, perhaps more accurately Anglo-British, feelings. At the same time, however, they also reflected between them contradictions at the heart of Englishness that fly in the face of any conventional national unity of purpose. Most of English power and wealth, influence and status, is centred on the City of London and the Home Counties; English self-imagery is bound up with essentially rural impulses whilst the large majority of English people live in an urban environment; and, finally, overlying all this, English identity is predominantly bound up with institutions – the monarch and Parliament – rather than with a more unifying, purposeful sense of territory and people. On all these questions Churchill and Priestley during the Second World War neatly represented the poles: Churchill the rural aristocratic tradition, Priestley the urban and democratic; Churchill the south-eastern metropolitan culture; Priestley the northern and provincial; Churchill closely bound up with loyalty to Crown and Parliament, Priestley representing a profound sense of the sovereignty of the people.

The clash was dramatized at the time by Churchill's declaring it intolerable for the BBC to broadcast criticism of the government and ordering Priestley to be taken off the air. It was confirmation that Priestley's message was felt to be deeply subversive to the dominant culture. A good example was his broadcast on 21 July 1940, which was an attack on perhaps the most sacred icon of the established order, property. Property, Priestley asserted, was an 'old-fashioned' idea which should be replaced by 'community':

> And I'll give you an instance of how this change should be working. Near where I live is a house with a large garden, that's not being used at all because the owner of it has gone to America. Now, according to the property view, this is all right, and we, who haven't gone to America, must fight to protect this absentee owner's property. But on the community's view, this is all wrong. There are hundreds of working men not far from here who urgently need ground for allotments so they can produce a bit more food. Also, we may soon need more houses for billeting. Therefore, I say, that house and garden ought to be used whether the owner, who's gone to America, likes it or not.[2]

In the second of his series of Postscripts, Priestley had proposed to talk further about such disturbing questions, about money, class and equality. 'I received', he wrote, 'two letters.' One was from the Ministry of Information telling him that 'the BBC was responsible for the decision to take me off the air'. The other was from the BBC saying that 'a directive had come from the Ministry of Information to end my broadcasting'.[3] Priestley's removal was widely greeted as a sign of government censorship. The *New Statesman* printed a selection of letters of protest, 'representative of the many others we have received'.

Yet Priestley's talks were hardly revolutionary. Though he articulated class and regional divisions, his talks submerged them beneath symbols of national unity. Thus, during the Blitz in the autumn of 1940 he remarked that Northerners like himself had imagined the Cockney spirit to be dead – but now the bombs had transformed London from a boring acreage of suburbs and commuters, a 'grey sea of a city', into an arena of beauty suffused with an all-transcendent Englishness:

> I saw the Dome and Cross of St Paul's, silhouetted in sharpest black against the red flames and orange fumes, and it looked like an enduring symbol of reason and Christian ethics seen against the crimson glare of unreason and savagery.

This image, of course is from London not from the North, and signifies Anglicanism rather than Nonconformism. Equally, in his talks, Priestley continually referred (in ten out of seventeen) to images of rural England, village communities and nature. For instance, as the Battle of Britain was starting, he found time to reflect, 'I don't think there has been a lovelier spring than this last one, now melting into summer.'[4]

And it is undeniably the case that idealized visions of long-lost village life have consistently been given greater precedence in the English psyche than urban realities. Examples are endless.[5] One of the most celebrated passages is this from Stanley Baldwin's *On England* (1926):

The sounds of England, the tinkle of the hammer on the anvil in the country smithy, the corncrake on a dewy morning, the sound of the scythe against the whetstone, and the sight of a plough team coming over the brow of a hill, the sight that had been seen in England since England was a land, and may be seen in England long after the Empire has perished and every works in England has ceased to function, for centuries the one eternal sight of England . . .

Or this from H. A. L. Fisher's essay on 'The Beauty of England' (1933):

The unique and incommunicable beauty of the English landscape constitutes for most Englishmen the strongest of all the ties that bind them to their country . . .

In his book *England is a Village* (1941) the journalist C. Henry Warren lovingly described life in East Anglia during the early months of the war – a story of community, the continuing importance of the squire, closeness to the past and nature:

. . . this is England, though 90 per cent of her population dwells in towns; for here the first condition of life is not gain but service – service of the land that feeds us and gathers us at last into its fecund darkness . . .

A more realistic picture of village life during World War II was provided by Richmal Crompton's volumes *William and the Evacuees*, *William Does His Bit*, *William Carries On*, and *William and the Brains Trust* – especially the first, with its description of village children gorging themselves at a spread in the knowledge that any left over would fall into the hands of the hated London toughs brought into their midst as evacuees.

The more idealized version of English village life is sustained daily by the radio serial *The Archers*. A former director general of the BBC, Sir William Haley, observed that 'whatever practical success *The Archers* had in rural England was far exceeded by its urban appeal'.[6] As the writer David White remarked, 'There is some corner in the English mind that is forever Ambridge: that half-real radio village . . .'[7] Evidently more illusory than Ambridge was Parkwood Hill, inhabited by Dr Dale and his family. That was an attempt to present an idealized suburb, but ultimately it was decided that it was no longer representative and taken off the air. *The Archers*, however, marches on.

By themselves such rural metaphors might be judged harmless romanticism; but when combined with a focusing of the imagery almost exclusively on southern England, then there is a distinct sense of a split opening deep into English society. One example of how England is thus typified was demonstrated by the Post Office which, between 1955 and 1970, issued four groups of four stamps carefully balancing views from the four countries of the United Kingdom. The four English views were in Windsor, Richmond (Surrey), Sussex and the Cotswolds. A fifth issue (British bridges, 1968) had two English, one Welsh and one Scottish example: both English bridges were in the South. The focus of English national identity is even more specific than just the South. The crucial area is the South-east, the English region so overwhelmingly dominant in English culture that all too easily it becomes synonymous with England. For as Oxford don L. J. Sharpe has expressed it:

Not only does London and the South-east dominate every sector of national life outside agriculture and certain extractive industries, it is also the home of practically every important institution, public or private, and if the whole institution is not located there its headquarters will almost certainly have to be. Even those in the upper reaches of the status system who do not live in the South-east were mainly educated there and in many senses feel themselves to be part of it. Their 'local' paper is *The Times*, they speak with a southern English accent and many of their values are rooted in the peculiar bogus-rural, rentier society of the Home Counties.[8]

Most parts of England present a distinctly physical image, whether the flatness of the Fens, the beaches of Cornwall, or the grandeur of the Lake District. But the image of the Home Counties is primarily a social one; they are not just a place, but a way of life. They are a belt of settled, affluent tranquillity that stretches in a wide arc around London, from the picturesque Essex villages to the north-east, through Hertfordshire in the north to the beech woods of the Chilterns where the Rothschilds built their mansions, and down to the Thames valley and Cliveden, home to the Astors and the 'Cliveden Set' in the 1920s. South of the river the ring of affluence continues through Windsor, and the wooded heathlands of Surrey to the Weald of Kent and the Sussex Downs. Areas like these represent the summit of the aspirations of a large number of the English: it is where they ideally would like to live. As Open University lecturer Chris Hammett put it:

> This is the land of large drives and even larger houses. The land of cocktails and G and Ts and the natural habitat of the Mercedes, BMW and Range Rover set. When the successful rock stars, stockbrokers and company directors set out to buy their country houses this is where they come. To Weybridge, Virginia Water and St George's Hill – the nearest British equivalent to Beverly Hills.[9]

It is here, too, that the key sporting and cultural events in the English calendar take place: Ascot, Henley, Glyndebourne, Lords and Wimbledon. Together they form a unique cultural, class and geographical symbolism. They locate a magic circle of social acceptance, wealth and power. In the words of R. W. Johnson, a Politics don at Magdalen College, Oxford:

> To be at the epicentre – in the royal enclosure at Ascot or on the boards of the great merchant banks – is not just a matter of being socially and economically more upper class, but also, in a sense, more English. The real outer groups are not just the poor, the black or the working class, but those furthest

from the geographical epicentre of the South-east. Thus the suburban professional from the South-east stands rather closer to this centre than say, a North-eastern entrepreneur, even if the latter is somewhat wealthier than the former . . .[10]

The Home Counties have a higher proportion of professional, managerial and other white-collar workers than any other part of Britain. Just over half of all its workers are white-collar, and almost two out of three households own or are buying their own homes. Income per head is also higher here than elsewhere and unemployment, of course, is lower.

The key to the dominance of the English South-east, and the explanation of its increasing divorce from the rest of Britain, is the City of London. At a time of generally recognized industrial decline in Britain, the City's commercial and financial institutions continue to generate wealth, operating as a world financial centre. As Geoffrey Ingham in his *Capitalism Divided?* (1984) concluded:

> The City is unique: no other international commercial banking and financial centre has ever enjoyed such a lengthy and continuous period of operation – over 250 years. And in this crucially important respect, Britain is consequently also unique: no other industrialized society has ever acted as host to a centre which has undertaken such a large share of the world capitalist system's commercial, banking and financial activities. Britain was not only the 'workshop of the world' but its 'clearing house', and whilst the former status has long been lost, the latter – despite some recent competition from other centres – has not. The consequences of this enduring economic activity for the development of the dominant classes, the state system, and the economy of Britain can scarcely be overstated.[11]

Ingham traces a history of more than 150 years of competitive struggle between the requirements of manufacturing industry and the City over investment policy which the City has consistently won:

. . . Successive British governments have maintained the political conditions for the City's existence as an international centre: an open economy (i.e. no restrictions on the inflow and outflow of money); a stable, high-value currency; attractive interest rates for the holders of sterling. All three policies have invariably clashed with plans to strengthen the productive economy.[12]

In each policy can be traced the clear gains for the City on the one hand and losses for manufacturing industry on the other. Keeping an open economy has been a major factor in London's ability to take the largest share in international currency transactions. In the late 1970s, for example, it was estimated that the daily turnover in foreign currency exchange was $50 billion in London, $40 billion in New York, $10 billion in Frankfurt and $2 billion in Tokyo.[13] Yet, keeping an open economy has also entailed forgoing restrictions on investment capital, which has tended to be placed abroad rather than at home. Within months of the abolition of exchange controls in 1979, the pension funds, for example, increased their overseas assets dramatically – from 7 per cent of their total holdings in early 1979 to 20 per cent by late 1980, and the trend has continued since.[14] Equally, maintaining sterling at a high value has decreased industry's price-competitiveness in world export markets, and high interest rates have had a depressing effect on investment at home. All of which has accelerated the divide between the financial economy, overwhelmingly located in south-eastern Britain, and the manufacturing economy, largely located in north-western Britain. As Anthony Sampson put it in *The Changing Anatomy of Britain* (1982):

> In the last two decades the contrast between the City and the rest of Britain has become more extreme. Bankers and dealers have become more international while industrialists and others have been bogged down in the country's economic constraints . . . The square mile of the City has become like an offshore island in the heart of the nation . . .
>
> The inhabitants of this extraordinary island – like those

other banking islands such as Hong Kong, Singapore or Manhattan – view the world very differently from those on the mainland. They can see across the whole globe, but they see it through money; they clearly perceive Britain's economic problems, but they see the British people in terms of balance sheets. They are constantly dealing with bits of British industry, restructuring companies, joining their boards, merging them or rationalizing them. But they still remain aloof from the real industrial problems; and their business is making money, not things.[15]

Around the Square Mile, and as a result of its particular and peculiar activities, has developed a specific culture which pervades the Home Counties. It is one which is primarily international in motivation so that its sense of national self-awareness lacks focus. In the centre of the Square Mile, opposite the Royal Exchanges and the Mansion House, stands the Bank of England, the centre-piece of the City's confidence and stability. As the Chairman of Citibank in New York told Anthony Sampson, 'The Eurodollar market exists in London because people believe that the British government is not about to close it down. That's the basic reason, and that took you a thousand years of history.'

Within a short distance of the Bank of England stand the headquarters of all the Big Four banks – Barclays, National Westminister, Midland and Lloyds – which live in a world defined by rigid hierarchy, easy profits and lack of competition. The dominance of the City – the merchant banks, insurance groups and investment institutions – has been mediated through the Bank of England and its relationship with the Treasury. Out of these relationships the City has maintained a direct and decisive influence on the formulation of economic policy.

For all these reasons the City has long been and remains the wealthiest sector of the British economy. At the top of the corporate ladder in industry, a handful of chairmen and managing directors earn more than £100,000 a year. In the City, even lower-level employees can earn this much. Add to this fringe-benefits like share options and 'tax efficient' extra pension contributions, and the scope for saving and investment is substantial: in 1986 58 per cent of those earning more than £50,000 a year lived in London and the Home Counties.[16] The contrast in wealth concentration between industrialists living in North-west Britain and financiers living in the South-east has been described by Bill Rubinstein in his *Men of Property* (1981):

> . . . although there were indeed a substantial number of wealthy fortunes in certain manufacturing and industrial trades like cotton manufacturing and engineering, the wealthy in Britain have disproportionately earned their fortunes in commerce and finance – that is, merchants, bankers, shipowners, merchant bankers and stock and insurance agents and brokers, rather than in manufacturing or industry. This is one of the keys to understanding not merely the wealth, but the anatomy of British élites and, through them, the social structure of modern British society since the eighteenth century.[17]

And the élites are, of course, self-perpetuating most notably through the public schools and the Universities of Oxford and Cambridge, all overwhelmingly located in the South-east. By far the most common social characteristics of City figures have been attendance at Eton and Oxbridge. In 1983 sixteen of the eighteen governors of the Bank of England had been to either Oxford or Cambridge; five of them had been to Eton and another six to public schools located in the South-east. And of the chairmen of the sixteen merchant banks in London, eleven had been to Oxford or Cambridge, seven to Eton and a further five to other public schools in the South-east. Oxbridge links extend from the City into the financial heart of the civil service and the government machine: in 1977, when a survey was conducted, 68 per cent of those at the level of Principal or above in the Treasury had received an Oxbridge education. It was significant that this very high percentage contrasted markedly with other civil service departments dealing directly with British manufacturing industry – the figures for the Trade and Industry and Employment Departments were respectively 25 and 20 per cent.[18]

The role of Oxbridge and the Clarendon schools, especially Eton, and their connections with the City/Bank of England/Treasury nexus have been of critical importance in projecting aristocratic traditions and values into modern Britain. The City has been the main economic basis on which the old British aristocratic class structure has been sustained in the geographic location of the South-east. Moreover, it has been a means whereby the social structure of an aristocratically dominated rural England – the denigration of urbanism and the idealization of country life – has been regenerated. The City has simultaneously reinforced the gentlemanly style of life and compounded the divorce between finance and industry. As an American observer, Martin J. Weiner, remarked, City-based wealth:

> . . . was 'clean' – well removed from the actual process of production. It involved the extraction of wealth by associating with people of one's own class in fashionable surrounding, not by dealing with things and the working and lower-middle classes, in perhaps grimy and ugly and certainly unfashionable locations . . . The City, in short, offered a way (more difficult in industry) to be a gentleman and still get rich.[19]

Anthony Sampson was making a similar point when he commented, 'The banks can offer clever and presentable young men more money and more exciting prospects than industry or Whitehall, with a cosmopolitan lifestyle very different from the rest of the country.'[20] The edifice still rests on a class structure established in the Home Counties over centuries. When the speculative property boom of the early 1970s broke in 1974, new and spectacularly profitable firms run by such men as Jim Slater collapsed, but the old houses weathered the storm with few outward signs of difficulty. When asked by Lord Cowdray how he had avoided financial entanglement with this 'arriviste' group of speculative wholesale bankers, and consequently had avoided trouble, Lord Poole of Lazards merchant bank replied: 'Quite simple, I only lent money to people who had been at Eton.'[21]

Few things indicate the dominance of the City/Home Counties ethos within England so well as accent. To have a Welsh or Scottish or Northern Ireland accent is an instant identifier within the United Kingdom system. On the whole, an Ulster accent is a distinct disadvantage and it is better not to have a Welsh accent (Roy Jenkins) than to have one (Neil Kinnock), while a Scots accent has to be very mild and ultra-civilized (David Steel, John Smith). Generally speaking, however, they are tolerated. But what is it to have an 'English' accent? Anyone who talks 'Geordie', 'West Country' or 'Birmingham' is identified as that – in effect, some brand of country yokel or working-class idiot. The sole acceptable English identifier within the United Kingdom system is, of course, 'Received Pronunciation': not an 'English' mode of speech, but the correct and commanding mode of speech as delivered by the upper orders of society concentrated in the Home Counties and mediated to the rest, the outlying hinterland. This accent was described by the late Raymond Williams as the product of an emerging bourgeoisie.

In the eighteenth century, when there was a new middle class, a new bourgeoisie coming through, a whole set of people started devising a standard accent. They got pronunciation coaches and made up rules about English pronunciation.

Curiously, before that the British ruling class spoke in their original accents. But received standard English was very much a bourgeois invention, largely based on the Southeast dialect that became a class dialect. After all, you can talk about the Oxford or Cambridge accent, but go out into the working-class areas of Oxford and Cambridge and you won't hear either.

Received standard English was developed through particular institutions – the prep schools, public schools and the universities – until it became the badge not simply of power but of knowledge. There was a convention that to speak in that way was to know something. People tended to think that something spoken in that way was more authoritative.

I think this is loosening now, particularly under American influence, but it was a successful thing for about two hundred years, and its effects still haven't gone.[22]

There is, of course, at least one important qualification in the social, economic and political domination of the South-east over the rest of the United Kingdom, and that is the position of much of inner London. The position is best measured by the unemployment statistics which in London soared astronomically in the late 1970s and early 1980s. A few comparative figures make the point: in 1964 the official number of unemployed in Wales, Scotland and the North (defined as England beyond the Midlands) collectively amounted to 143,000, compared with 77,200 in the South-east. By the end of 1985, however, the respective figures were 772,000 compared with 779,800.[23] Yet the high number of unemployed in the South-east did not match up to the North's overall concentration of unemployment in percentage terms or in general spread. Instead it was concentrated in just a few areas and, most notably in inner-London boroughs such as Tower Hamlets and Hackney. By the mid-1980s these had more in common with Consett in County Durham than with Throgmorton Street in the City.

At the heart of the Divided Kingdom is a divided city. By the mid-1980s employment levels in every part of London's manufacturing economy were as bad as the British average and often worse: manufacturing employment fell by 25 per cent between 1978 and 1985 compared with 24 per cent in Britain as a whole. At the end of this period, unemployment in Hackney, Islington, Southwark and Lambeth was 20 per cent, while for young blacks it was over 30 per cent. In a report produced in mid-1986 entitled *A City Divided*, the London Strategic Policy Unit pointed out that London had the highest concentration of unemployed people in the developed world. In the eight inner-London boroughs the average rate of unemployment had increased a full three percentage points more than in any other UK region since 1979:

> There are 25,000 more people on the register in just these eight boroughs than there are in the whole of Northern Ireland.[24]

The report added that the growth and prosperity of the rest of the South-east had obscured the problem in London. By the same token, inner London's plight highlights the relative affluence of the City and the Home Counties. London, in fact, is like a doughnut: it has a hole in the middle – the Square-Mile City with its own Mayor and administration that effectively insulate it from the concerns of the rest of the capital. The City has the resources and structure to prevent its wealth being appropriated to serve the needs of the surrounding boroughs. Instead, it reaches out through London (the Underground and South-east rail network radiating like spokes from a wheel hub) to the affluent Home Counties which, in turn, insulate it from the demands of the rest of the country.

The overwhelming identification of England and Englishness with just one area of the country explains the lack of territorial emphasis in English sensibility. There are, of course, historical explanations as well: for only one brief period (1042–1066) has there existed a kingdom similar in territory to modern England. The English State was created in something smaller than present-day England – Egbert's realm – and from the start it claimed a territory larger than England. There has been no English Parliament since 1536 and today there is no English Office or Secretary of State for English Affairs. There is, in fact, no keenly felt territorial sense of Englishness that is a common characteristic with other, more conventional nationalities. Instead, the dominant expression and location of Englishness is to be found in the South-east. Here, for historic and economic reasons, is an identity that thinks primarily in world terms. The world, of course, is viewed from the perspective of the British State, but the State is seen as institutionally located exclusively in the South-east. England in a territorial sense simply does not figure. This world identity has been carved out by the City financial institutions over 250 years. And, as L. J. Sharpe pointed out, it is in the South-east that all the key relationships that make up the identity occur:

It is the South-east which sets the national standard so that identifying with the South-east culture is essential to upward social mobility, and the ambitious and successful with provincial origins quickly assimilate to it, thus draining the rest of the country and further reinforcing South-eastern dominance. Such continuous assimilation of each generation of provincial thrusters, or their children, is powerfully aided by the élite private secondary schools – the majority of them in the South-east – the special task of which is to impart to their charges the appropriate South-eastern values and accent. Respectability, orthodoxy and prestige are indissolubly linked to the South-east culture, and above all, most of the symbols of nationhood are also South-eastern: the standard English accent, the two major homes of the Monarch, Parliament, the High Courts, and the senior institution of the established Church.[25]

This last emphasis on the role of institutions leads to the third great distortion in English culture – after the near total concentration of power and influence in the South-east, and its bogus association with a rural, *rentier* society. This is that the institutions of the State – Monarchy, Peerage, Houses of Parliament – have come to be regarded as synonymous with the nation itself. In this the monarchy is central, royal births, weddings and deaths being celebrated not just as incidents in royal personal life, but as 'State occasions'. At the same time, the idea of the strong State is something to be feared. It has given rise to the protective English cult of privacy, with the Englishman's home his castle. Ultimately in the (unwritten) constitution, there are no English people – only subjects under the Crown. Public records, for instance, are opened by a concession, not as of right – and then, normally only after thirty years have passed (and a hundred years in Scotland). Even MPs elected to the House of Commons can only take their seats after swearing an oath of allegiance to the Sovereign. An MP elected at a by-election must be sponsored by two other MPs to be admitted to the Chamber – it is not his or her right to be seated, for all that an election has taken place.

If the Welsh and Scots have a dual identity – Welsh and British, Scots and British – at least the Welsh and Scots part of their identity have the potential for their own democratic, republican integrity. The English, with their fused identity of Anglo-Britishness, cannot even partly break out of subject status. This was hinted at by G. K. Chesterton in his famous lines from 'The Secret People':

Smile at us, pay us, pass us; but do not quite
                              forget.
For we are the people of England, that never have
                              spoken yet.

R. W. Johnson has noted that the terms 'people' and 'popular' are not often found in English in their European or American sense. Instead, as he puts it, 'the curious word "public" is extensively employed'. This term is not the same as 'the people', rather it refers to a particular section or portion of the community.

Implicitly excluded, at least, are those at the bottom end of society – the poor, those wearing ragged clothes, lumpen elements of any kind, the unemployed and all those who are not 'respectable' . . . Perhaps the clearest sense of its non-inclusive quality is found in the still-current usage of 'public schools' – meaning schools exclusively reserved for the progeny of the well-to-do. The view is very much one of the population from the top down rather than the bottom up: the public is all those people whom the state and its Establishment wish to address or acknowledge as their own. This sense of state agency is perhaps most explicit in 'public prosecution', which is a prosecution by the Crown. In a social sense 'the public' is clearly coterminous with something like 'polite society'. Whether or not one is one of the elect of the polite, responsible, or respectable is, of course, a matter for judgement by one's betters.[26]

Of course, in one sense this is only another way of saying that England is a self-consciously class-ridden society. But the fact that in England class is defined from the top down and from the point of view of the State institutional structure, is extremely important. It means that this sense of class, necessarily exclusive within the society, is the primary identification of what Englishness means. And when the definition is also given a psychic location in the countryside and, further, a territorial location in the South-east, then exclusivity turns into divisiveness.

Such a sense of identity was ideally suited to England's role as the centre of a world-wide imperial system in which the Square Mile of the City of London was as significant as, if not more significant than, the territory of England itself. But in a situation where external circumstances – loss of Empire, relative economic decline, entry into the European Community, and emerging Scottish, Welsh and Ulster consciousness – are forcing the English to come to terms, perhaps for the first time, with the reality of England, then this primary sense of identity based on institutions and class in a specific geographical location, rather than on People, is a problem. It is a problem because it is inherently divisive rather than unifying; inherently regressive and stultifying rather than liberating and mobilizing; inherently authoritarian rather than democratic.

But under pressure of events in the last quarter of the twentieth century, the welding at the heart of the fused Anglo-British identity is threatening to break apart. The

English are being forced by circumstances to make a choice between who they think they are, perhaps even between who they would like to be, and who they really are. Perhaps at long last in our generation, the people of England will finally speak.

NOTES

1 Quotations in this section are taken from Anthony Aldgate and Jeffery Richards, *Britain Can Take It – The British Cinema in the Second World War*, Basil Blackwell, 1986, Chapter 3.
2 J. B. Priestley, *Postscripts*, Heinemann, 1940, p. 37–8.
3 J. B. Priestley, *Margin Released*, Heinemann, 1962, p. 221–2.
4 Quoted by Jean Seaton in 'Broadcasting and the Blitz' in *Power without Responsibility: The Press and Broadcasting in Britain*, Fontana, 1981, p. 175.
5 See Martin J. Wiener, *English Culture and the Decline of the Industrial Spirit*, Penguin, 1985. The following quotations are taken from Chapter 4.
6 *Times Literary Supplement*, 20 January 1978.
7 *New Society*, 26 September 1974.
8 L. J. Sharpe, *Devolution and Celtic Nationalism in the UK*, West European Politics Journal, July 1985, p. 94.
9 Chris Hammett, 'Life in the Cocktail Belt', *The Geographical Magazine*, October 1984.
10 R. W. Johnson, *The Politics of Recession*, Macmillan, 1985, p. 235.
11 Geoffrey Ingham, *Capitalism Divided? The City and Industry in British Social Development*, Macmillan, 1984, p. 40.
12 Ibid., p. 224.
13 William M. Clarke, *Inside the City*, Allen & Unwin, 1979, p. 142.
14 *Bank of England Quarterly Bulletin*, September 1981, p. 370.
15 Anthony Sampson, *The Changing Anatomy of Britain*, Coronet, 1983, p. 295–7.
16 *New Society* supplement, 'The Rich in Britain', 22 August 1986.
17 W. D. Rubinstein, *Men of Property*, Croom Helm, 1981, p. 61.
18 Peter Kellner and Lord Crowther-Hunt, *The Civil Servants: An Inquiry into Britain's Ruling Class*, Macdonald, 1980, p. 193.
19 Weiner, op. cit., p. 145.
20 Sampson, op. cit., p. 312.

21 Ibid., p. 313.
22 Raymond Williams, interviewed during April 1987.
23 The figures are quoted by Kevin Morgan in 'The Spectre of Two Nations in Contemporary Britain', in *Catalyst*, Vol. 2 No. 2, Summer 1986, p. 14.
24 London Strategic Policy Unit, *A City Divided*, August 1986, p. 4.
25 Sharpe, op. cit., p. 94–6.
26 Johnson, op. cit., p. 233.

7

Greater England

If, as has been argued in the previous chapter, the English class structure specifically disallows any republican sense of a People, can the English really be regarded as a nation at all? After all, there is confusion at the start over the very name of their country, a confusion that reflects the lack of clarity about their territory. Is England the same as Britain, Great Britain, the United Kingdom, or the United Kingdom of Great Britain and Northern Ireland? The last is the official title of the State the English inhabit, yet the description is rarely used. On the other hand, the agencies of Statehood – most notably monarchy, Parliament, police and armed forces – are a primary reference point for English identity in a way that territory is not. Moreover, as has been argued previously as well, when the English evoke a sense of territory it is invariably a rural idyll located somewhere in the deep south of England.

Then again, what kind of sensibility do the English have in relation to their 'national' flag? When England plays Scotland at football matches the English supporters wave not the flag of St George but the Union Jack – the flag of the United Kingdom which specifically combines the national flags of England and Scotland, though not of Ireland or Wales. It is commonly believed that the Union Jack also includes the Irish Cross of St Patrick, but this is not the case. The red saltire is, in fact, the arms of the Fitzgeralds, descendants of the Geraldine family, Welsh Marcher Lords sent by Henry II to conquer Ireland. Not having been a martyr, St Patrick was not heraldically entitled to a cross and, in any event, the symbol has never been used by the Irish people. Such details, however, have little meaning for the English who merely assume the Union Jack to be an English flag. The ambiguity is even more emphatic with the 'Royal' Navy's White Ensign where the Union Jack is relegated to a corner of what is otherwise the St George's Cross.

The key question is the relationship of England with Britain and how far that is changing. This is a central preoccupation for the identity of the Scots and the Welsh, not to say the Irish – both North and South. As has been explored in previous chapters, all of them have devised various ways of coming to terms with the problem. Usually these have taken the form of accepting, sometimes even celebrating, a dual nationality: Welsh and British, Scots and British, and so on. One consequence has been the awakening of such identity crises as the 'split mind' in Scotland, fear of being absorbed into a 'swallowing wind' of Britishness in Wales, communal strife in Ireland. But at least the issue is looked, if not squarely then partly, in the face. In England, the issue tends not be raised, but rather bypassed as an unnecessary topic that would only create embarrassment if considered. Yet, any analysis demands an exploration of the status of English nationhood. The late Hugh Seton-Watson, a Scot, put his finger on the nerve when, in the course of his panoramic survey of nations and states across the globe, he paused to remark:

I find it very hard to make up my mind as to whether a 'British nation' is a valid concept. 'Britain' is of course a much older word than 'England' or 'Scotland'; but if the word is used in its strictest historical sense, the only people entitled to call themselves 'British' are the Welsh. There has been at times a tendency for the English to interpret 'British' as English writ large, and to expect Scots and Welsh to become English if they are to be truly British. Yet it is also true that until recently the sense of belonging together to a British community, and pride in this community, have been extremely strong among the Scots and Welsh: indeed, one might argue that Scots and Welsh have been 'more British' than the English. Does this add up to a British national consciousness, or should some other word be found?[1]

Seton-Watson was writing during the mid-1970s, a period when, stimulated by the devolution politics of the time, the Welsh and Scots probed the identities particular to themselves to such an extent that parties, communities, even families, were divided. The issues occupied a large proportion of the time of the House of Commons. Yet the English, by and large, remained unmoved, distant and untouched by the debates, seemingly unaware that if they had come to fruition the impact on England would have been considerable.

To understand this paradox it is necessary to consider the fact that while the Welsh, and possibly the Scots and the Ulster Protestants, could at least contemplate merging their identities into 'a British national consciousness', it would never be possible for the English. They have long adopted a quite different, if seldom articulated relationship, with Britain. This can simply be regarded as an idea of Greater England, a kind of fusion of the two in which the resultant identity can best be described as Anglo-British. The process has been a consequence of a complex interaction of the geography and historical development of the British Isles with the institutions that have evolved, especially the monarchy and Parliament, and the relationship of the whole with the wider world. The critical period for the fusion of England with Britain and the creation of the idea of Greater England began with the Civil Wars of the mid-seventeenth century and the accommodation between monarchy and Parliament of 1688. At that moment a popular, democratic and republican idea of England and Englishness was smothered, as it were, at birth. What developed, as events unfolded, was a curious identity, reliant more on institutions than people and more on territory abroad than at home. It was an identity forged and tested through the period of the Napoleonic Wars when democratic and republican revolutionary France was faced down by monarchical and oligarchic Greater England. This was the heroic period of the Anglo-British whose twin gladiators, Wellington and Nelson, still dominate the high ramparts of the 'nation's' capital.

The victory, from 1793 to 1815, was the foundation for the industrial revolution and imperial expansion of the nineteenth century. The identity was maintained through the first half of the twentieth century by two World Wars. Since 1945, however, it has lapsed into a kind of nostalgic nationalism kept alive by the annual round of Parliamentary and royal occasions and commemorative ceremonies such as Remembrance Day. Reflecting on the developing vacuum at the core of the Anglo-British identity from the perspective of the mid-1970s, two perceptive writers provided the same hostage to fortune.

Anthony Birch, a political scientist, remarking on the youthful audience at the Albert Hall Promenade concerts (watched by about 8 million viewers) concluded that the fervour with which they joined in singing 'Land of Hope and Glory' 'suggests that younger people share the nostalgic nationalism of their elders' rather than finding a new source of national pride which he felt to be 'relatively weak in contemporary England'. However, he judged

> . . . another war of a conventional type would immediately rekindle the latent flames of English/British nationalism. But a conventional war is not imminent . . .[2]

Writing in the same period Tom Nairn made the same point, but more graphically:

> England needs another war. This alone would recreate the peculiar spirit of her nationalism, rally her renegade intelligentsia (as in the 1930s), and reconcile the workers to their lot. Unfortunately, war of that sort – like her empire – is a lost cause. The 'British' patriotic symbols are unlikely to receive further transfusions of blood. Nelson, Wellington, Haig and Churchill will – with any luck – never arise from rest to dance on our heads again . . .[3]

Within a few years of these judgements being penned, the Falklands/Malvinas melodrama provided just the conflict that the Anglo-British identity 'needed'. But the conflict was an attenuated creature: it could not even be a 'war'. Diplomatic necessity prevented a war being formally declared. Admiral Sir John Woodward, the leader of the Task Force, hardly appeared as some re-incarnated Nelson. 'Sovereignty' was a rather abstract principle to fight over and, in any event, was strongly contested. Apart from the sobering casualties (on both sides), there was the legacy of a cost that seemed disproportionate to defending a group of islands 8,000 miles away which previously had been known mainly to stamp collectors. As Ludovic Kennedy reflected, putting the best possible face upon it: 'This was not a war of national survival, rather the action of a man who finds a burglar in his house and proceeds to eject him. Ejecting a burglar is an unpleasant but necessary task and does not call for war-dances and whoops of joy.'[4]

At almost the same time as the Falklands, another event occurred which had something to say about the character of Greater England and the Anglo-British identity. On 23 March 1982 the film *Chariots of Fire* became the emissary and emblem of the 'British film renaissance' in California when it won the prize for Best Picture and three further Academy Awards. From the podium the film's writer, Colin Welland, patriotically declared, 'The British are coming!' Aside from the fact that, poignantly, it had been entirely financed by foreign backers, the film – based on a true story of the 1924 Paris Olympics – was a subtle evocation of the workings of the Anglo-British identity. This has operated by eschewing rigid demarcations, denying clear frontiers, and incorporating at appropriate moments subversive outsiders into its ruling oligarchy, its Establishment. Classically, the process has seduced ambitious Irish, Scots and Welsh who have, over the centuries, found no insuperable barriers to making their way through England's southern Establishment institutions, from Oxbridge and the House of Commons to the City and the Lords. The disproportionate number of expatriate Scots and Welsh – there are fewer Irish these days – in prominent positions in the City and Parliament is eloquent testimony to this absorption and its success. The same applies to Jews, as *Chariots of Fire* relates. Harold Abrahams, a Jew of Lithuanian extraction studying at Cambridge, and Eric Liddell, a Scot studying at Edinburgh, both keen runners, try for selection for the Paris Olympics team. Despite racial prejudice and disapproval of his ruthless professionalism, Abrahams runs and wins a gold medal in the prestigious 100-metres race. Liddell, a devout Sabbatarian hewn from Scottish Calvinist stock, refuses to take part in his heat, scheduled to be run on a Sunday – despite cajoling from the Prince of Wales in a wonderfully evocative scene. For the first time in his life Liddell finds himself in circumstances where Scottish Sabbatarianism cannot be assumed to be the norm, and, similarly, the Prince is faced with a situation in which religion, instead of being a kind of emotive glue reinforcing his own position, is something which threatens to undermine the meaning of Britishness as he sees it. Liddell sticks to his position and by implication rejects his Britishness. The position is only rescued when another runner, Lord Lindsey, a scion of the Establishment, stands down in his heat, the 400 metres, enabling Liddell to replace him there, win a gold and set a world record. However, as the critic Sheila Johnston put it:

It is around the figure of Abrahams, the foreigner who aspires to become a true Englishman, that the narrative is organized (the film opens and ends with his funeral) and that these questions most sharply cohere. Abrahams' naked ambition quickly incurs the displeasure of the doyens of the Establishment, the Masters of Trinity and Caius Colleges who, in a key confrontation, berate him for hiring the Italian-Arab Sam Massabini as his coach. The problem is that Massabini – and Abrahams – are not only aliens, but also grubby professionals, impudent parvenus. The questions of nationality and class are collapsed together: Englishness is identified by them with the inherited privilege of Cambridge's *jeunesse dorée*.

The chief representative of all this is Lindsey – born, as

Welland's screenplay neatly puts it, with a whole canteen of silver cutlery in his mouth. He is the gentleman sportsman whose typically idiosyncratic training method – jumping hurdles balanced with glasses that are brimming with champagne – offsets Massabini's more punishing and 'serious' programme. Charming, sybaritic, verging on the dissolute, Lindsey is none the less aware that changes are afoot, that aristocracy must cede to the new meritocracy, and he gallantly stands down for his chums (Abrahams in love, Liddell in his race) in a true act of *noblesse oblige*.

Thus nationality, and the social status that accompanies it, are honours that can be *earned*, not just acquired by inheritance. Abrahams 'becomes' an Englishman by virtue of his Olympic victory: symbolically, Massabini, waiting anxiously back at the hotel, learns of this by seeing the Union Jack hoisted aloft and hearing 'God Save the King' played in the distance. On their triumphant return, he and the rest of the team are greeted with newspaper headlines (now heavy with post-Falklands resonance) that declare: 'Our boys are home'. Returning, full cycle, to his funeral, we even find Abrahams described at his death as 'the Elder Statesman of British Athletics', as we hear the wonderfully traditional sound of the voices of choristers lifted in song. And what are they singing but the grand old Blakean hymn which lends the film its title and which, in calling for Jerusalem to be built in England's green and pleasant land, aptly stands for the synthesis of Abrahams' twin origins?[5]

The co-option of exterior, potentially competitive and alien excellence into the Greater English élite described here, fits better with the 1920s than the 1980s. Nevertheless, the theme is still distinctly recognizable, as the success of *Chariots of Fire* witnessed. At the same time its success was linked, like so many other contemporary films and television series – *Brideshead Revisited*, *The Jewel in the Crown*, *The Forsyte Saga*, *Ghandi*, *A Room With a View*, *Greystoke* – to a nostalgic celebration of the past. The same is true of two further life-support systems for the Anglo-British identity: royalty, and the sense of a global, 'White Anglo-Saxon Protestant', Anglo-British diaspora which remains the contemporary legacy of Empire and Commonwealth, and gives a world-wide reference for Greater England.

To gain a perspective on these key characteristics of Greater English (that is, Anglo-British) identity, a brief historical survey is necessary, though one that takes in the broad sweep of development from Roman times to the present day. The main objective is to highlight the brief moment when English national consciousness emerged and flowered, and to see how quickly this was metamorphosed, or to use the term suggested above, fused, into an Anglo-British consciousness. The political scientist, Michael Steed, has commented on the many paradoxes of England: that its State was first formed in an area smaller than that of present-day England – south of the Humber–Mersey line and east of Offa's Dyke – by Egbert, King of Wessex, 802–839; that from the start the State claimed an area larger than England; that the history of England is largely written as the history of the expansion and the political system of the State but not of the area of England itself; that the English language is shared with a good part of the world; and that, finally, when something is described as being typically English, it is all too often just typical of a region which is the South-east of both England and Britain.

The difficulty of pinning down what is English becomes clear if we run through some of the more popular heroes of English history, who tend noticeably to be military ones. King Alfred was a Wessex king fighting against the Danes, who were to form part of the subsequent population of England. Richard Lionheart and Henry V were fighting for their dynastic interests, that is maintaining a cross-Channel political entity (which had it survived into early modern times would doubtless have set about building up a cross-Channel popular national identity of the sort that Switzerland has successfully created but the Hapsburg Empire failed to). Turning the medieval Anglo-Norman-French kings into English national

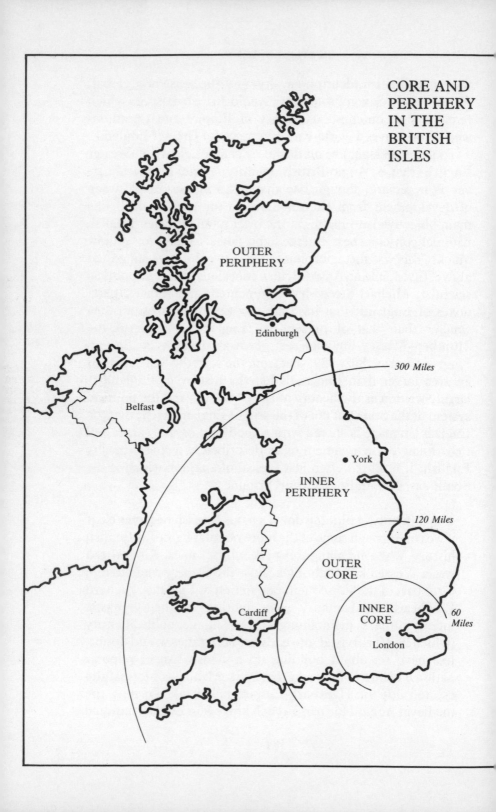

CORE AND
PERIPHERY
IN THE
BRITISH
ISLES

OUTER
PERIPHERY

Edinburgh

300 Miles

Belfast

York

INNER
PERIPHERY

120 Miles

OUTER
CORE

INNER
CORE

Cardiff

60
Miles

London

hero-figures was a Tudor (and especially Shakespearean) exercise in just such nation-building. Later military heroes like Marlborough, Nelson, Wellington or Churchill may sometimes be referred to as English but they indubitably fought for Great Britain or the United Kingdom. There is no English hero in the way that the Welsh have Glendower or the Scots Robert Bruce, no one who simply fought for or defended just England. Consequently the military heroes of English history all refer to battles for something less than or, usually, something more than England.[6]

Steed suggests that instead of a division of Britain's political geography three ways into England, Wales and Scotland, a core-periphery interpretation, focusing on the contrast between lowland and upland Britain, corresponds more accurately with historical development and present-day political realities. His pattern divides the British Isles into core and periphery, as illustrated on the map on p. 182. The core is sub-divided into an inner core (the South-east) and an outer core (East Anglia, the Midlands and the mid-South, or Wessex). The periphery is similarly sub-divided, into an inner periphery comprising the North, Wales and the South-west (Devon and Cornwall); and an outer periphery, Scotland and Ireland. The core area broadly corresponds to lowland Britain and the periphery to upland Britain.

This pattern certainly fits Roman Britain which established a clear division between a settled zone (the lowland Britain core) and the parts where British tribes were subject to military rule. It was, in fact, only the outer periphery that escaped any systematic occupation. The Anglo-Saxon phase of state-building can be seen as the gradual merging by conquest of the heptarchy of seven kingdoms, a combination of the inner and outer core areas. The Normans extended this outwards by creating quasi-militarized border zones, the Marches of the Northumberland highland region and along the Welsh border. The Tudor period saw the final creation of a centralized State governing the whole core and inner periphery. Steed remarks that it is symbolic that 1536 saw both the full incorporation of Wales into England (so far as legal and administrative processes were concerned) and the abolition of the last independent palatinate jurisdiction of Durham. Nevertheless, the Council in the North and the Council in the Marches of Wales acknowledged that for another century the core-state needed special arrangements to rule these two areas.

This core-periphery framework can be seen continually in the centuries that follow. Thus the seventeenth-century Civil War was a victory by the inner core over the inner periphery, most of the battles being fought in the outer core. With the coming of the industrial revolution, upland Britain suddenly discovered economic advantages – water power and then coal – reversing in the nineteenth century the long-standing economic advantage of lowland Britain and the South-east. Steed notes that the anti-Corn Law League represented the interests of those parts of Britain which focused on Manchester and Liverpool, traded westwards and wished to import cheap food, as opposed to those parts of southern Britain which were better able to produce food. Politically the shift was marked by the repeal of the Corn Laws in 1846 and the growing divergence from then on between upland peripheral Britain, mobilized for Gladstonian Liberalism, and lowland core Britain, mobilized for Tory Unionism. In the present century the same divergence has continued, with only the nuances of socialism and Conservatism added. Steed completes the picture of the contemporary relevance of his core-periphery historical analysis by referring to the distribution of the morning press in Britain, which he divides into the following five categories:

1 London-based 'national' dailies, doubling up as the only morning papers for the South-east inner core.
2 A changing situation in Manchester, with most major London dailies having distinctive Northern editions.
3 An almost fully separate Scottish press, with only limited penetration from papers published in England.
4 A zone, comprising most of the North, Wales, and the

South-west peninsula (the inner periphery), having its own
morning press competing with the London dailies.

5 An intermediate zone – roughly the outer core – where two
large cities (Bristol and Birmingham) maintain a morning
daily, but where the frequency of provincial papers per
head is less and the dominance of the London-based papers
is greater.

Despite the historical outline mentioned here, English national
consciousness only fully developed by the sixteenth century. It
was a long evolution of the growth of a monarchical centralized
State interacting with the slow emergence of the English language. The language grew out of a merging of the Saxon and
Norman-French streams. A symbolic date was 1362 when
English replaced Norman French in the law courts and the
opening of Parliament was conducted for the first time in
English. The Reformation of the sixteenth century became the
anvil of English national identity with the rejection by Henry
VIII of the religious domination of Rome. A generation later the
external military threats of France and Spain further defined
English national consciousness. And it was no coincidence that
the Elizabethan literary flowering gave the national mood full
expression. But even then, during what in retrospect can be
seen as the high point of English identity, the Greater England
dimension was never far away. It was a psychic sensibility
exemplified by the famous lines eulogizing England which
Shakespeare gave to John of Gaunt in *Richard II*:

This royal throne of kings, this scepter'd isle,
This earth of majesty, the seat of Mars,
This other Eden, demi-paradise,
This fortress built by nature for herself
Against infection and the hand of war,
This happy breed of men, this little world,
This precious stone set in the silver sea,
Which serves it in the office of a wall,
Or as a moat defensive to a house,

Against the envy of less happier lands;
This blessed plot, this earth, this realm, this England.

The undercurrent of Greater Englandism here is detectable in
the identification of England as an island – the English as an
'island race' as Churchill was later to echo. But in this period it
can be argued that there was a distinctive sense of a separate
English nation, generally undisturbed by the wider British
Isles, and that, despite Raleigh and Drake, the bordering sea
was seen more as a protective 'moat' than a trade route to
Empire. It was a brief moment, however. Within a generation
outside pressures, coupled with internal class and religious
differences, were destined to fracture the surface of Englishness, beginning most dramatically with the revolutionary
period of 1640 to 1688. The next crisis came a century later with
the American and French Revolutions. And a century after that
Greater England entered the long crisis of losing its world
pre-eminence which is still under way today. In all these great
movements the role of the monarchy is crucial, indeed has
become steadily more important in defining the Anglo-British
Greater England identity.

The most important outcome of the revolutionary period of
the Civil War and the republicanism of the Cromwellian inter-
regnum was that it ended with the Settlement of 1688 when the
monarchy under King William III was placed firmly within the
context of Parliamentary sovereignty. It was a compromise,
symbolized today by the placing of Cromwell's statue immediately outside but not within the Palace of Westminster. It
is, of course, true that Jacobite notions of an absolute monarchy
were put to the sword (or to the axe, in the case of Charles I) and
that the rising urban and commercial middle class in England
achieved a new prominence. But the popular democracy of
these events – recently, and significantly rediscovered by the
English Left – the debates in the Long Parliament, and the
Levellers, were quickly suppressed. This was the meaning of
the invitation given to William of Orange in 1688. An accommodation was reached in the creation of an aristocratic State in

which the interests of land-owners and a new commercial élite were united under a benign monarchy that gave precedence to Parliament. The men of property were in charge: they had wrested control from an absolute monarch without having to share power with the massed lower ranks in society. As Tom Nairn has put it, likening the outcome to the oligarchic Venetian Republic:

> British Royalism, Anglo-British national identity and the United Kingdom State are indeed all 'anachronistic' phenomena. However, the past which remains so stubbornly alive in them has nothing to do with feudalism or the 'immemorial', and still less to do with folk or ethnic tradi- tions. What it really connects with is one circumscribed era of early modern development reaching from 1688 up to the middle of the eighteenth century: the founding period in which England's patrician Revolution was consolidated and rendered 'British' by the assimilation of the Scottish State in 1707. That process created a pre-democratic class State distinct both from the Absolute Monarchies still dominating Europe and (later) from the lower-class, more emphatically *bourgeois* regimes aimed at by revolutionaries in the spirit of 1776 and 1789.[7]

The 1789 French Revolution stimulated a reactive nationalism everywhere else in Europe – either liberal (following the trend established in Paris), or conservative, State-sponsored national- ism defying the revolutionaries and arousing popular support for a safer variety of patriotism. It was Britain that took the lead in this latter reaction, leading the assault on revolutionary France in the wars between 1793 and 1815. The French bourgeois revolution, with its echoes of the Levellers' agitation a century earlier, threatened the compromise of 1688. What happened in Britain was, in effect, a State nationalization of national*ism*, with the chief beneficiary being the monarchy. Nairn notes how, in 1789, 'a frantic search of the records had to be conducted to establish just how the Nation ought properly to

celebrate King George's apparent recovery from illness'.[8] Over
the next decades, as well as increased prominence being given to
the round of State occasions, there was a huge growth (reminiscent of our own times) in popular tokens of loyalty to the
Throne: commemorative pottery, cheap prints and obsequious
ballads. In the face of external threat, a unique blend of
Anglo-British monarchic nationalism was defined, and
hardened into an identity that is still recognizable today.

In the immediate aftermath of the Napoleonic Wars the need
for nationalist mobilization on this basis receded. But not for
long. The progression towards a widening democracy after the
1832 Reform Act meant that new ways had to be found of
incorporating larger elements of the population into the regime.
More problematic still as the century progressed was the fact
that competing powers challenged Britain's industrial dominance and imperial supremacy. In this situation the monarchy
was increasingly deployed to bolster Anglo-British identity. As
David Cannadine observed in a seminal survey of the monarchy
from 1820 to 1977, a similar process happened elsewhere,
but in England/Britain there was a crucial difference:

From the 1870s onwards, in England as in other western
countries, the position of the head of state was ceremonially
enhanced. A venerated monarch, conveyed in a splendid
coach along triumphal thoroughfares was no longer, as his
predecessors had been, just the head of society, but was now
the head of the nation as well. In England, as elsewhere in
Europe, the unprecedented developments in industry and in
social relationships, and the massive expansion of the yellow
press, made it both necessary and possible to present the
monarch, in all the splendour of his ritual, in this essentially
new way, as a symbol of consensus and continuity to which all
might defer. And, as international relations became increasingly tense, this added a further inducement to the
'invention of tradition', as national rivalry was both expressed and sublimated in ceremonial competition. Only in
one major regard did the English experience differ from that

of the other western nations: in Russia, Germany, Italy, America and Austria, this efflorescence of ceremonial was centred on a head of state who still exercised real power. But in England, while the ceremonial shadow of power was cast over the monarch, the substance increasingly lay elsewhere.[9]

The consequence, as Cannadine goes on to point out, was that while in Austria, Russia and Germany this phase of royal ceremonial 'efflorescence' (between the 1870s and 1914) was founded on royal power (and in the United States on republican loyalties), in England it was centred on royal weakness. And in that paradox lies the secret of the English/British royal success. Elsewhere, royal rituals were swept away in the wake of the First World War. In Britain, where royal power was no threat – indeed, had not been since 1688 – and where, in any event, the sovereign was at the head of a 'victorious' nation, the monarchy survived with its reputation enhanced. Indeed, the place of the monarchy grew, in proportion it seemed to the decline of Britain as a world power and the diminution of Greater England. Here royalism became a substitute for a democratic nationalist identity for the Anglo-British. So far as this identity is concerned the 'people' do not exist as citizens in the conventional republican sense that applies in comparable countries. Instead, the people are thought of as 'average' or 'ordinary' – 'the man on the Clapham omnibus'. In contrast, in the popular press and on television, the extraordinary is continually defined by the royal persona, but defined subtly and paradoxically by the pretence that these people are actually quite ordinary. In this way the mass of 'ordinary people' become part of the royal nation. The point has been made by Judith Williamson who perceptively observes that the key to the significance and popularity of royalty is that they are at once like us, and not like us:

This combination of the ordinary and the special represented *by* Royalty is manifested in the representation *of* Royalty through two basic modes: the informal and the formal. There is the intimate and casual private moment on the one hand; the spectacle of State occasions, the glamour of wealth and national tradition on the other. In one form of imagery the Royals are just like ourselves, in the other they are delightfully different. To see either one of these alone as the crucial representation of the royal family would be a mistake; it is the combination of the two which makes each so powerful. The formal, official aspect of Royalty is seen not only in the more 'regal' portraits and photographs of ceremonial events, but in the hundreds of commemorative medallions, mugs, crests, posters etc which are in many ways the modern form of pageantry. Formal 'Royal' occasions such as coronations and weddings give rise to a coinage of heraldic household articles whose charm lies in their combination of the important and the everyday. Conversely, the informal imagery of Royalty takes its interest from the fact that it *is* 'Royals' who are shown in otherwise completely unremarkable situations – walking a dog, holding a child, being pregnant. The enormous effort the *Sun* photographers took to sneak photographs of Princess Diana bathing when pregnant on holiday is striking for the very banality of the product: the whole point was to get shockingly *ordinary* pictures, far from glamorous, of a woman looking exactly like any other pregnant mum . . .[10]

Judith Williamson's analysis has been amplified by Tom Nairn to explain why the monarchy has become the main reference point for Anglo-British identity:

The mystic radiance of these extraordinary beings is not dissipated by their becoming 'ordinary' and 'just like us'; on the contrary, the more this occurs the more (by unspoken implication) we become like them – a Royal and extraordinary Nation, illuminated by enchantment rather than by the grey daylight Republican peoples have to put up with.

This can be put in another way. The modern British Monarchy is an eccentric form of nationalist ideology, and all such idea-systems have to project some kind of populist equality to depict their national communities convincingly. But in Great Britain, where an élite authority-structure has been successfully preserved through the whole era of *égalité* and written constitutions, this can't be achieved by formal or literal means. It can only be done 'symbolically'. Only a totemic (or 'irrational') mode of identification can create the felt appearance of oneness: a sentimental common subject-hood in lieu of citizenship. Hence, this identity-dream has to be continuously enhanced and renewed roughly in propor-tion to the strains and threats facing the Nation, by a very active ideological apparatus of (so to speak) State folklore – a populism 'settled down' from above to the deferential classes below. The system has worked, because this lore *is* genuinely popular: people need a Nation, and (however regrettably, or conservatively) this has been the one on offer – the main available emblematic way of being 'English' or 'British'.[11]

If the monarchy is, by now, the chief symbol of Britishness it has, too, a curious and rather paradoxical relation to the idea of Greater England. This is because the Crown heartland, the geographical locus of the monarchy, is much smaller than territorial England. It is marked out by the metropolitan South-east, the Home Counties stretching perhaps as far as Sandringham in East Anglia but usually confined to London and Windsor. At the same time the monarchy retains its imperial resonance through the Commonwealth link and in this context one must include the Scottish Balmoral connection and perhaps Caernarfon in Wales (though interestingly, and significantly, nowhere in Northern Ireland). So, at one and the same time the monarchy has reference points that are smaller and yet larger than England itself. The present Queen takes her role as 'Head of the Commonwealth' extremely seriously, as the reported clash between herself and Mrs Thatcher over the South African sanctions issue in the summer of 1986 made clear. It was interesting, for the thesis being suggested here, that on this occasion Mrs Thatcher appeared to be on the defensive. It was not just that she seemed to be opposing the Queen, but opposing her on the issue of the Commonwealth and its psychic links with the Greater England identity. On another occasion, however, at the time of the Falklands/ Malvinas conflict, Mrs Thatcher was not slow to play the 'kith and kin' card. Though, as the Tory commentator Peregrine Worsthorne remarked at the time:

> If the Falkland Islanders were British citizens with black or brown skins, spoke with strange accents or worshipped different Gods it is doubtful whether the Royal Navy and Marines would today be fighting for their liberation.[12]

Nonetheless, it is clear that the role of the monarchy, typified by its intimate relationship with the Commonwealth, is the central sustaining point, the keystone in the arch of Greater England. As Cannadine concluded his essay:

> Just as, in previous periods of international change, the ritual of monarchy was of importance in legitimating the novelty of formal empire and in giving an impression of stability at a time of international bewilderment, so in the post-war world it has provided a comfortable palliative to the loss of world-power status. When watching a royal occasion, impeccably planned, faultlessly executed, and with a commentary stressing (however mistakenly) the historic continuity with those former days of Britain's greatness, it is almost possible to believe that they have not entirely vanished. As Richard Dimbleby noted condescendingly at the time of the coronation, the Americans might be 'a race of such vitality', but they were so 'lacking in tradition' that 'they must wait a thousand years before they can show the world anything so significant or so lovely' . . .[13]

An exploration of the Greater English or Anglo-British identity is important because it provides an explanation for many of the paradoxes that criss-cross the political cultures of the British Isles like fault lines. It can be immediately understood, for instance, how inimical Anglo-British identity – with its focus in the rulers above, the monarchy – is to the kind of Scottish and Welsh national consciousness being mobilized by the SNP and Plaid Cymru, which is based on territory, traditional culture and a republican sense of 'the people'. Then again, it provides an explanation for the fact that although the English have a highly developed sense of regional culture – articulated via literature, music and the visual arts – this is extremely weak in terms of any political expression.

There are, by now, well-worn clichés concerning the problems of Anglo-British identity and Greater England, summarized by Dean Acheson's 1950s aphorism that Britain had lost an Empire but was still 'to find a role'. Thirty years later it seemed Greater England might be superseded by a Greater European identity. If this were the case, it was clear that it would be a long, slow evolution lasting well into the next century. However, the Divided Kingdom perspective suggests an alternative scenario. This is that the process of change in the Anglo-British consciousness is finding its essential dynamic internally, rather than externally, and that this process is likely to be quicker. The case can be summarized, and illuminated, by a glance at the messages being relayed by the three main British political parties as they strive to establish a clear identity for themselves in 1980s Britain. All three – Labour, Democrats and Conservatives – are presenting separate and distinctive challenges to the idea of Greater England.

It is another paradox of British political culture that Labour – with its powerbase firmly located in the North of England, Scotland and Wales – vies with the Conservatives in being the most Anglo-British of the parties. A range of interlocking reasons impels Labour in a centralist/British direction: the influence of the trade unions which from the start were British in their orientation and organization; the ideological belief that greater equality demands centralization; and, not to be underestimated, the absorption of most Labour MPs into the metro-

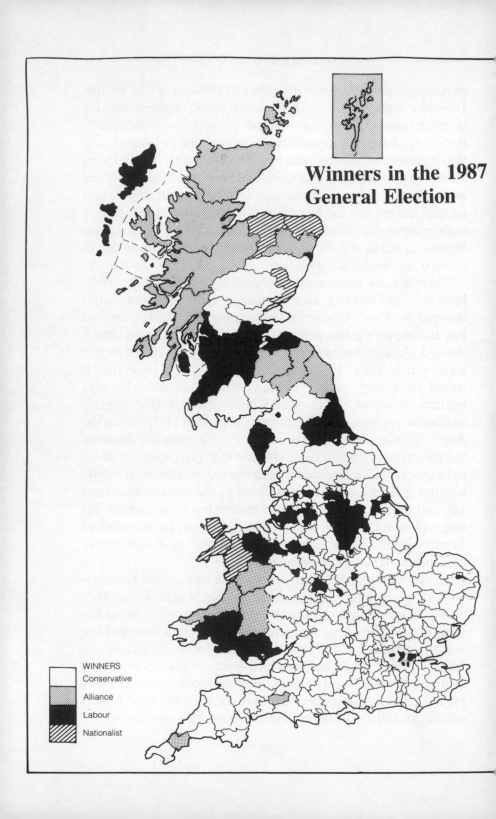

Winners in the 1987
General Election

WINNERS
Conservative
Alliance
Labour
Nationalist

politan/Westminster environment and culture. Yet although Labour's aspiration in the 1980s remained firmly to achieve power at the centre, the logic of electoral arithmetic was driving it to contemplate another strategy. Quite simply, this was to create alternative centres of power in those regions where it was strongest. In early 1987 the party unveiled a new policy for regional government in England. This would re-establish the Greater London Council and introduce a new tier of regional authorities, initially in the North-west (Lancashire, Cheshire, Merseyside, Greater Manchester), and in the North (Cumbria, Northumberland, Durham, Tyne-and-Wear and, possibly, Cleveland). Other regional authorities in England would follow, as demand and experience dictated, but most probably first in Yorkshire and Humberside, and the West Midlands. Labour was already committed to setting up a Scottish Assembly 'as early as possible' and hoped to 'establish a new authority for Wales'. These regional tiers of government would be responsible for regional economic planning, transport, water, fire and more than a dozen other functions including some developed from central government. They would probably be funded by a local income tax.[14]

Such wholesale devolution would, of course, entail a major assault on the Greater England identity sketched here. It would also run against the grain of more than sixty years of Labour ambition and sentiment. But it would build on the municipal socialism rediscovered by a new generation of Labour leaders in London and the other, northern, metropolitan authorities in England in the early 1980s. Moreover, it would reflect political realities. In the general elections of the 1980s Labour's vote collapsed nearly everywhere except inner London, northern England, south Wales, and the central belt of Scotland (see map opposite). Moreover, if another map were drawn to indicate whether Labour came second, it would merely show a widening band outwith these heartlands.

The Liberal and Social Democratic Party (Democrats) embraces, if anything, a range of policies that would more clearly undermine the Greater England identity. It is, of course, committed to a general 'decentralization' of central government power, the impact of which would be not unlike the Labour policy sketched above. But the Democrats have a more fundamental and wide-ranging commitment to constitutional change than Labour. Their central objective, of course, is proportional representation and, if implemented, this would have profound implications for the idea of Greater England in at least two ways. First, it would be a further extension of the electoral franchise movement begun in the early nineteenth century in that the vote of every individual would, in practice, count for more. Secondly, and following on from that, its result would be to break finally the two-party control of the House of Commons. This would be most significant since by enabling successive governments to be elected on a minority of the vote, the first-past-the-post electoral system, and the two-party power monopoly it fosters, is fundamentally undemocratic: it strengthens a culture in which 'the people' tend to focus their attention upwards, to the rulers above.

As well as these policies the Democrats are firmly committed to the idea of European integration. This is the closest the party has to a badge of identity and is the most salient characteristic distancing it from Anglo-Britishness and Greater England. Commitment to Europe is the foundation of the Democrats' whole project for modernizing Britain. As the SDP's biographer, Ian Bradley, put it:

It was opposition to the anti-EEC stance of the Labour Party in the early 1970s that brought 'the Gang of Four' together and forged the alliances that culminated in the launching of the new party ten years later. Of the ten original Social Democrat MPs who sat in the 1970 Parliament as Labour Members, only one, John Horam, did not defy a three-line whip and vote with the Conservatives on the crucial vote in October 1971 in favour of the principle of entry into the EEC . . . Every other prominent Social Democrat one meets seems to carry the battle scars of the 1975 referendum campaign.[15]

But what of the Conservatives, the party that in so many ways personifies and continues to articulate Anglo-British, Greater England identity? The ease with which the Conservative government was able to generate Anglo-British Churchillian-style patriotic fervour over the Falklands/Malvinas conflict in 1982 is a clear route to analysis of the Greater England sensibility. Nevertheless, some features of contemporary Conservatism are deeply inimical to Anglo-British identity. There is, of course, the fact that Conservative support in the 1980s has more and more concentrated in the South and South-east of England, making difficult the projection of an all-British identity and concern. As has been seen, however, this need not be a fundamental stumbling-block to a sense of Greater England since one of its characteristics is a lack of distinct territorial identification and, in any event, the Home Counties are its Crown-centred heartland.

It is in the presentation of a new modern Conservative image, and in some of the policies that flow from this, that the party has made the most subversive attack of all on Anglo–Britishness and Greater England in the 1980s. It has been subversive since it has tackled the royalist root of that identity. This has been the, perhaps unintentional, consequence of modern Conservatism's espousal of market forces as being the main criteria for decision-taking. Rather than any notion of royal sovereignty, or even sovereignty of Parliament, the market demands consumer sovereignty. And, as R. W. Johnson has pointed out in a penetrating analysis, market forces and consumer sovereignty are actively hostile to the old Tory aristocratic order. They demand greater openness, modernity and managerial competence. The result, according to Johnson, is an internal crisis for Tory culture, one which it seems incapable of overcoming.

For the fatal contradiction is that while Conservatism is committed to the promotion and encouragement of market forces, a Tory culture based upon the absence of any notion of popular culture can never really accommodate the notion of consumer sovereignty. If there really is no free lunch – if the market is the one great fundamental – and the people's choices and wishes are ultimately sovereign in that market, how can the people fail to be sovereign in the political and every other field? Moreover, the philosophy of the market is anarchic. It is hostile to the strong state. It respects only what is powerful in the market. It is antagonistic to monopoly, let alone a hereditary monopoly such as the monarchy . . .[16]

What Thatcherism – the new Conservatism – has attempted has been to place a popularly based, that is, *People*-based, nationalism at the centre of the political agenda.[17] Thus in her first leadership speech to the Conservative Party conference, in 1975, Mrs Thatcher declared:

We are witnessing a deliberate attack on our values, a deliberate attack on our heritage and our great past. And there are those who gnaw away at our national self-respect, rewriting British history as centuries of unrelieved gloom, oppression and failure – as days of hopelessness not days of hope.

Here Mrs Thatcher was referring to the need to defend a traditional patriotism, the one associated typically with the Dunkirk spirit. But her appeal was to the idea of the People as constituting the nation whose 'national self-respect' required sustaining. This was the underlying philosophical justification for the privatization measures of the later 1980s – though, of course, there were pragmatic financial considerations as well. Putting shares in the hands of the People and dismantling State ownership dovetails neatly with this approach. And so, for that matter, does using the proceeds to reduce the People's taxes – though here the dangerous ground of distribution and fairness looms. Another example of this approach is the new Conservative attitude to the trade unions, a further central preoccupation for Mrs Thatcher. In a speech to the Conservative Trade Unionists' Annual Conference in November 1979, she emphasized that trade unionists were also consumers and as such were as much interested in choice and 'value for money' as anyone else. Later in the speech she remarked:

Our belief in the secret ballot stems from our trust in the good sense of the twelve million British people who are members of trade unions.

The point Mrs Thatcher was stressing here is that the People are primarily citizens of the State, and only secondarily do they happen to be trade unionists. It is as citizens that they can be trusted with 'good sense' and not as trade unionists. In addressing 'the People' as citizens Mrs Thatcher is taking a fundamentally republican stance, one that undermines a monarchy-centred Anglo-British identity. This is likely to be the most far-reaching consequence of the so-called Thatcher revolution. For, as R. W. Johnson noted, it is provoking a crisis for the Tory culture. And it is the Tory culture that, ever since the counter-revolution of 1688, still known as 'glorious', has been the foundation of Greater England.

NOTES

1 Hugh Seton-Watson, *Nations and States – An inquiry into the origins of nations and the politics of nationalism*, Methuen, 1977, p. 487.
2 Anthony H. Birch, *Political Integration and Disintegration in the British Isles*, George Allen and Unwin, 1977, p. 138.
3 Tom Nairn, *The Break-Up of Britain*, Verso, 1981, p. 274.
4 Ludovic Kennedy in Cecil Woolf and Jean Moorcroft Wilson (eds.), *Authors take sides on the Falklands*, Cecil Woolf Publishers, 1982, p. 64–5.
5 Sheila Johnston, 'Charioteers and ploughmen' in Martin Auty and Nick Roddick (eds.), *British Cinema Now*, BFI Publishing, 1985, p. 100–102.
6 Michael Steed, 'The core-periphery dimension of British politics' in *Political Geography Quarterly*, Vol. 5, No. 4, October 1986, p. 93–4. This is a development of a mimeographed paper he presented to a UK Politics Workgroup conference at the University

of Warwick in August 1979, *The United Kingdom – What Components?*, which is also referred to here.

7 Communication to the author, June 1986. The theme is fully developed in Tom Nairn, *The Enchanted Glass – Britain and its Monarchy*, Chapter 2, 'The Nation', Radius/Century Hutchinson, 1988.

8 Tom Nairn, *The Enchanted Glass*, p. 168.

9 David Cannadine, 'The Context, Performance and Meaning of Ritual: The British Monarchy and the "Invention of Tradition"' in Eric Hobsbawm and Terence Ranger (eds.), *The Invention of Tradition*, Cambridge University Press, 1984, p. 133.

10 Judith Williamson, *Consuming Passions – The dynamics of popular culture*, Marion Boyars, 1986, p. 80–2.

11 Tom Nairn, *The British Monarchy: Bagehot and After*, unpublished mimeograph, July, 1987.

12 *Sunday Telegraph*, 23 May 1982.

13 Cannadine, op. cit., p. 157–8.

14 *Guardian*, 13 January 1987.

15 Ian Bradley, *Breaking the Mould?*, Martin Robertson, 1981, p. 124–5.

16 R. W. Johnson, *The Politics of Recession*, Macmillan, 1985, p. 239.

17 This theme is explored in Alan O'Shea, 'Trusting the People: How does Thatcherism Work?' in *Formations of Nation and People*, Routledge and Kegan Paul, 1984.

8

'Ain't no black in the Union Jack'*

No more dramatic instance of the Divided Kingdom could have occurred than the inner-city riots that took place first in 1981, and were repeated with increased ferocity and often in the same locations in 1985. In between although there was an outpouring of concern mixed with horror and anger, and a plethora of studies and reports – most notably Lord Scarman's inquiry into the Brixton disorders – the position of the people living in the inner cities worsened. Urban-aid programmes were directed at the inner cities, but most local authorities lost more than they gained through cuts in the rate support grant. Unemployment increased. Reflecting on the position in 1986 Lord Scarman noted:

> When I reported on the Brixton disturbances in 1981, there seemed to be a sense of urgency about implementing my recommendations. As far as the police reforms went, many were acted on very quickly. But when one comes to my suggestions for improving social and environmental conditions, I have to say that the government did not show the same sense of urgency until 1985 – when they suddenly learnt that more was needed to prevent a recurrence of Brixton than merely improving the quality of our policing. It took the

* This is the title of Paul Gilroy's book on the cultural politics of race and nation in Britain, published by Hutchinson in 1987. It is also a National Front slogan, most prevalent in the 1950s and 1960s.

NON-WHITE VOTERS IN THE 1987 GENERAL ELECTION
(statistics derived from the 1981 Census)

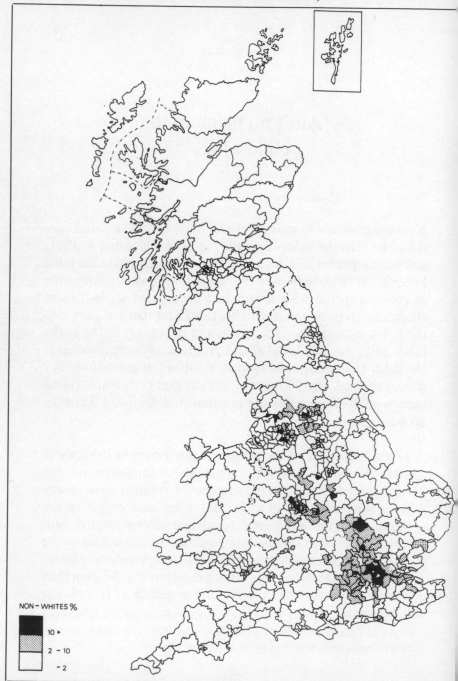

NON – WHITES %

10 +

2 – 10

– 2

From *The Atlas of British Politics* by Robert Walker, Croom Helm, 1984

Birmingham riots of 1985 to bring home the importance of implementing the social recommendations of my 1981 report . . .[1]

The Handsworth/Soho/Lozells area of Birmingham, with a population of 56,300, is regarded by the City Council as 'the most deprived district in the city'. Unemployment is a major affliction, and at the time of the riots, which were sparked on 9 September 1985, 36 per cent of the workforce in Handsworth was out of work, while the figure for people under twenty-four years was 50 per cent.[2]

Handsworth is an area which had been noted for reasonably good relations between young blacks and the police, based on the concept of community policing introduced by Superintendent David Webb in the late 1970s. However, at the end of 1981 he left the police service and although his approach was continued by his successor he, too, left the area in April 1985. The new superintendent instituted changes which included moving a number of the area's community police officers to other duties, and clamping down on activities by local youths which had previously been tolerated. In particular police attention turned to the use of cannabis by black youths, and a number of raids took place during the summer (for instance, on 10 July 150 police officers raided the Acapulco café on Villa Road, and seven people were arrested).

These changes in officers and tactics brought an increase in tension between youths and police. In July 1985 two serious disturbances occurred in Handsworth, but both were played down and went unreported by the media. In the first, about seventy youths rioted, attacking police vehicles and officers and looting a shop. It took more than two hours to restore order. A few days later police officers who were questioning a youth were attacked by a large group of young people. The context within which the eruption occurred on 9 September was thus one of deteriorating relations between the police and young people, especially blacks, as well as widespread unemployment and social disadvantage.

The tinder merely required a spark, which was provided when a black youth become involved in an altercation with an officer over a parking ticket. It is alleged that during the incident, at which more police arrived, a black woman was assaulted, but whether or not this occurred what is certain is that two hours later some forty-five buildings in Lozells Road were ablaze. The riots resulted in the deaths of two Asian men, Amir Ali Moledina and his brother Kassam Ali, who were asphyxiated in their burning post office. Thirty other people, mainly police, were reported injured and the value of damaged property was put at £10 million.

Brixton was the scene of the next outbreak of violent disorder, during the weekend 28–29 September 1985. More than 900 crimes were reported, forty-three members of the public and ten police officers were injured, and 230 arrests were made. As in Handsworth, the trigger event which led to the rioting involved police officers and a black person, on this occasion Mrs Cherry Groce. At 7 a.m. on 28 September, armed police entered her house in Normandy Road, Brixton, looking for her son. Two shots were fired by an officer, and a bullet damaged Mrs Groce's spine, causing permanent paralysis. At 6 p.m. the local police station was attacked with petrol bombs, and during the next eight hours large numbers of black and white people took part in burning and looting which caused damage estimated at £3 million. During the rioting a freelance photographer, David Hodge, sustained injuries from which he died three weeks later.

Two days after Mrs Groce was shot, rioting occurred in Liverpool 8. In this instance, the disturbances were precipitated when four black men were refused bail at Liverpool Magistrates' Court. They had been charged in connection with a fracas in August, but local youths claimed that they were being treated unfairly and picked upon by police. During the summer there were reports of rising tension in the area, and on 30 August a crowd demonstrated outside Toxteth police station, and then attacked police cars and the station itself. In the incident on 30 September a crowd of 300 youths armed with stones took to the streets after the four defendants were refused bail. Two streets in Toxteth – Princess Avenue and Upper Parliament Street – were sealed off by riot police and a number of cars and a post office van were set alight. The fire brigade were called out to deal with a blazing launderette.

As in Handsworth and Brixton, police relations with young people, and especially black youths, were a significant factor in the explosive mixture and the disorder was precipitated by an incident involving police officers and black people.

But the most serious of the disorders occurred at the Broadwater Farm Estate, in Tottenham, London. Rioting there began at about 6.45 p.m. on Sunday 6 October 1985, and during a night of extraordinary violence PC Keith Blakelock was stabbed to death, twenty members of the public and 255 police officers were injured, and a large number of cars and some buildings burned. Guns were fired at the police, causing injuries to several officers and reporters, and the police deployed CS gas and plastic bullets although these were not used.

In the immediate aftermath of the Handsworth riots Nicholas Deakin, Professor of Social Policy at the University of Birmingham, observed that compared with other inner-city areas Birmingham's had the highest unemployment rate among sixteen- to nineteen-year-olds, the fastest increase in unemployment between censuses, and the largest proportion of single-parent families. The West Midlands, he said, was the epitome of the collapse of British manufacturing industry under the impact of recession.

Four years ago 'it took a riot', as Michael Heseltine put it, for Merseyside to gain the nation's attention and ultimately its garden festival. In four years time no doubt Birmingham will have its sports stadium. Lord Scarman ended his report on the 1981 events by quoting President Johnson – 'the only genuine long range solution for what has happened lies in an attack – mounted at every level – upon the conditions that breed despair and violence. All of us know what those conditions are: ignorance, discrimination, poverty, disease, and not enough jobs.'

There is a limit to the amount of repetition fine phrases can stand without action to support them. Perhaps this time it may happen, but the smart money says that by the end of the decade we shall be no nearer solutions.[3]

Certainly this appeared to be the case in Handsworth in the late 1980s when the Handsworth local economy remained devastated and the area where the rioting occurred was still reminiscent of a bomb site. Basil Clarke, leader of the Lozells Road Trader Association which was set up after the riots to co-ordinate action – he himself lost one business in the riots and had another property badly damaged – said:

We are fed up with promises being made and nothing being done. We don't want to shake hands with big name politicians; we want jobs.[4]

In December 1985 the Church of England published the outcome of a two-year study into the problems of the inner cities, what the government defined in 1977 as Urban Priority Areas. The report, *Faith in the City*, emphasized that these had become 'separate territories' from the rest of the country, dependent entirely on the public sector and outside the mainstream of economic and social life.

. . . what has most astonished (and depressed) us has been a widespread feeling among those we have talked to in the Urban Priority Areas that 'nothing can be done' about unemployment. Not that nothing should be done – the feeling is that the 'social evil' is so widespread and unchanging, the problem so baffling, and the authorities apparently so unresponsive, that hope has been abandoned. We wonder whether some politicians really understand the despair which has become so widespread in many areas of the country.[5]

Perhaps what was most remarkable about the report, however, was the manner of its reception by the government. One Cabinet Minster (unnamed) was reported as describing it as 'pure Marxist ideology'. The Environment Secretary at the time, Kenneth Baker, declared it 'negative and out of date'.[6] Yet the despair in the inner cities was not acknowledged, nor their dependence on the public sector highlighted, in the report appreciated; instead public sector spending was withdrawn from the inner cities. In Liverpool, for example, under the inspiration of Michael Heseltine it seemed that public expenditure increased in the years leading up to the 1985 riots. And it was the case that the Urban Aid programme's spending in the city doubled between 1980/81 and 1983/84, from £6 million to £12 million. Yet Liverpool's housing subsidies in the same period were slashed by £13 million (from £18 million to £5 million), and its rate support grant by £23 million (from £141 million to £118 million).[7] A similar picture emerges from the other cities. After the 1981 riots Michael Heseltine tried to persuade the Cabinet to provide more help for the inner cities, and failed.

Ken Young of the London Policy Studies Institute, where a series of inner-cities studies have been carried out, pointed to the fact that investment was shifting from the cities to the outlying towns and shires:

The present epoch of counter-urbanization cannot be stopped. The trend is as powerful as the inward migration which built up our major cities in the nineteenth century. The big question which all policy-makers are ducking is what is going to happen to the big city in the modern western economy. The Government has failed to recognize that its cuts to inner-city budgets is compounding the difficulties created by the private market withdrawing when it should have been trying to counter market trends.

Enterprise agencies do very little for the inner-city resident. What jobs they create tend to be picked up by people commuting from outside the inner city. The most important element in the inner city for the main bulk of the unemployed – the unskilled and disadvantaged – is the public sector.

The key objective should have been trying to minimize the increase in unemployment rather than the creation of new jobs. The public sector cuts have had a disproportionate impact because the people who have been made unemployed are often trapped in the inner city without a house of their own to sell – and so are unable to move out to a new town to get a job.[8]

In 1985–86 the government was spending 60 per cent less on housing and renovation than six years previously, such building work being the most labour-intensive job provider available in the inner cities. And the impact is all too noticeable since council housing – which is 57 per cent of the housing stock in Hackney, for instance – tends to be cramped, in a poor state of repair and even then subject to impossibly long waiting lists. Bertha Turner, of the Housing Advisory Service, in a study of poverty in Hackney concluded:

Some people cannot afford more than one meal a day. They live in unheated and damp housing or have no homes, dressing themselves in cast-off clothes from jumble sales. Many spend 40 per cent to 60 per cent of their incomes on housing and fuel alone whereas the average family spends just 20 per cent . . . The London Electricity Board is not allowed to cut off electricity to families with young children during the winter months, so they do it in summer. And once cut off, it is impossible to stretch an insufficient income to cover the cost of arrears . . .

Many conscientious mothers living on council estates are frightened to let their children out to play. There is a serious lack of safe play spaces for children . . .

Largely for this reason, the television set, sometimes referred to as the 'one-eyed babysitter', has become the one most powerful medium of communication. Often more influential than parents in shaping social values, since it is cheap and available even to the poorest, it has become a common if sinister way to keep the kids quiet in crowded and cramped housing space. Idealized lifestyles, gratuitous violence, and rampant consumerism all serve to set up expectations and behaviour patterns that cannot be served or accommodated by present-day inner city realities. It is a chilling fact that in London, one murder in seven is committed in Hackney: ten times the national average . . .[9]

And, of course, it is in inner-city areas like Hackney, Brixton, Toxteth and Handsworth that black people are concentrated. Over the past thirty years, declining local economies led to the exodus of the more affluent residents, leaving generally poor and decaying housing to be occupied by immigrants. So, whereas just 6 per cent of Britain's white people are located in inner London, inner Birmingham and inner Manchester, 23 per cent of Asians and 43 per cent of West Indians live there.[10] For these people racism has to be added to the more general evils of unemployment and social deprivation. A 1982 Policy Studies Institute survey found considerably higher rates of unemployment among West Indians and Asians and reported that those who had managed to secure a job were likely to be in low-paid work: 'on average white men earn substantially more than black men'. Black people also suffered considerable disadvantage in housing.

Blacks are more often found in flats, and those in flats are more often at higher floor levels, and those with houses are less likely to have detached or semi-detached property; black families have smaller property on average, and their density of occupation is much higher . . .[11]

Realities such as these led Lord Scarman to state in his Brixton report:

. . . racial disadvantage is a fact of current British life. It was, I am equally sure, a significant factor in the causation of the Brixton disorders. Urgent action is needed if it is not to become an endemic ineradicable disease threatening the very survival of our society.[12]

When Euphemia Hamilton arrived in Brixton in 1955 she was among more than 24,000 West Indians who had travelled that year from British colonies.[13] For most of them the objective was simply to better themselves and return enriched to their corner of the Empire. The Nationality Act of 1948 had confirmed the right of colonials to settle in Britain. Enticed by a campaign by London Transport and the British Hotels and Restaurants Association, more than 125,000 West Indians came to Britain in the decade after 1948.

Initially Euphemia Hamilton aimed to stay no more than five years. Back home she had her own small clothes store and she wanted to accumulate some capital to build it up. In Jamaica she used to employ two assistants in the store and also a home help to look after her children and her house.

In England she was a worker in a sewing factory, and a tenant in an eight-roomed house with eight black families sharing two kitchens and two bathrooms. But she never returned to Jamaica. Her children followed her to England, she established new relationships and though the thought of returning remained, there was no longer a set time-limit. Euphemia Hamilton's life story hit the headlines when her daughter, Mrs Cherry Groce, was shot in the Brixton disorders of September 1985. Looking across the generations she commented:

When my generation came here we took a lot of abuse, and perhaps did not fight for our rights. This generation is more educated. They have not the faith nor the patience.[14]

If she had never left Jamaica her son, Mervyn Bartlett, would not have become an honours graduate in computer and micro-processor engineering at Essex University. He used not to think that the police have one law for the blacks and another for the whites. After the Brixton disorders he was not so sure:

My impression before the police shot my sister was that perhaps there was a criminal element in the area, and the police were simply trying to close down on it. But that is not the case. What they did to my sister and what they have done to black people in general is not justified.

Bartlett insists that he, and black people born here, are British: 'I think it is wrong when a black child born here is called West Indian.'[15]

This is the view of second-generation black people who have been educated and found work. What about the feelings of second-generation and, perhaps more emphatically and poignantly, third-generation black people without work? Devon Thomas had lived in Brixton since his family arrived from Jamaica in the 1950s and he was a prominent figure in the Brixton Defence Campaign which was set up to give support to those who were arrested, and their families, during the events of 1981. Today he works in the South Bank Inner-City Centre which he helped set up to focus on the employment and economic needs of inner-city communities. Looking back at the period of West Indian immigration after 1948 he reflected that the welcoming spirit in Britain soon came to an end:

The years from the late 1950s to the late 1970s were characterized by increasingly frantic attempts to prevent black people coming to this country, using legislation and any other means available. There was miseducation of those young blacks going through school, and a systematic attempt to blame blacks for the increasing economic problems of the country by fringe racist groups, and then by 'respectable' political organs of this society. This was the background against which I grew up and went to school . . .

In the early 1960s on reaching the age of eleven I took and passed my '11 plus' examination.This opened up the opportunity for me to attend grammar school, which pleased my parents greatly. I applied and was offered an interview to the local grammar school. This pleased me, as one of my best friends, a white boy, had also passed the exam. He had an interview at the same school a week after my own. I attended the interview along with my father where I answered all the questions asked by the headmaster, apparently to his satisfaction. At the end of the interview the head said: 'It is very interesting, we don't get many of you people coming here.

Your son seems to be a very bright chap. We've only ever had one chap like him attend this school, but he was rather naughty and we had to expel him.' He turned to me and said, 'I hope you're not like that.' This was typical of the kind of attitude that many teachers had towards their black pupils. Needless to say, my friend attended his interview the next week, and was offered a place. However, my father received a letter shortly afterwards informing us that the school was full and therefore could not take me. I consequently attended the local comprehensive school which catered largely for the locality of Brixton . . .[16]

Later, when he came to look for work, Devon Thomas found predictable difficulty.

The usual excuse from personnel officers for not appointing me would be: 'If we give you the job, you will have responsibility. Some of the people you have to work with are very touchy and might not be willing to take orders from a person like you. I wouldn't like to expose you to that kind of thing, so I think perhaps it might be better if I didn't offer you the job.' This put me in a position where they were trying to get me to collude with the racism implicit in the situation and literally agree to exclude myself . . . In the end most of us had to start off in jobs far below our ability and aspiration.[17]

Many, of course, could not find work at all. Thomas concluded:

It is now clear to me, reviewing my own personal history and that of the black community generally, that this society had attempted to reproduce in my generation, and those that have followed, a similar role for us as for my parents' generation – that of unskilled labourers at the bottom of the labour pile.[18]

This is a key issue identified by Lord Scarman. He says the answer must be a major educational and training campaign to equip black people, especially young blacks, for skilled work.

Ethnic minority opportunities should be created in the universities, business activities and industrial management, the civil service, the police, politics and public life.

> In other words, we must create a black British middle class. This was the strategy pursued in America. As in America so here, black and brown as well as white faces must be seen not only on the production line but also in positions of authority and influence at all levels in society . . . If we can create a black middle class, then we will also be creating a group that can exercise responsibility and creative leadership in their own community and in the nation . . .[19]

But given present circumstances how likely is the creation of Lord Scarman's 'black British middle class'? Consider just the 'British' part of this aspiration: life in the inner cities has produced a kind of counter-culture amongst black youth which is better defined as Afro–Caribbean than British, an identity often expressed through an exotic mix of Rastafarianism, reggae music, gospel churches, and cannabis. In economic terms it is leading to ideas of separate development, with black people establishing their own enterprises as the only way in which they can make progress. But opportunities for this are relatively rare and for many young blacks in the inner cities unemployment or, at the very most, under-employment, is the norm.

Back in 1977, when Handsworth in Birmingham was beginning to come out near the top in the country's crime statistics and youth problems generally, the Professor of Social Policy at Cranfield Institute of Technology, John Brown, in a specially commissioned report talked about the criminal sub-culture that flourished there. He identified a group of 200 West Indian youths who had rejected conventional society and were alienated from their families. Whenever they came into contact with the police there was a risk of confrontation and violence. He predicted that matters would worsen if the employment prospects in the area did not improve.[20]

Unemployment has, of course, worsened in the 1980s as have living conditions generally. The Church of England's *Faith in the City* report drew attention to the massive switch of housing wealth since 1979 from council renters to (richer) owner occupiers as marking out the growing gulf between the inner cities and the rest of the (generally) more affluent country. Since 1979, it pointed out, council rents had risen by 150 per cent – far more than inflation – to a level where they were no longer subsidized. The majority of councils now actually make a profit on housing, which is transferred to the general rate fund. Yet, at the same time as taxpayers' subsidy to council tenants was being eliminated, the cost to the Exchequer of mortgage-interest relief soared from £1.1 million in 1978–79 to an estimated £4.5 billion in 1985–86. And, of course, the higher the income, the higher the subsidy. The average tax relief for a mortgagor earning £9,000 in 1985–86 was £430 a year rising to £1,290 for someone earning £30,000.

Following the Handsworth disturbances three lengthy and highly contrasting reports appeared. The first, in November 1985, was by the Chief Constable for the West Midlands, Geoffrey Dear. It received wide publicity and its conclusions can be summed up in one word: drugs.

> There is firm evidence to suggest the disorders were at the outset orchestrated by local drug dealers who had become fearful for the demise of their livelihoods. Similarly, there is evidence that the riots were fuelled and organized by persons who require the supply of drugs to continue their normal lifestyle.[21]

The report suggested that owing to police effectiveness the dealers had become 'frustrated': their distribution points were being reduced, their freedom of movement curtailed. So what did they do? They 'planned and conceived' the riot. Chief Constable Dear conceded that there had been an 'overall increase' in police activity in the area, though he failed to emphasize the shift some six months prior to the riots from low-key community policing to high-profile law enforcement, particularly in relation to drugs.

The Chief Constable's unlikely explanation was challenged by another report, this time commissioned by Birmingham City Council and written by a former city Labour MP, Julius Silverman. He concluded in February 1986 that there was 'no evidence whatever of [Chief Constable Dear's] conclusion of a grand design to burn and destroy and loot a large portion of the Lozells road'. The root cause, Silverman stated, was unemployment, with 38 per cent on the dole and more than half of the sixteen- to eighteen-year-olds out of work:

> Without minimizing in any way the horror, destruction and distress of the events, the really important matter for the future is not who struck the match which set Handsworth alight but the evidence of the social conditions, the mass of hostility, frustration and potential violence which still exists in Handsworth.[22]

The most significant report on the disturbances had appeared a month earlier, however. Published by the West Midlands Metropolitan County (in its dying days) the report was called *A Different Reality: an account of black people's experiences and their grievances before and after the Handsworth rebellion of September 1985*. It was written by a panel of six black people, among them Stuart Hall, Professor of Sociology with the Open University; Herma Ouseley, an experienced local government administrator; and Keith Vaz, a solicitor and a prospective Labour parliamentary candidate (who was to gain a seat, along with several other black Labour candidates, in 1987). The report was a radical, passionate and bitter account of how black working-class people see their lives in Britain's inner cities. It quoted from local studies of job discrimination, not least in the Youth Training Scheme and not least by well-known private companies with household names. It recorded the incidence of overcrowding and young black homelessness in the area. On local schools it quoted the trenchant views of pupils and parents: 'We are only expected to be good at running and football – and to look at princesses with golden hair in our books.' But the primary view in the report was that Britain is a racist society:

> It is racist because all the power and control of resources and organizations is vested in white people who use their authority to ensure that black people remain second-class persons . . . [Theirs] is an experience of relative poverty, institutionalized discrimination, denied opportunity, denigrated pride, devalued culture and state harassment . . . The reality for black people living in Britain is that many of them see their existence as a form of apartheid. They are confined to the worst housing, they are predominantly among the unemployed, they are channelled into dead-end training schemes having endured schooling in education cul-de-sacs where they are expected to fail and tutored accordingly . . . Harsh policing on top of all this provides the chemistry for violent reaction.[23]

That racism is endemic in British society cannot be denied. The ease with which terms of racial abuse slip into the English language is only the most obvious illustration: wog, frog, kraut, dago, spic, yid, coon, nigger and, particularly indicative of the 1980s, Argie. But to describe this racism as 'institutionalized' reveals a failure of understanding of the British State that has a paralysing effect when it comes to thinking through approaches to change. The idea that British racism is 'institutionalized' has become accepted by black intellectuals. The above quotation is one example. Another was Salman Rushdie's Channel 4 broadcast on 'The New Empire' in 1982: 'The evidence of institutionalized racism is so voluminous that I cannot hope to do more than provide a few examples . . .'[24] Though racism permeates British institutions and even the government itself (when the Race Relations Act was passed the government specifically exempted itself and all its actions from its jurisdiction), this is quite different from allowing that racism is institutionalized. That would be tantamount to saying that British treatment of black people was comparable to genuine (that is, South African) apartheid.

There is in fact only one area where racism in Britain is institutionalized, and that is on the outer perimeter of State and society: the law and practice of nationality and immigration. The process began, significantly, at the point when the decline of Empire was incipient, if not imminent: the 1905 Aliens Act was the first to restrict entry into Britain and was aimed mainly at Jews. The definition of 'aliens' was widened in further legislation in 1914 and 1918. The 1948 Nationality Act set out to define the boundaries of the Empire rather than to restrict rights. However, in the 1960s a more urgent phase of restriction was set in train, with entry for work being the main target. The 1962 Commonwealth Immigrants Act withdrew the *right* to live in Britain from citizens of independent Commonwealth countries and the colonies. They could, however, apply for work vouchers which, unlike work permits for aliens, granted them an indefinite right to live in Britain and to bring in their families. In 1965, under a Labour government, the number of work vouchers available was reduced by two-thirds to 8,500 (of which 1,000 were reserved for Malta) – this in the wake of the loss of the safe Labour seat of Smethwick in the 1964 by-election to a Tory who campaigned on the slogan 'Vote Liberal or Labour for a nigger neighbour'. Richard Crossman confided frankly to his diary:

> This has been one of the most difficult and unpleasant jobs the government has had to do. We have become illiberal and lowered the quotas at a time when we have an acute shortage of labour. No wonder all the weekend liberal papers have been bitterly attacking us. Nevertheless I am convinced that if we hadn't done this we would have been faced with certain electoral defeat in the West Midlands and the South East. Politically, fear of immigration is the most powerful under-tow today.[25]

In 1968 a further Immigration Act removed the right of free entry to Britain for people from the colonies who had not been born in the country and who lacked a parent or grandparent who had been – a specifically segregationist measure. The doors were finally closed on black primary legislation with the 1971 Immigration Act, though citizens of other countries who had a parent or grandparent born in Britain (mainly white) were called 'patrial' and given entry. The process was completed with the 1981 Nationality Act which, with a kind of ultimate absurdity, removed the automatic right of all children born in Britain to be British citizens. In its anxiety to deprive black people of their citizenship right, the government removed the auto,atic citizenship rights of everybody. Henceforth, citizenship was in the gift of the State.

Immigration and the concentration of communities of blacks in the inner cities has exposed the most sensitive point of the ramshackle British State structure: how can incomers be treated like actual or potential citizens, regardless of race, colour, etc., when none of the natives are truly citizens either? The incomers are not 'second-class citizens' since there are no citizens in the British system, first-class or otherwise. The inhabitants are actually what the British Constitution textbooks say – 'subjects'. As a consequence there is no formal or statutory apparatus of equal rights and treatment, no 'Bill of Rights', no formal, written constitution to which the individual can refer when resisting the demands of the State. In this situation it becomes more comprehensible why so often the flashpoint in the inner cities is provided by the relationship of black people with the police. The racism of the police (and the courts) enrages the black population because there is nothing they can do to fight back. There is, of course, a 'Police Complaints Procedure' but in practice the police are unassailable, a law unto themselves, virtually free from outside, constitutionally supported inquiry, censure or discipline. This affects all the peoples of the British State. In particular circumstances it bears heavily on the Welsh, Scots and Irish – but never so acutely as on the black population confronting a system of authority shot through with the most extreme manifestation of their host society's racial prejudice, most extreme because it almost daily expresses itself in physical violence, somewhere in the inner cities scattered across England.

Thus, to accuse the British political culture of harbouring 'institutionalized racism' is to miss the point. There is in a key sense no institutional structure in which this can happen or be redressed. The black population, like everybody else, is dependent upon an assemblage of conventions, or customs held in common and variously expressed through notions of 'decency', 'moderation' or 'playing the game'. Their liberties are dependent upon those in authority abiding by these traditional values. Yet in *their* confrontation with the problems of the inner cities 'those in authority' are not inherently predisposed to deploy these virtues; rather the reverse. Black demands for 'equal rights' founder, ultimately, on there being no basis for citizenship rights for anybody within the legal, constitutional State structure. This is the essential context in which the stark question raised by Lord Scarman, looking back at the two phases of inner-city rioting in the 1980s, should be viewed.

The inner city is critical for the future of the British nation. The inner cities are the testing ground where the character of Britain will be determined.

This is because of their population mix, their high rate of unemployment and their substandard physical environment. Most importantly, our fellow citizens who live there see themselves at a disadvantage, compared with the rest of us, and many of them attribute their disadvantage to racial prejudice. The question the inner cities raise, therefore, is: are we to become a successful, multi-racial nation, or are we on course for a revolutionary phase in our history?[26]

A popular image of the Handsworth riot was encapsulated in a photograph that appeared the next day on the front pages of all the tabloid newspapers. It was of a young, casually dressed black man with an angry scowl on his face and a petrol bomb in his hand. The *Sun*'s headline was: HATE OF BLACK BOMBER. The story began: 'A black thug stalks a Birmingham street with hate in his eyes and a petrol bomb in his hand. The prowling West Indian was one of the hoodlums who brought new race terror to riot-torn Handsworth . . .'

A different way of perceiving this image was articulated in the West Midlands Metropolitan County Report, which referred to the 'riot' as a 'rebellion'.

> Most people who were spoken to expressed great fears about the future of the area if real changes are not forthcoming. In such circumstances this rebellion is perceived as a beginning and not the end . . .
>
> Violent resistance is now permanently on the agenda while the oppression and the denial of rights and resources continues. That is the clear message emerging from the black people of the inner cities.[27]

The government's response, following a review of the 1985 riots in London by the Metropolitan Police Commissioner, Sir Kenneth Newman, in June 1986, was to arm the police with more powerful weaponry. The Home Secretary, Douglas Hurd, told the House of Commons he had agreed that Scotland Yard could buy twenty-four armoured Land Rovers, of the type familiar in Northern Ireland, eighty personnel carriers, 1,500 truncheons (28 ins long instead of the standard 16 ins) and 700 radios.[28] A week later, however, an independent report commissioned by Haringey Council (which includes the Broadwater Farm Estate) and chaired by Lord Gifford, accused the police of glaring irregularities and a history of abuse against black people on the estate. Lord Gifford said his inquiry team was 'very concerned with the increasing militarization of the police'.[29]

Were the immigrant communities to encounter genuine 'institutionalized' racism, an ideologically developed and politically organized system of rejection – as in South Africa – their situation would be quite different. What they have actually met is steady, grudging antagonism punctuated by moments of violence. The result is a kind of stalemate which both sides are expected to endure until such time as they can grow used to each other, the black communities patiently waiting for the racism endemic in their environment to diminish. This is unlikely to occur so long as all involved fail to appreciate that the inner cities in the 1990s are a 'testing ground' for something far deeper than Lord Scarman suggested. This is what the black experience there has thrown into relief: the absence of a truly democratic basis for individual rights in Britain; the absence, that is, of a principled and formal constitutional structure in which conflicts such as those that are occurring in the inner cities can be regulated.

In this respect the black communities of the inner cities can be compared with the projection within the United Kingdom of separate Ulster, Scots and Welsh identities, as well as the regionalist stirrings in the English North. All these expose the hopelessly old-fashioned and *ad hoc* structures of the dominant Anglo-British identity: its 'irrational' and piecemeal nature, its dependence on monarchy and an imperially projected military tradition, its sense of bourgeois class values emanating from the Home Counties, its official secrecy, and, above all, its inability to modernize which is epitomized by the tired procedures of Lords and Commons at Westminster. The conflicts of the inner cities, perhaps the sharpest and most precipitous edge of the Divided Kingdom, are telling us as much about the character of the Anglo-British State as the black identities of those who are forced to endure them.

NOTES

1 Lord Scarman, 'Injustice in the Cities', *New Society*, 14 February 1986.
2 Full details of the background to the riots in Handsworth and elsewhere are contained in John Benyon, *A Tale of Failure – Race and Policing*, Centre for Research in Ethnic Relations, University of Warwick, March 1986.
3 *Guardian*, 11 September 1985.
4 *Guardian*, 2 October 1985.
5 *Faith in the City*, Church House Publishing, London, December 1985.

6 *Guardian*, 3 December 1985.
7 *Guardian*, 'The Cities of Inner Despair', 3 October 1985.
8 Ibid.
9 *Whose Responsibility? Reclaiming the inner cities*, Town and Country Planning Association report, April 1986, p. 11–12.
10 Colin Brown, *Black and White Britain: The Third PSI Survey*, Heinemann, 1984, pp. 55 and 61–63.
11 Ibid., p. 305–306.
12 Lord Scarman, *The Brixton Disorders*, HMSO (comd. 8427), para 9.1.
13 See Leslie Goffe, 'Casualties of the Impossible Dream', *Guardian*, 4 January 1986.
14 Ibid.
15 Ibid.
16 Devon Thomas, 'Black initiatives in Brixton', in John Benyon (ed.), *Scarman and After*, Pergamon, 1984, p. 185–6.
17 Ibid., p. 187
18 Ibid., p. 186.
19 Scarman, 'Injustice in the Cities', op.cit.
20 Reported by Paul Brown, 'The bleeding heart of England', *Guardian*, 11 September 1985.
21 Reported by John Clare, 'Things are likely to get worse before they get better', *Listener*, 6 March 1986.
22 *Guardian*, 28 February 1986.
23 John Clare, op.cit.
24 Salman Rushdie, 'The New Empire', broadcast in the *Opinions* series on Channel 4, 6 December 1982, and printed in *New Society*, 9 December 1982.
25 Richard Crossman, *Diaries of a Cabinet Minister*, Vol. 1, Hamish Hamilton and Jonathan Cape, 1975, p. 299.
26 Scarman, op.cit.
27 Clare, op.cit.
28 *The Times*, 3 July 1986.
29 *Guardian*, 8 July 1986.

—9—

Images of identity

In his 1977 report, *The Future of Broadcasting*, Lord Annan judged that the BBC 'is arguably the single most important cultural organization in the nation'.[1] And it is not difficult to trace the reasons why. Starting in the 1930s, when broadcasting began its sustained national impact – though this can be traced back to the coverage of the 1926 General Strike – broadcasting transformed a whole range of public occasions and ceremonies from being isolated events available only to a few into moments available to all. As Paddy Scannell, of the Polytechnic of Central London, has written:

> They took place in the BBC's calendar as broadcast events that recurred regularly, year in year out, at the appropriate time. Civic and sacred ceremonies, sporting and cultural events, entered into a new relationship with each other, woven together in the National Programme (commenced 1930) as idioms of national identity, moments in which the whole of society was able for the first time to participate . . .
>
> Their combination in a single national channel worked to stabilize the national culture, the British way of life, as a knowable settled organic community. The BBC constructed its national audience as individual family members with private pleasures and public duties as citizen-members of a democracy. The nation-state was distinguished from government, and its values and loyalties, embodied in the

monarchy, transcended politics. Both were presumed to be in harmony with each other. If government and people had a common interest in the effective and efficient working of democracy, then this secured the preservation and continuity of the nation in unity. Together they constituted the national interest in which rulers and ruled had a common stake.[2]

It is difficult to over-emphasize the relationship between the media – especially television – and the monarchy in knitting together the idea of national unity described here.

A study of public attitudes to the monarchy in the wake of the 1969 Investiture of Prince Charles pointed up what were suggested to be incompatible or contradictory feelings about the royal family: 'They would like the Queen to be at one and the same time grand and common, extraordinary and ordinary, grave and informal, mysterious and accessible, royal and democratic.'[3] But, as was suggested in Chapter VII, it is the very combination of these apparent opposites that accounts for the appeal, success and power of the monarchy as an institution. And in this process the media play a key role. It is broadcasting's ability to personalize the monarchy, together with its powerful projection of royal ceremonial events, that has fused the image of a rather 'ordinary' family into a symbol of nationhood. It is unlikely, for instance, that the wedding of the Prince and Princess of Wales would have been as effective as a spectacle if it had not been preceded by the purely journalistic and personalized coverage of the secular romance between Charles and Diana. As David Cardiff and Paddy Scannell observed:

Ritual always works to transform and, if it is to be effective, the spectator must have the opportunity to witness the object of ritual in its earlier, untransformed state. By purveying images of royalty in both its secular and sacred state, television enables this chemistry to work at a national level. Allowing for both personal identification and collective awe, it binds together the private and public spheres, thus fulfilling what has always been an underlying aim of public service broadcasting.[4]

The conjunction of the sacred with the profane has long had a resonance with the peoples of Britain, and particularly the English. It goes some way to explain public acceptability of Central Television's lampooning of royal personalities in its satirical puppet show *Spitting Image*. The delicious profanity of a puppet image of the Queen holding a toilet seat has to be seen alongside the sacred images of her at the Cenotaph, opening Parliament, or reviewing the Household Cavalry in Horse-guards Parade.

Broadcasting has revitalized the power of the monarchy as a transcending value which is above the levels of social and political strife, and which unites all classes. The examples of this process in action are as endless as the daily round of political crises and royal occasions themselves. Thus, in July 1981, as the inner-city riots in Toxteth and Brixton sent a shock wave through the body politic, the impact was cauterized by the reassuring build-up and then excitement and climax of the royal event of the decade, the wedding of Charles and Diana. Not long after that, the national unity and purpose necessary to sustaining the Falklands adventure was supported by the presence of Prince Andrew himself as a helicopter pilot with the Task Force. In 1986 the Queen's sixtieth birthday celebrations neatly competed for headlines with the American bombing of Libya, using British bases.

There is no conspiracy in all this: it is just the combination of the natural rhythm of family life – albeit royal – with its projection by the media. In this the BBC has long played a special role, symbolized by the Christmas Day broadcast which, as Scannell put it:

. . . forged a new intimacy between monarch, people and nation. From the very beginning Christmas on radio was a celebration of 'Home, Hearth and Happiness' (*Radio Times*, 18 December 1924), and the royal broadcasts which began in

1932, after years of diplomacy by Reith, seemed to put a crowning seal on the work of binding the nation together by giving it a particular form and content: the family audience, the royal family, the nation as family.[5]

By now the ITV network plays a role as important as, if not more important than, the BBC, with Sir Alistair Burnett and ITN being, almost by royal appointment, purveyors of the monarchical embrace to the nation. Equally, both the BBC and ITV have similar codes for reflecting and projecting the 'national interest' – a mission reinforced by the legal requirements for 'balance' and 'impartiality' in their coverage of politics, and by the government appointment of the governors of the BBC and the board of the IBA. There is a sense, however, in which the BBC is closer to being an arm of government than the ITV system. As Lord Annan has stated:

> BBC staff have to be more aware than other journalists that their first commitment is to serve the national community and the national interest. To do this, while remaining loyal to the facts, requires political sophistication. Without a commitment to this kind of distinctive public service journalism, how can the BBC really justify its claim to have a special place in our broadcasting system and a privileged form of funding from the licence fee?[6]

British television has been particularly good at feeding and promoting a national nostalgia for the glories of the past, constantly escaping from contemporary problems to a retreat down memory lane, classically to Edwardian costume dramas, the British Raj, and endless reworking of popular memories of World War II, from *Tenko* to *Dad's Army*. Anthony Sampson remarked in the early 1980s how news and current affairs on British television concentrated – much more than on other European TV networks – on 'national' events and personalities, 'keeping away foreigners who did not speak English':

Who could believe, watching the nightly news of British strikes, debates or human interest stories, that this was a country which had been part of the European Community for years, dependent on it for its trade and sharing most of its problems, including recession, unemployment and inflation?[7]

Alongside the narrowness and provinciality of much of the programming, there is a generally held conviction that 'British television is the best in the world', a view sustained by its relative economic success. Hence the following declaration from the chairman of Granada Television, Sir Denis Forman, in 1984:

Our most important colleague and adversary in matters of trade is the USA. In all respects save one we are outgunned: we have not the size of China, the military power of Russia or the industrial power of Japan. But in the matter of entertainment and the performing arts we are top dogs. British theatre, British television, British films have built a respect for British values which has an incalculable effect upon the psychology of the transatlantic relationship. It is the last field of world leadership left to us . . .[8]

Taken together, therefore, television's role in forging images of identity, especially around the royal family and memories of an imperial past, in promoting unity and the national interest, and finally in projecting Britain in the world, make it a powerful focus for national consciousness. Yet in the 1980s there were signs that the structure was creaking at the seams. The image of national identity relayed by television came under pressure on at least three fronts: first, the difficulties inherent in a London-based television's coming to terms with regional diversity within the United Kingdom; secondly, the breakdown of consensus politics since the mid-1970s, which placed under increasing strain definitions of 'the national interest', a factor highlighted in the 1980s by media disputes over the inner-city riots, the Falklands, the miners' strike and Northern Ireland; and lastly, changes in technology, especially the advent of satellite television, which threatened to undermine the structure of a centralized, networked 'national' service.

It has always been part of the BBC's ethos that, as its evidence to the Annan Committee put it, '. . . local and regional services are an essential part of a truly national broadcasting system'. The difficulty has always been to reconcile the regional with the national, particularly as the 'national' invariably comes down to a metropolitan or at most South-east/Home Counties perspective, faithfully reflecting the divide at the heart of English culture and society discussed in Chapter VI. The most sustained effort at reconciliation made by the BBC was with its programme *Nationwide* launched in 1966 and transmitted continuously until 1980. The period neatly encompasses the years in which peripheral nationalism in Wales, Scotland and Northern Ireland most preoccupied successive administrations in London. But the main impetus behind the programme was an effort to combat accusations that the BBC was too London-dominated. Indeed, when *Nationwide* looked at London in its film 'Our Secret Capital', the presenter, Julian Pettifer, specifically acknowledged the brief:

On *Nationwide* we try desperately not to be a metropolitan programme. Tonight is an exception. For the next twenty-five minutes we're looking at life in London: but we offer no excuse, because after all, wherever you live in the UK, London is your capital . . .[9]

The uneasy problems in relating London first to the English regions, and then to outlying Wales, Scotland and Northern Ireland, were analysed in the mid-1970s by two media academics, Charlotte Brunsdon and David Morley, in their BFI booklet, *Everyday Television: 'Nationwide'*.

When *Nationwide* was first established it had enough on its plate to rake up the dying embers of 'regional' consciousness, but this is now doubly problematic. Firstly because of the weakening of English regionalism, and secondly, ironically, because of the vitality of a regional 'awakening' on the Celtic fringes. In the present context *Nationwide* has both to rub the lamp to conjure up the dead spirits in the counties, and to try and control the wild spirits beyond them.[10]

The characteristic visual image of the programme was a shot of the presenter (typically Michael Barratt) facing a bank of screens relaying impressions of regional variations on a 'national' theme from the four corners of England and beyond. As Brunsdon and Morley stated:

If *Nationwide* constructs the 'nation' as a representative or imaginary whole, it does so through the construction of regional viewpoints . . . if the principal anchoring role is that provided by the central figure in the London studio, the programme nevertheless is constantly 'going out' to the regions from this point and 'returning' to home base: the 'nation' is always 'dropping in' on the regions.[11]

So even in this programme designed to placate criticisms of the BBC's metropolitan bias, the output was London-orchestrated and imbued with London evaluations of the 'news of the day'. There was, for instance, no regional autonomy in deciding topics to be covered. Each region had a *Nationwide* researcher allocated it and from time to time the whole team would 'drop in' on a particular region to give it blanket coverage. As Brunsdon and Morley concluded: 'London is the absent region, the invisible bearer of national unity. It is both technologically and ideologically the heart of the programme.'[12]

When *Nationwide* went off the air in 1980 it was interesting that the successor programme, *60 Minutes*, which aimed at producing a thoroughly 'national' early evening magazine programme, failed very rapidly, and the BBC resorted to the pre-1966 pattern of complete regional opt-outs for news/magazine programmes in this time slot. But the general trend, during

THE BBC'S 'FEDERAL' ORGANIZATION IN ENGLAND

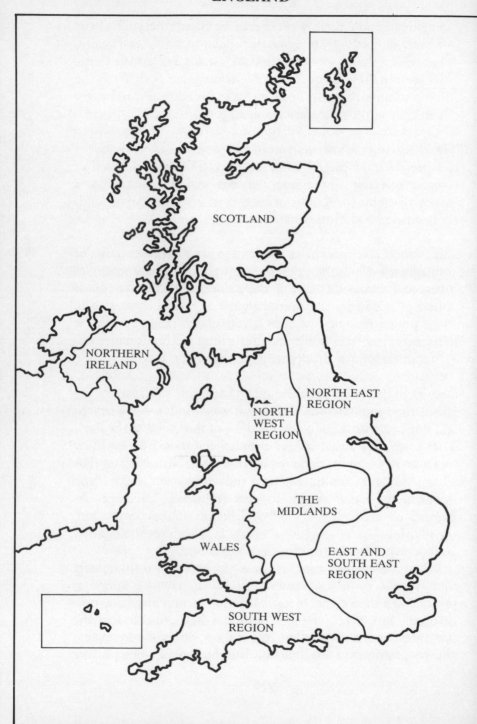

a time of financial stringency, was towards greater centralization. It brought a *cri de coeur* in 1984 from the former head of
the BBC's network production centre at Birmingham's Pebble
Mill studios, Phil Sidey:

> The huge populations in England outside the metropolitan
> area have little of their licence money spent in their neck of
> the woods; and even that much depends on the skill of a tiny
> handful of would-be entrepreneurs seeking to win pro-
> grammes from London in place of London's own produc-
> tions, with London as the judge, jury, paymaster and critic.
> It is a completely uneven contest.[13]

Sidey went on to bemoan the attenuation of resources in the
English regions at the very time when 'the miners' strike had
once more demonstrated the vital need of their grassroots
coverage to BBC television news'. Noting that management
reorganization in the 1970s had resulted in the abolition of
regional controllers along with their power-base, regional radio,
he judged that in any further cutbacks the BBC outside London
would 'have no real champion at the centre to fight for them'.
By way of remedy he pointed to ITV's federal structure of
autonomous companies.

> If I am right in my pessimistic belief that London will not
> surrender more programmes to the non-metropolitan
> studios, then the only way to get a fair share of the action is to
> federalize the BBC on geographical grounds.[14]

It was significant, therefore, that in 1986 the BBC reorganized
its regional structure in England, replacing eight areas with five
(see map opposite). Five regional heads of broadcasting were
created, each having responsibility for regional television and
local radio in their areas (and, in three cases, for network
production centres). The new arrangement was modelled on
the 'national region' structures already well-established in
Wales, Scotland and Northern Ireland and, indeed, was

masterminded by the former Controller of BBC Wales, Geraint Stanley Jones, now the BBC's Managing Director, Regional Broadcasting. He declared:

> We must, at the end of the day, be publicly accountable on the ground across the nation, and we must also be in a better position to reflect the nation to itself and the world in *totality*.
>
> Regional broadcasting in England must gain a new confidence in itself in the way which it has undoubtedly done in Scotland, Wales and Northern Ireland in recent years. Perhaps we should all banish the term 'provincial' from our vocabularies.[15]

But it was noticeable that the five large regions were created on the basis of the BBC's organizational convenience (dictated, too, by the location of transmitters) and not for reasons of regional identity or cultural affinity. Quite apart from the hopelessly large East and South-east Region (though now, for the first time, the South-east was included as a 'region' in its own right and not elided with the 'nation' as a whole), the definition of the Midlands region ignored a campaign that had gathered pace in the 1970s: to create an East Midlands television identity separate from that of the West Midlands centred on Birmingham. The campaign was led in the House of Commons by Philip Whitehead, then Labour MP for Derby and a member of the Annan Committee, and on the ground by the East Midlands Forum of County Councils. Aimed primarily at the IBA, which at the end of the 1970s was poised in any event to shake up the ITV system in its contract renewals, the campaign had some success. In 1980 the IBA announced that the contract for the Midlands would be awarded as a dual franchise, requiring recognition of the separate identities of the East and West Midlands and the establishment of major studio facilities in the East Midlands area to serve its distinctive needs.

By the mid-1980s Central Television had a £21-million new studio complex in place on a seventeen-acre site in Nottingham, employing some 600 people and producing a separate news and current affairs service for the East Midlands. The BBC responded by increasing its news coverage in the area but, in the face of major cut-backs to the English regional service (staff reductions of 110 and a loss of output by twenty programmes per region), it did not follow suit with an East Midlands BBC region.

Apart from financial considerations, the contrast between the BBC and ITV networks reflects their different structures. While the BBC is a monolithic organization with a hierarchical management system leading from the most-far-flung outpost up an administrative ladder to the London-based Director General, ITV is a federal network of fifteen regionally based, autonomous companies (see p. 234). Though in practice these are dominated by the 'Big Five' – Granada, Yorkshire, Central, Thames and London Weekend* – what evidence there is suggests that this federal structure more accurately reflects the wishes of the viewers than the BBC's centralized monolith. Before awarding the franchises for the ITV contract areas in 1981, the IBA conducted a major public relations exercise to gauge audience reaction to 'the size, shape and number of regions constituting the mosaic of Independent Television'. More than 250 public meetings were held throughout the country, together with an opinion poll survey. Commenting on the outcome, the IBA's contracts officer, John Harriott, remarked:

No subject was raised as often or as passionately as the subject of regional television. Speaker after speaker in every region pressed for more coverage of their own locality, more local news and current affairs, more coverage of local culture, history and achievements. There were complaints that some regions are so large that no particular town or village receives as much attention on the screen as the inhabitants would like.

* It is an interesting reflection of the North/South economic divide that Yorkshire Television's membership of the 'Big Five' was being challenged by Television South (TVS) as the 1980s drew to a close. It was achieving a higher advertising income and making an increasing contribution to network programming.

THE INDEPENDENT BROADCASTING AUTHORITY'S NETWORK OF AUTONOMOUS ITV COMPANIES

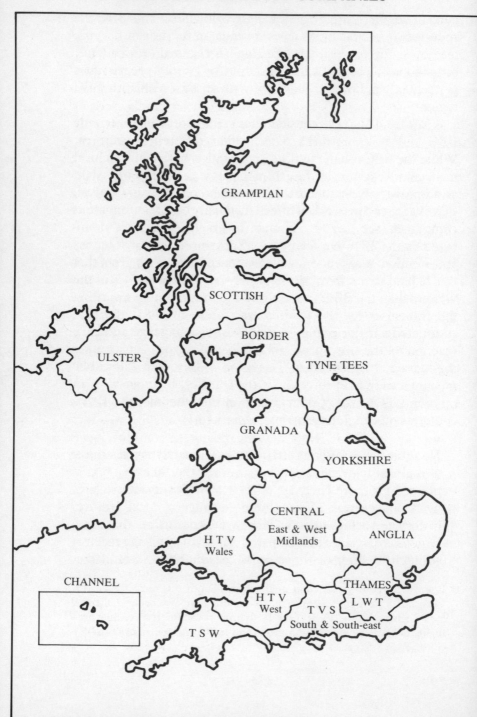

There were complaints along the regional frontiers that the area around the studio centre often seems remote and yet attracts a disproportionate amount of television coverage. There were complaints that television regional boundaries do not match political or social boundaries. There were frequent calls for smaller areas or more channels or special area or opt-out services. At times these expressions of local pride seemed more reminiscent of feudal Italy than modern, undevolved, socially mobile Britain.[16]

However, the BBC – if not ITV – argues that first and foremost it is a national institution, provides a national service and serves the national interest. The change in British political culture in the 1980s compared, say, with the 1950s, is that at least the latter two of these claims no longer command a ready consensus. Thus, when towards the end of the 1970s the BBC was reorganizing its radio coverage and establishing Radio Wales and Radio Scotland – largely in response to the devolution politics of the time – discussions were held in London about the implications for radio broadcasting in England. Geraint Stanley Jones, then Controller of BBC Wales, recalled:

Both I and Scottish colleagues tried to persuade our English counterparts simply to set up Radio England. But this idea was received, frankly, with puzzlement. I don't think it was possible for them to think in those terms. What happened instead was that we established Radio 4 UK.[17]

There is even less clarity so far as the concept of 'the national interest' is concerned. Who defines it? The simplest answer was that provided by the judge during the trial of Clive Ponting in 1985: 'The national interest is what the government of the day says it is.' However, it is doubtful whether even the BBC would accept this definition. In the 1980s the pressure of events forced it to confront the question in uncomfortable ways. Its dilemma was similar to the one it faced in the 1930s when, against government opposition, it struggled to present a balanced view of the build-up of German military forces and to prepare people for the possibility of all-out war – and failed. As Scannell observed:

> After the general strike, Reith had rationalized the role of radio in the matter by arguing that 'since Government in the crisis was acting for the people . . . the BBC was for the Government in the crisis too'. Munich was the first test of that syllogism as a precedent for the role of broadcasting in a national crisis. The BBC was confronted with the fundamental dilemma as to whose interests it had a priority to serve and it rightly decided that its final responsibility was to society, not the state. But what compounded its difficulties in breaking the deafening silence was its own absorption in the state domain . . .[18]

There was little sign that the position had altered in the 1980s. A succession of events, sometimes unwittingly, led television reportage, and often subsequent reaction to it within television hierarchies, to take tendentious stances on 'the national interest'. The first big occasion was coverage of the 1981 inner-city riots. The main thrust of discussion at the time was worry that the television coverage was creating 'copycat' violence. Lord Scarman, in his report, declared: '. . . the media, particularly the broadcasting media, do in my view bear a responsibility for the escalation of the disorders . . .'[19]

But a more fundamental issue concerned television failure to explain why the riots were happening. To a great extent, perhaps, this was inevitable: the dramatic and violent clashes between the police and rioters contained all the classic ingredients of a 'good visual story'. Nevertheless, little attention was paid to allegations of a build-up of resentment at the way Toxteth had been policed which, it was claimed, caused the incident that triggered the riots and so lay behind the disorders. As a result, as the BBC television presenter John Humphreys pointed out, later, neither television 'nor anybody else were able adequately to explain why the riots were happening'.[20]

The main impact of the television coverage, in fact, was to stress the impression of irrational and criminal mob behaviour by the rioters and to intensify demands for tougher police action. As Graham Murdock of the Centre for Mass Communication Research at Leicester University concluded, the reporting of the riots may well have helped to make 'militarization of policing acceptable to the majority of the population'. He noted that popular participation is dominated by two opposed images, the public and the crowd:

> The public is composed of individuals, each one making rational political choices and expressing their preferences through an electoral system based on universal franchise. By contrast the crowd appears as a degenerate form of political expression . . .
>
> Against this, some commentators have argued that the British political system is currently undergoing a crisis of representation in which increasing numbers of people, particularly young people, no longer feel that the traditional parties and political organizations adequately articulate their interests and aspirations, and that consequently the riots must be seen, in part, as an alternative means of drawing attention to grievances and securing a political hearing.[21]

The outstanding feature of broadcast coverage of the Falklands/Malvinas conflict was the absence of any debate about whether the enterprise was in 'the national interest'. Television news programmes carried endless discussions of military strategy, involving, it seemed, Britain's entire population of admirals, both retired and still in service. Opponents of the war, whether elected politicians or commentators, were conspicuous by their absence from the screen. Enormous controversy was generated when the BBC's *Panorama* programme briefly interviewed four backbench critics of the war, including two Tories.[22] There were charges of treason and subversion and the government invoked a neglected clause in the BBC Charter to take over the Corporation's powerful transmitters on

Ascension Island. The Establishment attitude was summarized by Lord Annan in 1986 when, with the benefit of four years' hindsight, he declared:

> The other day I was talking to a journalist in ITV. He complained that during the Falklands War he had been forbidden to interview – while the fighting was still going on – the widows of servicemen who had been killed. I asked why he wanted to. 'Oh,' he said, 'lots of us were against the war, and I didn't see why it should be left to Tony Benn alone to make the case on TV against it. We wanted to ask the widows whether they felt the war was worth it.' Yet this was a war, unlike Suez, supported by both the government and the opposition. In a war, you have to keep up the morale of those in the front line and those at home . . .[23]

Annan, however, went on to commend the BBC's coverage of the 1984–5 mining dispute which, he said, was handled 'admirably'.

> It remembered that during the General Strike of 1926 the government had refused to allow any trade unionist to broadcast. Reith had even felt bound to refuse the Archbishop of Canterbury permission to appeal to both sides to resume negotiations. This time, archbishops and bishops gave their views, and Arthur Scargill day in day out was given a lot of time to put the NUM case and comment on events. Yet what does the BBC *Yearbook* say? It says the BBC 'faced the major difficulty in reporting the strike to a polarized audience, which sometimes found it difficult to recognize BBC neutrality'.
>
> That passage is written by someone who doesn't understand the difference between neutrality and impartiality. You cannot be neutral when the law is being broken, though you can be impartial in giving those who support the lawbreakers an opportunity to explain why they did so. The BBC could not be neutral and fail to reveal that the leaders of the NUM

were determined to dictate to their members, and to the nation, what its economic policies should be.[24]

Yet how 'neutral' were the broadcast media in their coverage of the dispute? A critical moment was the confrontation between police and pickets at Orgreave on 18 June 1984. The police maintained, and still do, that this was a riot and was treated by them accordingly. The subsequent riot trial, abandoned by the prosecution on its forty-eighth day, suggested otherwise. And the shocking treatment of the affair by television news on the day is further evidence. The most telling pictures were those of one man being repeatedly truncheoned by a police officer. These were shown by ITN but not by the BBC. However, ITN treated it as an isolated incident. More insidious was the fact that the television news reversed the order of the footage available in order to show men throwing missiles and then police charging when, in fact, it was the other way about. This theme was taken up in court by the prosecution – but failed through the contradiction of the evidence provided by the police's own film of the affair, obtained in court only as a result of a defence subpoena.[25]

Controversy over the role of the media in 'mirroring the nation' and representing 'the national interest' in the early 1980s culminated with the 'Real Lives Affair' of August 1985, described by Yorkshire Television's Managing Director, Paul Fox, as the BBC's 'biggest crisis since 1926'.[26] This brought the central dilemma of Northern Ireland, so far as the government is concerned, to the heart of the broadcasting establishment: the fact that, given a free vote in Northern Ireland, thousands of people cast it for Sinn Fein candidates who openly supported armed violence. The BBC's Northern Ireland Governor, Lady Faulkner, expressed her opposition to the programme in graphic terms.

The shots of McGuinness – who says he would be proud to be the Chief of Staff of the IRA – were like those foxes produced years ago for the anti-blood sports campaigners, pretty animals, like collie dogs. What one didn't see were the fowl in the hen-run with their heads pulled off.[27]

This was one of the arguments that evidently persuaded the rest of the BBC Governors, apart from Alwyn Roberts from Wales, to agree with the then Home Secretary, Leon Brittan, and ban the film portrait of two Ulster politicians – Republican Martin McGuinness and hardline Loyalist Gregory Campbell. Aubrey Singer, Managing Director of BBC Television, 1982–84, stated that the underlying explanation was that the Governors had been packed with pro-government supporters since 1979.

Whatever arguments swayed the Governors, the collective decision smacks of pusillanimous sycophancy. By any standards, an error of the first magnitude has been committed. It took twenty years to expiate *The War Game* and seven hours to divest the BBC of its reputation for independence. If the BBC is to allow itself to be turned into another organ of the public relations state, the source of its funding, which should be the origin of its independence, is of no import.[28]

Aubrey Singer may have judged the Governors of the BBC to be guided by 'pusillanimous sycophancy' but the record of the following eighteen months in the run-up to the 1987 general election gave no hint that the government remained complacent. Two episodes, surrounding the BBC's coverage of the American raid on Libya in April 1986 and the preparation of a BBC Scotland series *The Secret Society* revealing the existence of a British spy satellite called Zircon, provoked extraordinary responses. In October 1986 the Conservative Central Office issued an astonishing twenty-one-page attack on the BBC's coverage of the Libyan affair, claiming it to be straightforward Libyan propaganda. The attack was easily dismissed in a line-by-line rebuttal from BBC executives.[29] More serious was a police night raid on BBC Scotland's Glasgow headquarters in early February 1987 when tapes of *The Secret Society* series were seized. The legality of the procedure was doubtful and the nature of the action reminiscent itself of a police state: what was clearly under way was an effort in both instances to create an atmosphere of intimidation in which the broadcasting authorities would err on the side of caution whenever issues involving criticism of the government arose. Looking back on the argument over the BBC's coverage of the Libyan bombing raid, the reporter at the centre of the affair, Kate Adie, reflected that the government of the day typically accuses the broadcasting authorities of being 'disloyal':

I've always found that loyalty and patriotism tends by some people to be used as an excuse for ignoring reality and honesty. In times of war and national emergency, loyalty, patriotism and the national interest do come first. But when we're not under those very specific circumstances the facts, honesty and reality come first. It never occurs to me that one is being disloyal by delivering the facts, unpatriotic by being straightforward and honest.[30]

Looking ahead Kate Adie foresaw these conflicts being intensified and made more complex by the coming of satellite television:

There's going to be in the next few years an almighty fight on the international television front. More and more countries are acquiring the facilities through cable and satellite broadcasting to reach around the world. Just as now with a radio you can tune across the dial to stations from Moscow to Buenos Aires, before long you'll be able to do the same with your television set. This means that governments will become even more aware of the power of television and just who is running television stations. It will be easier in future for people to know what the outside world is both seeing and saying. So, for example, during a war it will be perfectly possible to receive pictures from another country of your soldiers losing a battle. Such things are nowadays normally subject to rigid national censorship. Well, where does that leave us? We're the BBC, and the British government likes to take a position in the world which we as a country, as a people, like as well. What are we going to put out as our image in the future? I think the question of the BBC being British and getting into so many homes around the world is going to be very acute in the not too distant future.[31]

The key to the immediate impact of transnational satellite television will be its effect on the quota system that operates within British broadcasting. Quite simply this is a government-imposed regulation, operated through the Independent Broadcasting Authority and the Charter of the BBC, requiring a high percentage (around 80 per cent) of all broadcast material to originate within Britain itself. The precise percentage varies, mainly according to the timing of transmissions so that at night, for example, the figure drops to nearer 70 per cent. The objective of the quota system is to ensure that the programmes transmitted on British television reflect an indigenous cultural perspective and are not overwhelmed by generally cheaper bought-in programmes from elsewhere in the world, most commonly America and Australia. It is just these kind of programmes that typically fill the air-time of the commercially orientated satellite channels which operate outside the legal and institutional framework of land-based television.

Only by imposing Continent-wide regulations can control be exerted over satellite broadcasts. For Britain this means a European dimension with controls exercised through the institutions of the European Community. During the 1980s a debate on this question began to open up.[32] The main question, so far as the argument here is concerned, however, is this: what will be the role of British television in forging a national identity, promoting the national interest, and projecting the country abroad in an era when the medium has broken the boundaries of the nation state and is operating Europe-wide?

Writing in 1982 Brian Wenham, then Controller of BBC2, depicted the history of broadcasting in three ages: the first age, dominated by radio, came to an end when the coronation in

1953 showed the full power of television. The age of the mass television audience was launched, an age 'deliberately and delicately regulated by Parliament, through the aegis of the BBC and IBA'. The third age, beginning in the 1980s, declared Wenham, would be marked by the weakening of regulation and control; by the opening of more channels, starting with Channel 4; by the breaking of the BBC/ITV duopoly of programme production; and by new forms of signal distribution via satellite and cable.[33] Looking back through this historical perspective it becomes plain that the images of national identity communicated by broadcasting in the first two periods up to the 1980s were not initiated or in any sense manufactured by broadcasting itself. It did not, in this sense, extend an existing culture, merely amplified it. All the deepest and most commanding images of identity transmitted by radio and television in this period were in place before broadcasting existed: Westminster, the rustic/urban idyll of the Home Counties, the imperial sense of 'greatness', and, above all, the monarchy. The dawn of the age of television in Britain, in 1953, was marked by the communion of the viewing nation with the most medieval-possible image of national identity in the form of the coronation. Henceforth, the second 'age' was regulated – largely, in fact, self-regulated by the broadcasters themselves – to prevent 'the best television in the world' committing any psychic damage to this addictive image of identity.

Only now, with the dawning of Wenham's third age of broadcasting, is this image of who we are, perhaps more accurately who we think we are in Britain, coming under the simultaneous challenge of divisions within and alternative messages delivered from without.

NOTES

1 Quoted by Lord Annan in 'To BBC or not to BBC', *New Society*, 31 January 1986. In the Annan Committee report, *Report of the Committee on the Future of Broadcasting*, Cmnd 6753, HMSO,

1977, Sir Michael Swann, chairman of the BBC in the mid-1970s, is quoted as saying (p. 263), 'an enormous amount of the BBC's work [is] in fact social cement of one sort or another. Royal occasions, religious services, sports coverage, and police series, all reinforce the sense of belonging to our country, being involved in its celebrations, and accepting what it stands for.'

2 Paddy Scannell, 'A conspiracy of silence: the state, the BBC and public opinion in the formative years of British broadcasting', in Gregor McLennan et al. (ed.), *State and Society in Contemporary Britain*, Basil Blackwell, 1984, p. 152–3.

3 J. G. Blumler et al., 'Attitudes to the monarchy: their structure and development during a ceremonial occasion', *Political Studies*, XIX, 2 (1971), p. 150.

4 David Cardiff and Paddy Scannell, 'Broadcasting and national unity' in J. Curran et al., *The Impact of the Mass Media*, Constable, 1984, p. 169.

5 Scannell, op. cit., p. 152.

6 Annan, op. cit.

7 Anthony Sampson, *The Changing Anatomy of Britain*, Coronet, 1982, p. 441.

8 Sir Dennis Forman, 'It is time we came out of our state of technological shock', *Listener*, 30 August 1984.

9 Quoted in Charlotte Brunsdon and David Morley, *Everyday Television: 'Nationwide'*, British Film Institute, 1978, p. 3. The film 'Our Secret Capital' was broadcast by BBC1 on 16 August 1976.

10 Ibid., p. 80.

11 Ibid., p. 81.

12 Ibid., p. 4.

13 Phil Sidey, 'BBC is abandoning regional role for mass entertainment', *Television Today*, 13 July 1984.

14 Ibid.

15 Personal communication, 4 June 1986.

16 John Harriott, 'The Regional Area and ITV', *Independent Broadcasting Magazine*, No. 29, June 1980.

17 Interview, February 1986.

18 Scannell, op. cit., p. 172–3.

19 Lord Scarman, *The Brixton Disorders*, HMSO (cmnd. 8427), para 2.30.

20 John Humphreys, 'Duty to inform – in pictures', *Television: The*

Journal of the Royal Television Society, September/October 1981, p. 15.

21 Graham Murdock, 'Reporting the riots: images and impact' in John Benyon (ed.), *Scarman and After*, Pergamon, 1984, p. 81.

22 *Panorama*, broadcast 10 May 1982. See Tam Dalyell's account in *One Man's Falklands*, Cecil Woolf, 1982, especially Appendix D.

23 Annan, op. cit.

24 Ibid.

25 See Gareth Peirce, 'How they rewrote the law at Orgreave', *Guardian*, 12 August 1985. See also Len Masterman, 'The Battle of Orgreave' in Len Masterman (ed.), *Television Mythologies*, Comedia/MK Media Press, 1984.

26 *Listener*, 8 August 1985.

27 Ibid.

28 Ibid.

29 'Conservative Central Office Media Monitoring – the BBC Response', 5 November 1986. See also *The Times* for 20 November 1986 for a 'judgement' from Lord Denning, former Master of the Rolls, on the affair, in which he 'acquitted the BBC on all counts'.

30 Kate Adie, interview, October 1987.

31 Ibid.

32 See the EEC Commission's Green Paper, 'Television Without Frontiers', adopted on 23 May 1984 (document Com(84)300). Also the House of Lords' Select Committee on European Affairs' detailed report in response with the same title, HMSO, 17 December 1985.

33 Brian Wenham, 'Third Age of Broadcasting', *Observer*, 21 March 1982.

—10—

A country
of the imagination

There is some logic in arriving near the end of a survey of the identities of the peoples of Britain and Northern Ireland with an account of the way these are mediated through the cold eye of television. For this, by now, is the main medium which provides people with an idea of who they are or, at least, who they think they are, and where they are heading. In this sense images are extremely important. They relate to aspirations and desires, to the nature of society and how it can be preserved or changed. They are powerful mobilizers of feeling because they speak to people in an emotional way which cannot be understood in terms of reason alone but has to take into account the world of fantasy as well. This is particularly the case when coming to terms with English and Anglo-British identity. As Enoch Powell who, more than any English political figure since World War II has grappled with the subliminal concerns of the English, once declared, 'The life of nations no less than that of men is lived largely in the imagination.'[1]

That statement, the opening of an extraordinary analysis of the idea of Empire in the English imagination since the nineteenth century, was made in a speech at Trinity College, Dublin in 1946. It was to be another decade before there was any fundamental questioning of Anglo-British identity, its imperial world role, and its foundation in the institutions of monarchy, church and Parliament. The spell was broken in 1956 by the Suez débâcle which triggered an immediate crisis of identity for the Anglo-British. It compelled them at last to begin the painful task of reassessing their sense of themselves and their position in the world. In April 1956, several months before the political crisis, the BBC launched a television series called 'We The British' to examine the following questions:

> Can a people be in decline? Can a nation be in decline? Is, in fact, Britain in decline? And if you say, 'Why ask such questions?' just listen to the talk you hear around you – to the people who say 'We can't win at anything nowadays – not even at football' or 'We get pushed out of Egypt, we leave the Sudan, they've dismissed Glubb Pasha, everyone thinks today that the British can be pushed around. Why don't we stand up for ourselves?'; to the foreigners, Americans, Germans and Swiss, who complain that British workmanship isn't what it was, that the English have forgotten how to do an honest day's work; to the voices at home that declare that delinquency is going up and morals going down; that family respect is dying; that religious faith is moribund.[2]

The myth and reality, symbolism and substance of British identity since 1945 was traced, if unconsciously, by Ian Fleming in his James Bond novels which all appeared in a key period between 1953 and 1965. As analysed by David Cannadine, a history don at Cambridge, the first seven of the novels, up to *Goldfinger* in 1959, persist with the myth of Britain's great-power status, and put Bond in the front line against the Russians. In *Casino Royale*, the first novel to appear, in 1953:

> . . . Bond is helped by 'our French friends' and 'our American colleagues' in his attempt to discredit Le Chiffre, the Communist trade unionist who would be a powerful fifth columnist in France 'in the event of a war with redland'. But in attacking the Russians in this way, Bond and the British Secret Service are in fact asserting their primacy within the Western alliance. For the job is one which the French should

have done, and which the Americans wanted to do. But the British get there first. 'Washington's pretty sick we're not running the show . . .' Leiter explains to Bond. 'Anyway, I'm under your orders, and I'm to give you any help you ask for.'

There is, then, in these early novels no trace of the reality of that 'special relationship' by which Britain was effectively subordinate to, and dependent on, America in the post-war period. On the contrary, the situation in the Bond novels is in fact the exact reverse . . .[3]

The plots of the early Bond novels are heavily nostalgic, reminiscent of Bulldog Drummond and Dr Fu-Manchu, with a little seasoning from the upmarket Somerset Maugham and Eric Ambler. In this they refer back to an earlier pre-World War II period when Britain's imperial identity was less ambiguous. Bond himself, of course, is Scottish, again summoning up an essential component of this imperial vision. The choice of Sean Connery to play Bond in the films later made of the books was appropriate in this connection, too, a choice said to have had Ian Fleming's approval. But by the early 1960s even Fleming had to come to terms with Britain's changing status in the world, a reality which is reflected in the Bond novels of this period.

In *On Her Majesty's Secret Service*, the College of Arms is preoccupied with designing the arms, stamps and currency of the newly independent African nations; and even Bond himself is nostalgic for past glories. M's naval stories, he realizes, are 'about a great navy that was no more, and a great breed of seamen and officers that would never be seen again'. And by 1964 (in *You Only Live Twice*) M is pictured as the head of a service recently discredited by scandal, so that the Americans are now 'worried about our security'.

In this last novel the reality of Britain's place in the world, and the myth so easily continued, is beautifully encapsulated in an exchange where Tiger Tanaka, head of the Japanese

Secret Service, taunts Bond with the enfeebled state of his country:

You have not only lost an Empire, you have seemed almost anxious to throw it away with both hands . . . When you apparently sought to arrest this slide into impotence at Suez, you succeeded only in stage-managing one of the most pitiful bungles in the history of the world . . . Your governments have shown themselves successively incapable of ruling, and have handed over effective control of the country to the trade unions, who appear to be dedicated to the principle of doing less and less work for more money. This feather-bedding, this shirking of an honest day's work, is sapping at ever-increasing speed the moral fibre of the British, a quality the world once so admired. In its place, we now see a vacuous, aimless horde of seekers after pleasure . . .

To this onslaught, Bond replies with spirit:

England [sic] may have been bled pretty thin by a couple of world wars, our Welfare State policies may have made us expect too much for free, and the liberation of our Colonies may have gone too fast, but we still climb Everest and beat plenty of the world at sports, and win plenty of Nobel Prizes . . . There's nothing wrong with the British people . . .

Cannadine points out that the year the first Bond novel appeared saw the coronation of Elizabeth II – which was the last great ceremony to connect the monarchy with Empire. It was distinctly an *imperial* occasion, with the Queen's dress containing embroidered emblems of the Dominions, and with regiments of Commonwealth and colonial troops marching in procession.

However, when the last Bond novel was published, in 1965, there occurred an event that, even at the time, was recognized as being a requiem for Britain as a great power. And, fittingly, the funeral of Winston Churchill was a world event watched on television, via direct satellite transmission, by an estimated 360 million people. It was a moment, as Bernard Levin commented, that marked the end of an old world and the emergence of a new one which was even more uncertain and insecure. Here was a man who had taken part in a cavalry charge and lived to make, in what was almost his last speech as Prime Minister, the announcement that Britain was to manufacture the hydrogen bomb. On television, half the population of Britain, some 25 million people, saw the whole ceremony.

> . . . step by step of the way, from the moment when Big Ben, early in the morning struck for the last time that day, and then fell silent until midnight, to the moment when the cameras, perched in an eyrie high above Waterloo station, showed the train bearing the body and the family mourners to Churchill's final, private resting place, steaming out of the station and between the houses, following it on and on and on, until it seemed as though the camera, must be flying behind the train to keep it in view for so long . . .
> . . . Yet the day was won by an unexpected sight. Unannounced, a camera swung its fishy eye up towards the whispering gallery of St Paul's and there picked out the silhouette of the trumpeter, sounding the Last Post.[4]

But though Churchill's funeral was in reality a requiem for Britain's imperial identity and world role – and a delayed requiem at that – the myth of this definition still endures. The popularity of the Bond movies in the 1970s and 1980s testified to that. So, too, did the majority Anglo-British response to the extraordinary events in the south Atlantic in 1982. In their wake Mrs Thatcher declared the victory meant that Britain had 'ceased to be a nation in defeat'. Instead the campaign had injected a new confidence that 'comes from the rediscovery of ourselves, and grows with the recovery of our self-respect'. The speech betrayed something of the real reasons why Britain fought the Falklands/Malvinas war, reasons that had little to do with the Falkland Islands themselves.

When we started out, there were the waverers and the fainthearts. The people who thought that Britain could no longer seize the initiative for herself. The people who thought we could no longer do the great things which we once did. Those who believed that our decline was irreversible – that we could never again be what we were.

There were those who would not admit it – even perhaps some here today – people who would have strenuously denied the suggestion but – in their heart of hearts – they too had their secret fears that it was true: that Britain was no longer the nation that had built an Empire and ruled a quarter of the world.

Well they were wrong. The lesson of the Falklands is that Britain has not changed and that this nation still has those sterling qualities which shine through our history.[5]

Events on the scale of, and with the fortunate outcome of, the Falklands/Malvinas conflict cannot be relied upon to bolster the Anglo-British fantasy world on a regular basis, however. The agency which most effectively and continuously carries the myth is the monarchy. It is no coincidence that as Britain's power in the world has waned, the role of the royal family has blossomed by way of compensation. Royalty and royal occasions now head a diminishing list of what the British do best in the world. Britain has the best actors, runners youth culture and rock music, still the best broadcasting system, and . . . the spectacle of royal ceremony. As the list dwindles, each item has to carry a heavier load of symbolic meaning. And it is significant that the list of the 'Best of British' is confined to the cultural sphere, with little or nothing of political or economic significance – in itself an indication of the post-war decline. Even Parliament and the House of Commons, once a democratic institution to be emulated around the globe, have lost their gloss compared with the monarchy. According to Norman St John-Stevas (now Lord St John of Fawsley):

The monarchy has become our only truly popular institution at a time when the House of Commons has declined in public esteem and the House of Lords is a matter of controversy. The monarchy is, in a real sense, underpinning the other two estates of the realm.[6]

The full weight of the monarchy's role in sustaining British identity was illustrated by the international spectacular that was made of the wedding of Prince Charles and Lady Diana Spencer in 1981. The international flavour of the event, and the importance of this dimension in adding to the royal myth of identity, were most clearly seen in the American coverage. *Newsweek*'s story, for instance, began:

> And so the Prince finally claimed his Princess, with every dash of clockwork spectacle and storybook splendour at England's matchless command . . .[7]

The piece ended:

> For a few shining days, the handsome heir to the throne and the lissome Princess had burnished British glory to majestic brilliance once again.

The *Sunday Times* carried a caption across a two-page spread of the vast crowd that walked down the Mall:

> Only the Victory Parade and the coronations of 1937 and 1953 have witnessed crowds as dense as this. In spite of fears in an age that has grown used to bitterness, riots and mindless assassination, the people of Britain and many visitors to London from abroad gave the world a visible demonstration of the power of a great royal event to unite the nation. In a sense it was a wedding to which we were all invited. Even if we were not able to join the hundreds of thousands who jammed the Mall, we could be part of the great audience of 750 million people around the world who could watch it all on television.

The problem is that royal occasions confine national unity to the ceremonial and symbolic plane alone. As the kingdom becomes more divided the myth is harder to sustain. But as the *Sunday Times* makes clear, British identity relies heavily on the royal myth of nationhood. It is interconnected, however, with a rigidly centralized and formalized political culture that, so far, has been successful in maintaining a framework for British identity and the appearance, at least, of continuity. The centralization is mediated through a variety of formal and informal constitutional conventions: the role of Parliament and its relationship with local government; the metropolitan character of representation in Parliament and the two-party system.

The only constitution that Britain has comprises the complete sovereignty of the Crown in Parliament, the power of the Crown exercised through the monarch's ministers. Herein lies the formal importance of the monarchy in the British institutional structure. Most specifically, it means that only the monarch's ministers in Parliament can propose raising and spending money. Parliament as such – that is, the institution representing the People – can take no initiative over money whatever. Sovereignty in Britain rests ultimately on a mystification, not on a democratic base. Therein is the formal, constitutional source of the unitary, centralized State. And it is much more than a constitutional point since it has profound implications for the whole political culture, for the character of British democracy, and for the ways in which the peoples of Britain imagine their country. It underpins, too, the peculiar character of class relationships in British, and especially English, society – the way the whole is controlled and mediated by deference. Walter Bagehot in his classic work *The English Constitution* identified England as a 'deferential nation', one that had a structure of its own. 'Certain persons', he wrote, 'are by common consent agreed to be wiser than others, and their opinion is, by consent, to rank for much more than its numerical value.'[8] A century later, in 1968, the same point was picked up by Robert McKenzie and Alan Silver in their volume *Angels in Marble: Working-Class Conservatives in Urban England.* Discussing the 'deference' ideology of lower-class conservatism, they pointed out:

> One of the pervasive conditions promoting the survival of deference is the modest role accorded 'the people' in British political culture. Although it is a commonplace of research on stable democracies that general electorates are typically uninvolved in politics . . . it is only in Britain that this is so largely consistent with the prevailing climate of political values. Though modern constitutions typically locate the source of sovereignty in 'the people', in Britain it is the Crown in Parliament that is sovereign. Nor is that a merely technical point. The political culture of democratic Britain assigns to ordinary people the role, not of citizens, but of subjects . . .[9]

This attenuated sense of citizenship, and the absence of a republican sense of 'the people' in British political culture, have a deeply distorting effect on the way the English (leaving the Scots, Welsh and Irish to one side) imagine their country.

> We English are indeed a curious breed and quite adept at concealing our deep love of country and culture from others. Patriotism is somewhat embarrassing and never talked about, except with polite disinterest, to the point where a foreigner might well wonder if it exists in an Englishman's breast at all . . .

Thus opens the 'Editor's Letter' in the Spring 1987 issue of *This England*, a glossy magazine published out of, where else but, Cheltenham. A glance through its pages reveals that once let loose, the imaginings of the English have a dream-like quality that make Welsh, Irish and 'Scotch' myths pragmatic by comparison. England is overwhelmingly urban in its culture, yet the nearest this issue of the magazine comes to considering town or city is an article profiling 'the Cathedral towns' of

Chelmsford and Guildford, both firmly located in 'the Home Counties'. For the rest the constant impression, tumbling out of the pages, is rolling hills whose greenness is 'breathtaking in its splendour'; charming thatched cottages which are 'the envy of the world'; bluebell woods, 'a riot of beauty in the deep folds of the English countryside'; and sheep still safely grazing in 'English villages far from the madding crowd'. This intense rural arcadia is shot through with a deep sadness and nostalgia for the lost generation of the First World War. So an article on Edward Thomas, part of a series on 'heroic soldier poets', opens:

> Spring came to England 70 years ago just as bright and beautiful as it had ever done before. The daffodils were golden on the edges of green woodland and amongst the wild hedgerows of quiet country lanes; cuckoos sang and church bells chimed, sending their lovely music soaring across farmers' fields where seeds were being patiently sown; and the skies were as blue as thrushes' eggs, dappled here and there with wisps of white cloud. But all was not quite the same. It was 1917, England was still at war and there wasn't a family in the land that tragedy had not touched in some way by the loss of a dear father, son or friend . . .

Another regular series in the magazine is on 'English county regiments', reinforcing the sense conveyed in its pages that the England of this imagination is imbued with past military prowess. The issue in question features The King's Shropshire Light Infantry (the 53rd/85th Foot) whose profile begins with a literary note: 'It is interesting to see how often the particular beauty of some or other English county has inspired writers and poets to compose outstanding work . . .' We are reminded that Sussex had this influence on Rudyard Kipling and Hilaire Belloc. Shropshire's poet was A. E. Housman who, despite his 'love of peaceful pastoral pursuits', was also a 'realist'. He wrote of men who said, 'I will go where I am wanted as a soldier of the Queen . . .'

This England imagines a ceremonial, rural, courageous and, above all, honourable society and hierarchical culture with the monarch at its pinnacle. In the keynote 'Editor's Letter' already referred to, the ringing appeal is to the 'Spirit of St George'. To those that scoff at its possibility in contemporary times the editor, Roy Faiers, responds that he recognizes it in 'the shiny pink faces of our young nurses', in 'the patient eyes of a young policeman dealing calmly with an ugly street incident' and 'in the courage of a young expectant mother who shuts her ears to the gloomy forebodings of the faint-hearts around her and instead sits knitting and thinking and planning in an England that, with the help of a loving husband, she will try to make even better than before'.

If you are English, whether by birth, adoption or descent; if there is a strong love of freedom, peace and Christian justice in your heart; if you believe in upholding the law and rooting out evil wherever it lurks; if you fear God, acknowledge the Queen as ruler in His name, and are prepared to place our nation's needs before your personal desires, then you can rightly claim to have inherited the Spirit of St George.

This, no doubt, is a caricature, but there is still a sense in which evocations along these lines resonate for an important stratum in Anglo-British society, for the million-plus regular readers of the *Daily Telegraph*, for instance. This England of the imagination still has a world-wide reference. Though the formal attributes of Empire have long gone, the 'White' Commonwealth (Canada, New Zealand, Australia . . . South Africa) still remains, the imagination here fortified by many real family links. In appearance it resembles the more affluent parts of the Home Counties stock-broker belt – often with the additions of a third car, better weather, and poolside telephone. One important aspect of the Falklands/Malvinas war was the ease with which the 'kith and kin' ideology was evoked, despite the absence of poolside telephones in Port Stanley. These familial ties and links with the Commonwealth are steadily weakening, but they still loom large in this particular English – or, more accurately Anglo-British – imagining. Indeed, as with the monarchy, it may be that they are more important in decline than they were in the days of expansion and imperial power.

Ultimately, however, this way of imagining the country rests on a fantasy that is less and less based in reality. Yet its powers of endurance should not be underestimated. It was suggested towards the end of Chapter VII that the modern Conservative image was subtly undermining this sense of identification, with its emphasis on consumerism and the sovereignty of the market place. But there is no democracy in the sense of 'government by popular consent' in this project. In the politics of consumerist sovereignty 'choice' is counterposed to 'democracy' precisely because, whereas the latter is public and social, the former can be defined in wholly private and individual – and perhaps family – terms. In a memorable interview in *Woman's Own* in October 1987, Mrs Thatcher declared, 'There is no such thing as society. There are individual men and women and there are families.' Nonetheless, Mrs Thatcher has been the first to mobilize the Anglo-British myth of shared belonging and collective action when this is required. Her use of the Falklands episode in this respect has already been emphasized. A less well-known, but revealing, example was her instruction in 1984 that the underground Cabinet War Rooms in Whitehall, used by Churchill during the early years of World War II, should be opened up to the public. During the next few years they were visited by more than a million people.

This country of the imagination has been as seductive for the Left in British politics as for the Right. It finds its most characteristic expression in the idea that Britain can somehow 'lead the world' in getting rid of nuclear weapons. There seems no end to the Anglo-British fantasy of leading the world in one way or another. So, for example, E. P. Thompson, a champion of the Anglo-British extra-Parliamentary Left, in an article entitled 'How Britain Could Break the Ice in the Cold War' in November 1987, offered:

I think it is in the power of Britain to break the Cold War stalemate, not because – after two terms of Mrs Thatcher – Britain qualifies as the moral leader of anything, but for other reasons . . . because of a weight of inherited history, a history which sometimes seems to smother us with inertia and guilt, but which on this occasion might serve to furnish us with resources in a crisis. History has left us uncertainly at a crossroads, between Europe, the United States (with whom we share a language) and a former empire, which even Mrs Thatcher has been unable to drive out of the Commonwealth. These conjunctions offer a mediating role, in which several of our Commonwealth partners . . . have more experience than ourselves. And despite Britain's role as an architect of NATO, we might prove to be acceptable . . . to the Soviet bloc.[10]

This, of course, is none other than Winston Churchill's old definition of Great Britain's geo-political destiny at the intersection point of the 'three circles', Europe, the USA and Empire (see Chapter I). Even in the context of disarmament politics the Churchillian destiny remains an inheritance through which the likes of E. P. Thompson qualify the country for, if not exactly a world role of moral leadership, then at least one of honest broker. Part of the explanation for the English Left's paralysis within this framework has been the historical problems it has had in imagining and projecting for itself a clear vision of democracy. A root cause, as argued earlier, is the monarchy-centred political culture which allows no place for 'the people', the building blocks of democracy. As Raymond Williams pointed out in *The Long Revolution*:

Democracy has never established a really deep social image, of a distinct kind, in Britain. Just because in the main it grew slowly, and by gradual constitutional amendment and compromise, it has always been difficult to separate the principle of democracy from the habitual loyalty to an establishment. The symbols of democracy, in the English mind, are . . .

likely to be institutions of power and antiquity, such as the Palace of Westminster.[11]

In a penetrating analysis Williams goes on to argue that the central vision of brotherhood or fraternity as the foundation of democratic sentiment and a popular-democratic identity has been overlain in the history of the British Labour movement by a corporate and defensive identity of 'class'. 'It can hardly be denied,' he says, that

> while socialism's long-term version of human society is brotherhood, its short-term version is of a very deep conflict . . . [and] the stage has been reached when the emphasis on class has been seen as the most obvious denial of brotherhood.[12]

The one thing such an overwhelmingly class-orientated version of socialism could not provide for was the idea of democracy as a primary requirement. Such a democratic-national identity, drawing on an image of popular sovereignty – that is active authority from below – should have been the ground on which socialism was constructed. In England, because of the particular development of State institutions from 1688 onwards, as outlined in Chapter VII, it was not. 'The image of human brotherhood is still there,' Williams concluded sombrely,

> but so darkened by the real process of attempting to create it out of societies powerfully organized in other terms that it has been radically confused.[13]

Such a radically confused socialism was bound to become the dominant lower-class oppositional identity in most areas of industrialization. In the North of England, South Wales and Lowland Scotland it imposed a class ideology which has also been a powerful vehicle for an overweening British identity based upon a rhetoric of class unity. This was ventilated to full effect during the devolution politics of the 1970s by such diverse figures as Neil Kinnock, Eric Heffer and Tam Dalyell.

The radical confusion resulting from socialism confronting a culturally secure hierarchical state system with an ancient but depoliticized monarchy at its pinnacle meant that the vision of socialism as a democratic brotherhood became hoplessly intertwined with Raymond Williams' 'institutions of power and antiquity' – the Crown and Parliament. What the combination produced was a non-democratic Labour movement. How else can one explain the fact that in the 1980s the key problems this movement has confronted have been those of democratic form? The fights within the Labour Party over its constitution in 1980–82; the NUM strike of 1984–5; the grudging yet inevitable acceptance by Party and unions of elementary forms of balloting – imposed by a right-wing government; the GCHQ affair; the Labour leadership's wrong-footedness over the Spycatcher secrets case . . . all these have been essentially issues of democratic and civil rights, demonstrating 'radical confusion' indeed, within the ranks of the British Left.

The lack of a clear democratic vision at the centre of the British Left also goes a long way towards explaining its difficulties, even embarrassment, in embracing any uninhibited sense of patriotism. If there is one area during the 1980s where the Labour Movement has been side-stepped at every point by the Right, it is here. It is not just a question of the defence debate and the nuclear issue which in this arena have been merely symptomatic of a deeper underlying reality. The clearest indication was the way the Conservative Party in the 1980s managed to hijack the Union Jack. During this period it was impossible to imagine the Labour Party Conference draped in the Union Jack and impossible to imagine the Conservative Party conference not draped in the Union Jack. Labour attempted to respond, in a muted way during the 1987 general election by adopting as its symbol a red rose. It was possible for the Conservatives to flaunt an Anglo-British image of themselves unashamedly in a way that Labour simply could not.

A combination of factors are at work here. The Anglo-British demonstrations typical of the Conservatives – 'Land of Hope and Glory', the Union Jack and so on – emerge naturally, if in a refracted way, out of a sense of the Greater England that Chapter VII attempted to delineate. This is, indeed, a country of the imagination, not territorially based, at once bigger and smaller than England itself. Affiliation to this, however, is impossible for the Labour Party: its roots in the Home Counties are tenuous; it approaches the institutions of the British State from the periphery; and its strongest bases are in Scotland and Wales where the Anglo-British identity is disputed. Then again, the imperial dimension of Anglo-British patriotism is no source of embarrassment for the Conservative Party, whereas for Labour it most definitely is.

But more fundamental than any of these points is Labour's failure to develop an alternative, clear idea of a patriotism to which it can adhere unambiguously and with enthusiasm. As charted above, the roots of this failure lie in the Labour movement's lack of identification with democracy and the idea of popular sovereignty based on 'the People' rather than the institutions of a hierarchical State. This is not to deny the existence of an honourable People-based tradition on the English Left that can be traced back through Thomas Paine at least to the Levellers.[14] But there has never yet been a moment when this tradition achieved decisive influence. A key moment in this century was the Second World War, which, because it involved total mobilization, was truly 'a people's war'. Movements towards greater equality and social justice were accelerated by the war, but in general the British political system, capitalism and the hierarchical State structure were fortified by the experience of the 1940s, not weakened by it. George Orwell graphically defined this difficulty in his celebrated evocation of England and the English written in 1941, *The Lion and the Unicorn*:

England is perhaps the only great country whose intellectuals are ashamed of their own nationality. In left-wing circles it is always felt that there is something slightly disgraceful in being an Englishman and that it is a duty to snigger at every English institution, from horse-racing to suet puddings. It is a strange fact, but it is unquestionably true, that almost any English intellectual would feel more ashamed of standing to attention during 'God Save the King' than of stealing from a poor box.[15]

Orwell ended this chapter a few paragraphs later with the plea that 'patriotism and intelligence will have to come together again'. However, he offered no clue as to how this might be achieved. His main theme was that England was a family with the wrong members in control:

England is not the jewelled isle of Shakespeare's much-quoted message, nor is it the inferno depicted by Dr Goebbels. More than either it resembles a family, a rather stuffy Victorian family, with not many black sheep in it but with all its cupboards bursting with skeletons. It has rich relations who have to be kow-towed to and poor relations who are horribly sat upon, and there is a deep conspiracy of silence about the source of the family income. It is a family in which the young are generally thwarted and most of the power is in the hands of irresponsible uncles and bedridden aunts . . .[16]

The main message, therefore, is – get rid of the aunts and uncles, and let some of the younger, more decent, more modern and educated members take over. Arguably this happened in 1945, 1964 and even perhaps in 1974. But the family set-up remained largely intact – a system still built on hierarchy and deference in which most members of the 'family' remained subjects not citizens. Orwell himself hinted at the reality obscured by his image of a family when he declared near the end of the book:

The heirs of Nelson and of Cromwell are not in the House of Lords. They are in the fields and the streets, in the factories and the armed forces, in the four-ale bar and the suburban back garden; and at present they are still kept under by a generation of ghosts . . .[17]

Few would deny that the 1945 Labour government presided over great and on the whole desirable changes. But the need for and direction of the changes had been perceived and generally initiated during the war years under Churchill's coalition government. The notion that the welfare state was created by Labour after 1945 in accordance with a democratic socialist ideology bears no examination: the proposals had already been agreed by enlightened managerialists of all parties. In 1964 Labour came to power with a promise to take economic planning away from the Treasury, to go for growth at all costs, without letting sterling crises impede the way, and to contain inflation with an incomes policy. The plan was perfectly feasible – and was instantly jettisoned in favour of maintaining the sterling rate, imposing a wage freeze, letting the Treasury have its way and returning to the 'stop-go' of the 1950s. As R. W. Johnson commented, 'Harold Wilson was shrewd enough to understand that neither the party nor the country had the stomach for an anti-capitalist crusade but could be coaxed – just – into a preference for scientific managerialism over feudalism.'[18]

The confrontation of the Heath government with the miners in the early 1970s produced what superficially appeared to be a major crisis for the British Establishment. However the impact of Arthur Scargill's flying pickets at Birmingham's Saltley coal depot and the subsequent fall of the Heath government in 1974 only served to illustrate the underlying resilience of the structure. There can be few societies in the contemporary world where such a flagrant and direct victory by workers over the State would not have produced either a political revolution or a counter-revolution. In Britain it produced a Labour government. The Wilson/Callaghan administration was one of calculated emollience, devoted to healing the wounds and restoring consensus once more. Not only that, within two years and in league with the International Monetary Fund, it began clearing the ground to make way for the Thatcher 'counter-revolution' of the 1980s. The 1984–5 re-run of the miners' strike never got as far as 1974; that is, there was no need this time for Labourite first-aid and reconstruction of the consensus under Neil Kinnock. The Anglo-British sense of a class war with the working class led by Arthur Scargill was less mobilizable than a decade before and in itself this was a significant shift, if a negative one. The result was, however, that the Anglo-British regime remained intact, indeed was strengthened by the struggle.

What this sketch of the history of the British Left since the 1940s reveals is a failure of the imagination, a failure to identify with a country and a patriotism other than that set in a mould by the Anglo-British Right. The majority of the Labour movement has traditionally pinned its hopes on being elected to control the operations of the British State. It has never planned in any real sense to change the nature of the State. In its imagination it has continually confused the identities of Britain and England, and generally ignored those of Wales, Scotland and Ireland. Consequently, it has failed to develop a notion of democracy as depending on the sovereignty of the people, and failed to embrace an authentic patriotism. Instead it has been left deracinated, unable to project even in its imagination the idea of a fully democratic society rooted in national communities where the people are sovereign.

What the British Left has consistently failed to see and imagine is that within the frame of the British State there exists a diversity of communities – Black British, Welsh British, Scots British, and in various formations English British, whose Britishness exists only to provide them with a passport, but whose real community of identity is expressed through their sense of place, their distinctive cultures and their social relationships. An exploration of the diversity and strength of these identities has been one theme of this book. Taken together they provide the basis for a different, more human, radical and democratic way of imagining Britain. A prime requirement in this project is the necessity of the English to think through the real meaning of being English, especially in a political context. The reality now, as it has been for most of the twentieth century, is that being English in a political sense means belonging to a medium-sized European nation and not just a declining imperial state.

The challenge here is that British participation in Europe in the 1980s has been pursued in the interests of a Greater England, Anglo-British identity. It can be called Channel Tunnel Europeanization and is a formidable new effort to bolster up South-east, or heartland, England by giving it a new territorial definition within Europe. It is accompanied and balanced by the post-Big Bang City's attempt to restore itself as a centre of international capital. And in this way British non-industrial capital will become even less involved with the needs of the rest of the country, servicing industrial and general economic development elsewhere. The renovation threatens to combine economic 'radicalism' – individualism, the enterprise culture and so on – with continued Anglo-British higher state traditionalism, with the monarchy, as ever, assigned a pivotal role. Though the mix is apparently contradictory, it simultaneously promotes the interests of heartland capital and its historical Greater England identity – a mix perfectly articulated by the politics of Mrs Thatcher. Numbers of *This England* magazine will issue forth from Cheltenham undisturbed.

What alternative is there to this appalling prospect? An inescapable conclusion from this book's survey of the various identities to be found inside the British State is that the dominant, heartland one is still immensely powerful – powerful, and hostile to all change affecting the superstructures of the State and its culture. It is difficult to envisage even a combination of the North of England, Scotland and Wales (Ulster is probably out of the reckoning) mounting a successful assault on it. This is another way of saying that, from the vantage point of the end of the 1980s, it is difficult to envisage another old-style Labour government in Westminster again.

But there is an alternative way of looking at, of imagining

Britain. This is to begin the task of dismantling the superstructure of the State from below, to campaign for effective regional government within England as well as for Scotland, Wales and Ulster. This perhaps is the major significance of the regional/national movements in Scotland and Wales, in providing the people of England with the idea that there is an alternative way forward. A programme of regional government would liberate the people of the North of England from the domination of the South-east, and it would provide the opportunity for cultural initiatives as well as the economic ones that are already beginning to emerge. It would be the only effective response to the dangerously anti-democratic centralization of power in Whitehall. In all this a European perspective is entirely logical and coherent. It simultaneously provides a setting for the diminution of classical nation-state sovereignty, and for greater acceptance, as in West Germany, Italy, and now even France, of devolution of power.

This book opened with the assertion that a clear image of British identity, as the twenty-first century approaches, remains that of a nuclear submarine sailing down the Clyde. The forces of the Left must learn that there is no way of ridding ourselves of nuclear weapons without first ridding ourselves of the idea of Britain in its present centralist, authoritarian and anti-democratic form. To achieve this we must first imagine a different kind of Britain, one containing a patchwork of self-governing communities relating not only to each other but to a wider European context as well. The most important and urgent step in making this a reality will be to reclaim sovereignty from the present State institutions of Britain and place it back where it belongs, with the people of the various countries and communities that make up our presently Divided Kingdom.

NOTES

1 Enoch Powell, speech at Dublin, 1946, in *Freedom and Reality* (*Selected Speeches*, ed. J. Wood, 1969), p. 245.

2 *Radio Times*, 20 April 1956, p. 5.
3 David Cannadine, 'James Bond and the Decline of England', *Encounter*, September 1979, from which the following quotations are also taken.
4 Bernard Levin, *The Pendulum Years – Britain and the Sixties*, Jonathan Cape, 1970.
5 Margaret Thatcher, speech to a Conservative Party rally at Cheltenham Race Course, 3 July 1982. Quoted in full as an appendix in Anthony Barnett, *Iron Britannia*, Allison and Busby, 1982.
6 *The Times*, 1 February 1982.
7 This and the following quotations taken from Rosalind Brunt's article, 'The Changing Face of Royalty', in *Marxism Today*, July 1984.
8 W. Bagehot, *The English Constitution*, Fontana 1963 ed., first published 1867.
9 R. McKenzie and A. Silver, *Angels in Marble: Working-Class Conservatives in Urban England*, Heinemann, 1968, p. 251.
10 *Independent*, 25 February 1987.
11 Raymond Williams, *The Long Revolution*, first published 1961, reference Pelican edition, 1971, p. 123.
12 Ibid., p. 128.
13 Ibid., p. 128.
14 A good and succinct survey of this tradition, a reprint of a series of articles from *Tribune* 1969–72, can be found in David Rubinstein (ed.), *People for the People*, London: Ithaca Press, 1973.
15 George Orwell, *The Lion and the Unicorn*, first published in the Searchlight Books series by Secker and Warburg, 1941. These quotations taken from the Penguin 1984 edition, p. 63–4.
16 Ibid., p. 53–4. Raymond Williams' *Orwell*, Fontana, 1971, contains a useful discussion of the factors that conditioned Orwell's thinking and prevented his taking his ideas to the kind of conclusion developed in this chapter.
17 Ibid., 122–3.
18 R. W. Johnson, *The Politics of Recession*, Macmillan, 1985, p. 262.

INDEX

working class, 32, 33, 67, 93, 97, 98, 101, 106, 115, 215, 254, 264; *see also* class

work vouchers, 217

World War I, 125

World War II, 22, 24, 25, 29, 153–4, 155, 156, 158, 257, 261

Worsthorne, Peregrine, 192

Wright, Patrick, 28

'Y Fro Gymraeg', 129, 130, 138, 140

Young, Ken, 207